RSVP RICE AND STEW VERY PLENTY

The Story of an Ismaili Girl's Expulsion from Uganda
and Acceptance in Canada

by Nazlin Rahemtulla

with Margaret Fairweather

Published by:

FriesenPress

Suite 300 – 852 Fort Street
Victoria, BC, Canada V8W 1H8

www.friesenpress.com

Distributed to the trade by The Ingram Book Company

Cover artwork by Narmin Kassam (née Rahemtulla). Titled "Aleem's Elephant," it is dedicated to the artist's son as a gift and celebration of his birth. The elephant pays tribute to Aleem's African roots and represents strength, honour, stability, patience, luck, fortune, and protection.

Table of Contents

PREFACE

I've long wanted to write my story, and that of my family, as a record for our future generations. Through the years, though, my friends and people I've met through my work and my travels have expressed an interest in a broader portrait of Ismailism; the settings of India and Africa; the human and economic carnage wreaked by Idi Amin, not just upon Asians but upon the Ugandan nation; and the successful emergence of Ismailis in Canada.

As well, I've thought that members of our Ismaili community, and other Asians from Uganda, might be interested in this story because our shared experiences are so similar.

So, I've expanded my original idea of a book for just my family's use to include some religious, historical, cultural, and geographic background that I hope will be of more general interest to readers.

I also wish to address a comment from a Price Waterhouse Africa report (see Appendix), written several years ago, about my father's business success in Uganda, which said:

> Not much is known about the Rahemtulla family or the founder of Jubilee Ice, Mr. Mohamed Rahemtulla, or their present whereabouts since their forced expulsion out of Uganda during the brutal regime of Idi Amin.

This book is my response.

Nazlin Rahemtulla

ACKNOWLEDGEMENTS

My heartfelt thanks to the members of my family who have contributed their recollections, and my deepest gratitude to Margaret Fairweather who has given so generously of her time to help me research and write this book, and without whom it would not have come to fruition.

CHAPTER ONE

My Ismaili and Indian Heritage

August 5, 1972—to paraphrase Charles Dickens, it was the best of days, and the worst of days.

I was sixteen years old, and all of our family and friends had gathered in Jinja, Uganda for the marriage of my sister, Zebby, and her fiancé, Rustam.

Our pre-wedding festivities had lasted into the wee hours but I arose at first light, to the lingering aroma of *oudh* (a smoky wood scent), which permeated the house. Awash in anticipation of the coming day, I slipped outside into our courtyard.

The cream, gold, and orange of dawn's first rays tinted the sky above Lake Victoria. Vibrant bougainvillea, jasmine, and frangipani festooned the gardens of our neighbourhood and the nearby hills.

Despite the hostile and savage environment in which we lived, I remember, in that moment, being exquisitely happy.

Looking back, almost forty years later, on that pivotal day, I marvel at the confluence of circumstances that led to the exodus of my family from India, our revival in Africa, our expulsion from Uganda, and our resurgence in Canada.

The Ismaili Path to the Gujarat

What I know of my family's story begins in the late nineteenth century. My great grandparents were *Ismailis* who lived in Madhapur in the Kutch District in the State of Gujarat, India. How my ancestors arrived in Madhapur will remain forever a mystery but a brief excursion into the enthralling saga of *Ismailism* offers clues to their possible roots.

All *Muslims* believe that *Allah* chose the *Holy Prophet Muhammad* (peace be upon him and His family) to deliver His divine message to the world. But, after the death of Prophet Muhammad, the smouldering debate among Muslims, which erupted on more than one occasion into civil war, was whether the Prophet's role as spiritual guide should pass to his own family or to his loyal followers. This controversy divided the Muslim community between *Shi'a* and *Sunni*.

The Shi'a, who believe that the Prophet's lineage is continuous, split, many centuries ago, into various sects, one of which was Ismailism. The Ismailis themselves suffered various schisms, the most notable being that which resulted in the advent of the *Nizari* Ismailis. My family belongs to the branch of the Nizaris known as *Khojas*.

Nizari Ismailis believe that after the Prophet's death, Hazrat Ali, his cousin and son-in-law, became the first *Imam* (spiritual leader) of the Muslim community; and that the Prophet's spiritual leadership continues, by hereditary succession, through Hazrat Ali and his wife Fatima, the Prophet's daughter. The lineage of Prophet Muhammad lives today in Prince Karim Aga Khan IV, the current leader of our faith.

By the final years of the ninth century, Ismaili missionaries were active, both religiously and politically, in many regions including North Africa. The early success of the Ismaili mission there climaxed, in the latter years of the tenth century, in the creation of an Ismaili dominion, the *Fatimid Caliphate*.

The Fatimid Caliphate, named in honour of Fatima, marked the zenith of the Ismaili empire, and also of Ismaili scholarly and religious development. During this period, Ismaili academics and intellectuals authored classic Ismaili literature, codified Ismaili law, and contributed substantially to Ismaili philosophic and religious thought.

These early Ismailis developed Cairo as the capital of the Caliphate, and it became a symbolic centre of education and enlightenment. The Al-Azhar University, established at that time and still existing today, is one of the oldest universities in the world. Under Fatimid rule, Cairo became the repository for vast library collections.

Religious forbearance was a hallmark of the Fatimid Empire. Egypt, in those long ago days, was home to diverse clusters of Christians, Jews, Shiite Muslims, and Sunni Muslims, all of whom worked in unison for the glory of the Egyptian empire.

The Fatimids solidified a burgeoning economic base in Egypt, and built up an impressive system of international commerce. Their trading vessels sailed through the Red Sea and Mediterranean Sea. They imported spices and luxury items from India and China, and exported linen, glassware, and other goods to Europe.

Hand in hand with the expansion of trade and commerce, the Fatimid missionaries spread their religious beliefs into various regions of the Middle East and Asia. Their reach extended to the Gujarat, the future home of my great-grandparents.

By the twelfth century, though, famine, internecine strife, racial tensions in the military, and attacks by Christian Crusaders and other invaders proved crippling. Then, in A.D. 1171, a Turkish army invaded Cairo, and ruthlessly toppled the Fatimid Caliphate.

After the demise of the Caliphate, the Ismaili faithful sought sanctuary in Persian and Syrian mountain strongholds. Their most famous retreat was the stony peak of *Alamut* in the Elburz Mountains of Persia. The Nizaris who conquered and governed Alamut fortified it against attacks until they thought it impregnable. They also laid out an ingenious irrigation system that allowed them to create wondrous gardens. And, being of an academic bent, they compiled copious collections of astronomical instruments and library books. Academics and scientific scholars from a host of countries visited and studied at Alamut.

History and legend record the infiltration and occupation of the fortress, at the end of the eleventh century, by a powerful Nizari splinter group called the *Hashshashins*. The western world at the time believed the Hashshashins responsible for the systematic elimination of political and other opponents of the Ismailis, and dubbed them the *Assassins*.

In 1256, Mongol hordes, led by the grandson of Ghengis Khan, overthrew the Ismaili enclave at Alamut, and destroyed the fortress. During their rampage, they burned all that was in their path including the collected works of the library. The irreplaceable loss of Ismaili historical and religious writings was a devastating consequence.

For the next few hundred years, Ismailis blended into the woodwork in Asian and African communities. Ultimately, though, the Nizari Imams re-established their authority in those communities, and missionaries succeeded in converting new devotees to their faith. Many of those converts were Hindus who lived in the Gujarat.

Some of the Gujarati Hindus were of a caste known as *Kshatriyas* or *Mistris*. They had migrated from the State of Rajasthan in northern India to the District of Kutch in the seventh and twelfth centuries. These migrants were soldiers of war but many of the later ones were also stone masons and architects. They established a series of nineteen villages around the Town of Bhuj. One of those villages was Madhapur, the birthplace of my *Ma* (mother) and my *Bapa* (father).

The direct descendants of Prophet Muhammad have possessed the Ismaili *Imamate* (spiritual leadership) for more than fourteen centuries. In the 1830s, the Shah of Iran bestowed the title *Aga Khan* (Commander-in-Chief) on Hasan Ali Shah, the forty-sixth Imam. In the 1840s, the Aga Khan moved from Persia to India, and established his Nizari religious and administrative headquarters principally in Bombay.

Sir Sultan Muhammad Shah, Aga Khan III, the forty-eighth Imam, was the spiritual leader of the Nizari Ismailis from 1885 to 1957, an astonishing seventy-two years. He was a figure of legendary stature—a prominent statesman on the world stage who served as President of the League of Nations. He was also a breeder of some of the world's finest race horses.

Aga Khan III was a hands-on administrator of his scattered Nizari communities. Bapa once had the privilege of meeting him in Kampala, the capital of Uganda. A request Aga Khan III made of Bapa and a promise he made to him, at that time, were to impact our family's fortunes significantly.

Through the centuries since the demise of the Fatimid Caliphate, military, political and religious oppressors, Sunnis and other Shiite sects not the least among them, have mercilessly persecuted Ismailis. That is not to say that Ismaili conduct, through the course of history, has been without blemish or blame. But, I believe that the discrimination and maltreatment by outsiders have served as coalescing agents in keeping our community close-knit and our faith stalwart.

The Backdrop of the Gujarat

In the late nineteenth century, Mark Twain embarked on an adventuresome odyssey which he recorded in *Following the Equator*. Of the great Indian subcontinent, he wrote:

> So far as I am able to judge, nothing has been left undone, either by man or nature, to make India the most extra-ordinary country that the sun visits on his rounds. Nothing seems to have been forgotten, nothing overlooked.

The remarkable geography, culture, and history of the State of Gujarat bears testament to that observation. In western India, the Arabian Sea to the south, and the Great Indian Desert in the State of Rajasthan to the northeast, border the Gujarat. Its plains comprise almost 34,000 square kilometres. Despite the state's physical isolation from the rest of India and from other countries, the people of the Gujarat have both enjoyed and endured relations with outsiders for eons.

The Indus Valley civilization of the Gujarat dates back more than 4,000 years. Its principal city, Lothal, was a flourishing ancient centre of commerce. The artisans of Lothal crafted agate, gold, and copper beads and ornaments, and produced striking red ware pottery jars. Lothal imported raw materials from various regions of Asia, and carried on trade with Mesopotamia, Arabia, and parts of the African continent.

Through the centuries, Gujaratis continued to trade extensively on the world market, and enjoyed far-reaching commercial ties. Oxford University possesses a rare Gujarati map from the eighteenth century that includes sailing directions, and a list of ports on the Indian Ocean.

The Gujarat, over the course of several hundred years, was subject to conquest and domination by Asian and European empire builders. By the middle years of the second millennium, the Portuguese empire had spread its tentacles through both Africa and India. Its aim was to control the extraordinarily lucrative spice trade. To further that goal, Portugal became the first European nation to descend upon the Gujarat, seizing and occupying several ports along the Arabian Sea.

One of those hungry empire builders was Great Britain. The British East India Company set up shop in the Gujarat, and, early in the nineteenth century, the British army gained dominion over the territory. A primary purpose of the British was to control the raw cotton industry for export to China and other countries. To carry out their goal, the British, in the second half of the nineteenth and first third of the twentieth century, built railways across the state on the backs of Indian labourers.

In the course of its occupation, the British established a military base in the Kutch District. The name *Kutch* means "turtle" or "tortoise," so called because of its shape. The Gulf of Kutch, on the Arabian Sea, and two deserts, the Great Rann of Kutch and Little Rann of Kutch, effectively separate the district from Pakistan to the north and the remainder of the Gujarat to the east.

The *ranns* (deserts) are immense salt plains subject to extreme temperatures. During the rainy season, water can submerge the Little Rann of Kutch but, during the dry season, it reverts to a dry, dusty, salty wasteland. The Little Rann supports a massive population of lesser flamingos, and is home to the endangered Indian wild ass. The government has now designated the entire rann as the Indian Wild Ass Sanctuary.

The history of Kutch is captivating. Archaeological evidence indicates the prehistoric settlement of human beings in Kutch; and, later, it was home to the Indus Valley civilization. For many centuries, caravans of merchants plied the trade routes across the ranns to and from the Far East. Nomadic cattle, sheep, and camel breeders and shepherds were, and still are, traditional occupants of the area.

While they held sway over Kutch, British forces occupied Bhuj, an isolated medieval fort near the Gulf of Kutch and the most westerly city in India. Bhuj, founded in the sixteenth century, was a near impregnable stronghold fortified by thick stone walls.

Maharao Lakhpatji ruled Bhuj in the mid-eighteenth century. During his reign, foreign trade burgeoned; performing artists, writers, and poets prospered; and a unique style of architecture stamped a lasting imprint on the city and nearby villages. The spectacular legacy Maharao Lakhpatji created was a city of dazzling, dramatic, and colourful *Jamatkhanas* (Ismaili mosques), palaces, and temples along with a heritage of exquisite artistry.

The artisans of Bhuj and its surrounding villages were renowned for their superb crafts. They included uniquely stitched embroidery, precious metal engraving, ivory carving, weaving, block printing, and wood carving.

Musical extravaganzas, camel races, bazaars, and the sale of their handicrafts attracted nearby villagers to Bhuj on a regular basis. I like to imagine that these events drew my family's ancestors, and perhaps even my great-grandparents, from Madhapur to this vibrant metropolis.

During this period, the export and import trade between Kutch and Great Britain, China, the Middle East, and Africa flourished.

Tragically, in 2001, a catastrophic earthquake caused a dreadful loss of human life, and the destruction of architecturally priceless edifices in Bhuj and its environs. Another dire result was the loss of vital records of births, deaths, marriages, and property holdings through which I might have been able to trace my family's origins more accurately.

Low hills surround Bhuj, and beyond one of them, a few kilometres to the east, lies the village of Madhapur which various sources describe as a "railroad station." Its location is near the coast, and it is only about three metres above sea level. Because of its proximity to the ranns of the Gujarat, Madhapur's weather is extreme. The summer months are searing, and the winter months cooler and milder. During late spring, monsoons flay the area with drenching downpours. To make matters worse, cyclones often couple with monsoons to wreak mayhem. The countryside is bleak.

Behind the Scenes in Madhapur

All four of my grandparents were born in Madhapur in the last years of the nineteenth century. My paternal grandparents were likely born in the 1870s, and my maternal grandparents in the 1880s. They were all Nizari Ismailis.

My paternal grandfather, Rahemtulla Devji, married Rehmatbai, who bore him six children. Bapa, whose name was Mohamed Rahemtulla, was born in Madhapur in 1912. Bapa's siblings were Ali, Karmali, Salemohamed, Sajabai, and Fatmabai.

Rahemtulla Devji, My Paternal Grandfather

My maternal grandfather, Abdulla Bhimji, was the only child of Fatmabai and Bhimjibhai. My maternal grandmother, Sekinabai, was the eighth child and only daughter of Sajabai and Sachedina. I believe that all her brothers, Karim, Mohamed, Hirji, Ali, Fazal, Ahmed, and Gulamussein remained in India.

Abdulla and Sekinabai, who were dear to me, married in about 1918. They had three daughters. Ma, whose name was Jenabai, was born in Madhapur on January 19, 1920. Her sisters were Kharunissa (whom my family has always called Mariam), and Malek.

We called Ma's parents *Nanabapa* (grandfather) and *Nanima* (grandmother). Had we known Bapa's parents, we would have referred to them as *Dadabapa* and *Dadima*. Ma was the spitting image of Nanima, and Ma's sister, Mariam, looked exactly like Nanabapa.

Dadabapa and his family were neighbours of Nanabapa and his family in Madhapur. My parents would have known one another although Ma would have been just a baby when Bapa left for Africa.

Life in Madhapur was likely a hard-scrabble existence with little opportunity for improvement, and I can only speculate about what it was like for my family. Nanima, Nanabapa, Dadima, Dadabapa, Ma and Bapa, and the other children, likely lived in *bhungas*. They were round dwellings constructed of stone, mud, and dung with conical roofs. The walls were thick so as to keep the inside cool during the sweltering weather, and warm when the weather was chilly. In the morning and late in the day, Nanima and Dadima probably sat outside their bhungas discussing daily affairs with the other women.

Like most Indians in small villages, my grandparents would have fashioned earthenware vessels which they used for their food, and ground grain using stones activated by oxen. Their food staples would have consisted of corn and red rice.

Bapa and his friends likely played street games like *gilli-danda*, a primitive form of cricket. Spiders and reptiles were a constant menace around the village. None of the kids would have slid into shoes without shaking them in case a scorpion was hiding, and they would have avoided the long grass that concealed venomous snakes.

Ma did not receive any schooling in Madhapur. I believe Bapa obtained a minimal elementary school education.

I don't know how Nanabapa and Dadabapa supported their families but they may have fished in long canoe-like boats; tended cattle, buffalo, or camels; or raised corn, cotton, or sugar cane. Given the pervasive British presence in the area, they may have worked for the families of the British military and railway workers as gardeners, sweepers, or bearers. Nanima and Dadima may have found employment as nursemaids or cooks to the British families. Another possibility is that they may have been merchants, tailors, or cobblers because, historically, Ismailis were noted for their business acumen. Or, they may have toiled as artisans of the crafts for which the region was so famous.

However hard the lives of Dadabapa and Dadima may have been, they must have instilled in their children a sense of adventure and a desire for a richer life because all six of them immigrated to Africa. Their parents, though, remained in Madhapur. Dadabapa died in the 1930s, and Dadima in about 1940.

Nanabapa and Nanima, along with their three daughters, and Nanabapa's mother, Fatmabai, also migrated to Africa, and on that riveting continent the second part of my family's saga begins.

CHAPTER TWO

Outward Bound to the Dark Continent

The Allure of East Africa

The 1920s saw waves of young men from China, Japan, Austria, Great Britain, India, and a host of other nations leave their ancestral homes to search out new horizons, adventures, and opportunities. They immigrated to continents and countries as far-flung as Asia, Africa, Australia, Canada, and the United States.

I can only hypothesize as to why my relatives left the safe familiarity of their lives in Madhapur to face the unknown perils of the "dark continent." They must have known little of the world beyond the stifling confines of their village in that remote region of western India. I'm sure, though, that, in order to act upon their dreams, they must have possessed incredible courage and a remarkable pioneering spirit. Likewise, I can only surmise what led them to choose East Africa but the inextricably linked histories of Africa, India, and Great Britain offer many pointers.

The ties between East Africa and India, and the presence of Indians in East Africa, span thousands of years. The *Arabian Nights*, for example, offer many tales of merchant voyages along the African coast and across to India.

Sailors and traders in *dhows* (triangular sailing vessels) bravely plied the Indian Ocean between India and Africa, taking advantage of the monsoon winds to propel them toward the East African coast in winter, and back to the Indian sub-continent in spring.

As I've mentioned, the commercial, cultural, and religious cross-currents between India and Africa were prolific. The Indus Valley civilization, which settled in the Gujarat more than 4,000 years ago, traded with African territories. In the tenth and eleventh centuries, trade between

India and the Fatimid Caliphate in Egypt mushroomed, and Ismaili Fatimid missionaries carried their religious message to the Gujarat.

Vasco da Gama, a Portuguese explorer, was the first voyager from Europe to sail directly to India. In the early years of the fifteenth century, he commanded a fleet which rounded Cape Horn, and ventured up the East African coast. Da Gama and his crew were the first Europeans to set anchor in Mombasa, Kenya. He then sailed on to India, the first of several voyages he made there, and, on behalf of Portugal, delved into the Indian Ocean trade.

In the middle and later years of the second millennium, Portugal and Great Britain, who were both attempting to establish hegemony in Africa, dominated the Gujarat. Their interactions with Gujaratis almost certainly raised the profile of East Africa in Kutch.

In the seventeenth century, if not before, Nizari Ismailis from Kutch began to participate in the trade network between the Gujarat and East Africa. In the nineteenth century, they began immigrating to East Africa in greater numbers. Droughts and the resulting dearth of food in the Gujarat undoubtedly spurred them on. At the beginning of the Nizari exodus, they settled primarily in Zanzibar. Later, taking advantage of new roads and railways, they followed increasingly accessible trade routes to Kenya, Tanganyika, and Uganda. In 1964, Tanganyika and Zanzibar united to form the United Republic of Tanzania.

In the last part of the nineteenth century, Great Britain contracted with more than 30,000 Indians to come to Africa. Their task was to construct the British East African Railroad from Mombasa, through Kenya and Uganda, and in time to Kampala.

A significant reason for this wave of immigration was the passage by the British government of the *Slavery Abolition Act* of 1834. As a result of this legislation, many former slaves who were working on the railroad departed their forced servitude, leaving an acute labour shortage. The British had no choice but to import replacement workers, many of whom came from the Gujarat.

Construction of the railroad opened up an abundance of commercial opportunities for Indian immigrants. As the rail line advanced, many of them established *dukas* (small shops) to sell goods to the railway workers and to Africans who lived nearby.

Because Great Britain did not consider Uganda a healthy territory in which to settle, primarily because of the pervasiveness of sleeping sickness, the Indians, after completion of the railway, were able to expand their commercial enterprises. The British encouraged them to enter the cotton industry as middlemen, purchasing cotton from native Africans and selling it to cotton ginneries. As time went by, some Indians established or bought their own ginneries, and, as well, made inroads into the sugar industry. Other Indians immigrated to Uganda to work on the plantations.

The late 1800s and early 1900s saw the emergence, in East Africa, of several exceptional Indians worthy of individual mention. By dint of remarkable hard work and entrepreneurial genius, they became business and philanthropic titans whose ethos laid the foundations for the growth, in the whole region, of commerce and industry, which they complemented with open-handed charity.

One such pioneer was Allidina Visram, an Ismaili from the Gujarat, who arrived in Zanzibar by dhow in 1863 when he was only twelve years old. He began trading by caravan in Tanganyika, and soon expanded to Uganda and other areas of East Africa. He built dukas along the railway line, and eventually enlarged his empire to include ventures such as sugar cane and rubber plantations. His well-earned sobriquets were "King of Ivory" and "Uncrowned King of Uganda." Visram's charitable works were legendary, not the least of which was his construction of the first Jamakhana in Kisumu, Uganda. Aga Khan III honoured him with the title of *Vazier* for his beneficence.

In 1835, a ragged and penurious twelve year old Ismaili by the name of Tharia Topan left Kutch for Zanzibar where he snagged a job at a financial firm as a garden sweeper. By virtue of his work ethic and honesty, he climbed the firm's employment ladder, and, by his early twenties, was already a wealthy man. He branched into the provision of financing for caravans, and supplies for European explorers. He once had the honour of entertaining both Dr. Livingstone and Henry Morton Stanley at his home, and Stanley famously said of Topan:

> One of the most honest men among all individuals, white or black, red or yellow, is a Mahometan Hindi called Tarya Topan. Among the Europeans at Zanzibar he had become a proverb for honesty and strict business integrity. He is enormously wealthy, owns several shops and dhows, and is a prominent man in the councils of Seyyid Burgash.

Tapan was renowned for his generosity. Among many other charitable endeavours, he built the Sir Tharia Topan Jubilee Hospital in Zanzibar to memorialize Queen Victoria's Golden Jubilee. In recognition of his exceptional services, Queen Victoria granted him a knighthood, the first Indian to receive such an accolade.

Sewa Haji Paroo, born in Zanzibar to an Ismaili immigrant, made his fortune in the caravan trade as well. The goods he conveyed included mericani (the popular Massachusetts cloth), gunpowder, and beads. Paroo was devoutly religious, and extended his bounty to the ailing and the poor of all races. He donated land and buildings for, or funded, missions, schools, hospitals, and a refuge for lepers.

Nanji Kalidas Mehta immigrated to Uganda at the turn of the century at the age of thirteen. He also based his business empire on trading, and then expanded into agriculture, sugar manufacturing, and tea and coffee plantations. He founded the Mehta Group, a multi-national conglomerate which still flourishes today, the global assets of which exceed US $400 million. Mehta was a Hindu, held in the highest regard for his beneficence in establishing schools, hospitals, and temples in East Africa and India.

Not the least of these magnificent Indian entrepreneurs was Muljibhai Prabhudas Madhvani. He was a Hindu from the Gujarat whose business acumen and philanthropic nature impacted my family significantly, and about whom I shall relate more later.

Aga Khan III was passionately devoted to Africa. He undertook his first sojourn to the continent in 1899, and paid many more visits there during the course of his reign. Because of his love for the region, he tirelessly promoted East Africa to his Ismaili adherents, and convinced many of them to settle there. The harsh farming and weather conditions in the Gujarat, and the political foment in India over the campaign for home rule, also contributed to the Indian migration to East Africa.

Both Nanabapa and Nanima, and Bapa and his siblings, may have left the familiarity of the Gujrat based on any one or more of these intricate links between India and Africa. Or, the puzzle of their journey to a new land may have been as simple as relatives, who had moved there already, urging them to come.

A Snapshot of Uganda

I wish I were a poet to better describe the mysterious allure of Uganda—its majesty and might, the terrible sense of awe it inspires, the gently undulating hills and valleys, the diamond lakes, the lush foliage, the brilliant hues of the tropical flowers, the magnificent sunsets, and even the comedic hippopotami. Once you have lived there, and despite the atrocities committed against one another by so-called human beings, the glory of Uganda clutches your soul and never releases you. Sir Winston Churchill was so enthralled with Uganda's magnificent landscapes and wildlife that he proclaimed the nation to be the "Pearl of Africa."

Uganda lies at the centre of the continent, and consists of close to 236,000 square kilometres. It is a landlocked country that straddles the equator. Today, its neighbours are Kenya to the east, Rwanda and Tanzania to the south, Zaire to the west, and Sudan to the north.

Uganda's climate is tropical, and the heat in the middle of the day can be enervating. However, because of its location several thousand metres above sea level, the evenings bring a cool and welcome breeze. Southern Uganda, where I lived with my family, is subject to onslaughts of afternoon thunderstorms during the rainy seasons.

The terrain of Uganda is panoramic and varied in its sweep. The north-eastern territory consists of arid plains and savannahs. Dense forests dominate the southern landscape. The nexus of Lake Victoria and the River Nile makes the south a rich, fertile area for agriculture. The western realms of Uganda boast the legendary glacier-tipped Rwenzori Mountains, formerly called Ruwenzori Range and popularly known as the Mountains of the Moon.

Lake Victoria is the largest body of water in Africa, and from its northern shore rushes the River Nile. The Nile is the longest watercourse in the world, and flows more than 6,400 kilometres to the Mediterranean Sea.

Uganda's incredible diversity of wildlife features lions, zebras, buffaloes, elephants, leopards, baboons, gorillas, giraffes, cheetahs, antelopes, water bucks, bush bucks, bush pigs, chimpanzees, and untold varieties of birds, insects, and snakes.

East Africa has the reputation of being the "cradle of humanity." Anthropological finds in Kenya and Tanzania provide evidence that hominids roamed these territories millions of years ago.

Historically, the African region which became Uganda was home to a multitude of kingdoms and tribes. The *Nilotic* people, in about AD 400, were likely the first to inhabit it. They were hunter-gatherers. During the following centuries, the *Bantu* people, who were skilled at agricultural cultivation and iron working, migrated to the area around Lake Victoria, and forced the Nilotics northward into more mountainous terrain. However, the Bantus and Nilotics found ways to co-exist. The Nilotic people were warriors, and protected the Bantus. In return, the Bantus established territorial realms for the Nilotic chieftains to govern.

From the 1500s to the 1800s, the *Bunyoro* kingdom dominated a good portion of Uganda north of Lake Victoria. The *Buganda* tribe, though, began to colonize the northern shore of Lake Victoria and gradually enlarged its holdings. By the middle of the nineteenth century, the Bugandans were the prevailing power in what was to become central Uganda. They maintained sway over their expanded dominion with an immense army. But, despite these advantages, they never totally eclipsed the other tribes.

The mid-1800s heralded enormous upheaval in Uganda. The root causes were the emergence of ivory as a sought after commodity in world markets; the pursuit of slaves; the thirst for empire building; and the potential for the conversion of natives to Christianity or Islam. These material and religious enticements led a host of foreign powers and influences to overrun and besiege what until then had been an isolated and primitive country.

Backed by Indian financial interests, Arab traders based in Zanzibar paraded into Uganda by caravan. They sought ivory tusks and slaves. They offered in trade guns, gunpowder, and *mericani*, a cloth woven in Massachusetts, which was a hot ticket item among both the Bunyoro and Bugandan tribes. The Arabs also sought to convert the tribes to Islam.

The Egyptians engaged in similar trading enterprises, and hoped to expand their domain. The second half of the nineteenth century witnessed increasing incursions by a maelstrom of British, French, German, and Muslim explorers, traders, missionaries, *mullahs* (Muslim religious leaders), and soldiers. All were convinced of the righteousness of their political, economic, or religious missions, and the result was a civil war that tore the territory asunder for four agonizing years.

Meanwhile, in 1862, John Hanning Speke, an audacious explorer and an officer in the British Indian Army, discovered that Lake Victoria was the source of the mighty River Nile.

John Hanning Speke Monument—Source of River Nile at Lake Victoria

Great Britain emerged triumphant from the years of war and con-quest, and, in 1894, claimed the Ugandan region as a protectorate of the British Empire.

The last few years of the nineteenth century were no kinder to the indigenous tribes of Uganda. They suffered from a series of appall-ing sleeping sickness, smallpox, and rinderpest epidemics that cut a destructive swath through both the people and the cattle on which they were reliant.

During the years of military strife, the Bugandans allied themselves with the British while the Bunyoro defied them. In return, the British treated the Bugandans generously. They rewarded them with a substan-tial portion of Bunyoro lands, and recruited them to assist in governing the protectorate. As a result, the Bugandans exercised considerable power as tax collectors and labour organizers. In addition, they dominated the commercial and agricultural sectors. By 1901, when the British com-pleted the extension of the railway from Nairobi to Lake Victoria, cotton became a lucrative cash crop, and the Bugandans prospered even more.

In 1907, the Bunyoro people had suffered enough under the conde-scending rule of the Bugandans. They revolted, and forced the British to abandon their use of Bugandans as colonial administrators and agents. The British utilized the Nilotic and other tribes situate in northern Uganda, as well, by enlisting them in the local military and police forces.

This setting was the stage upon which Nanabapa's mother, Nanabapa and Nanima, their children, and, later, Bapa, made their African debut.

Steamship Bound for Uganda

Nanabapa and Nanima, and their family, journeyed to Africa in the 1920s. They crossed the Indian Ocean by steamship, and landed at Mombasa in Kenya. I don't know how they made their way to Uganda but, somehow, they managed to do so.

When Nanabapa arrived, he toiled as a labourer in Bujuta at a cotton ginnery owned by the Bandali Jaffer family. The Bandali Jaffer family themselves started out as plantation workers but, in due course, saved enough money to buy their own plantations. As well as being the employers of Nanabapa, the Jaffers were related to Bapa, and well-known to him.

Nanabapa, Nanima, and the girls had to learn Swahili in order to communicate with the African workers on the plantation. However, they were never able to master the English language, probably because they had little exposure to it.

Bapa's Trek to Jinja

Bapa and his siblings all immigrated to East Africa in the 1920s. Karmali and Fatma arrived first at the Port of Dar-es-Salaam, and then migrated to Tabora in Tanganyika. Ali, Salemohamed, Saja, and Bapa followed by steamship, and arrived at the Port of Mombasa in Kenya. The other three siblings followed Karmali and Fatma to Tabora but Bapa decided to press on to Uganda to look for work. He made the journey by foot with a travelling party. Walking from Mombasa to Uganda must have required almost superhuman stamina.

In my mind's eye, I can see him marching ramrod straight; planting a wooden walking stick firmly with each step; listening to the roar of lions; and being ever cautious of the formidable predators that roamed the dense jungles through which he trekked.

When Bapa reached a small town on the north shore of Lake Victoria, he stopped. Jinja, he decided, was where he would forge his new life.

CHAPTER THREE

Bapa and Ma in the Place of Flat Rocks

Jinja in the Early Days

The town of Jinja lies in south-eastern Uganda on the northern shore of Lake Victoria at the source of the River Nile. It is about eighty-six kilometres east of Kampala.

Historically, the Buganda and Basoga tribes lived near Lake Victoria on either side of the Nile. Close by Ripon Falls on the river were a series of large flat rocks which allowed tribesmen to cross the river. The name *Jinja* is a derivative of the word both groups used, in their dialects, for "rock." Hence, they described the area as "the place of flat rocks."

Jinja originated as a fishing village but flourished as the cross-roads for various trade routes. In 1907, the British established the town as an administrative centre. It was a strategic railway station, and a port for steamship services. Because it lay in a lush agricultural sector, plantations of sugar cane, cotton, and tea developed around it, and the town grew apace. Cotton ginning became a lucrative industry.

The year 1928 was pivotal in the development of Jinja as both an industrial and transportation centre. The British American Tobacco Uganda Company founded a plant for processing tobacco, and the British completed construction of a direct railway line linking Jinja with Kenya and its coastal ports on the Indian Ocean.

Bapa appeared on the Jinja scene during an unprecedented period of agricultural and industrial growth marked by buoyant economic optimism. Being a remarkably bright man, he must have seen abundant opportunity for wealth and success.

The Marriage of Bapa and Ma

Sometime after Bapa arrived in Jinja, he reunited with Nanima and Nanabapa, and their three daughters, his old neighbours from Madhapur. At the time, they still lived in Bujuta. When Ma was seventeen, Bapa was smart enough to begin courting her, and they married in 1937. Bandali Jaffer, Nanabapa's plantation boss, served as matchmaker. I know nothing of the details of their wedding or even if they indulged in a honeymoon. They possessed little money at the time, so they likely partook of a small wedding at the Jamatkhana in the presence of family and a few close friends. Bapa couldn't afford a fancy ring but, until the day she died, Ma wore the small, inexpensive wedding band with which he had honoured her, and which symbolized her marriage vows.

Ma and Bapa in their 70's

The Copious Offspring

Bapa and Ma "got busy" right away, and Ma gave birth to seven children, the first six within a ten-year span. Bearing so many children was not a religious issue. It was simply traditional. Fortunately for me, a lack of birth control may have been a contributing factor.

Their first beloved child, my eldest sister, Khatun, arrived in 1938. Her name comes from the Arabic language, and means "lady" or "noble woman." My sister, Rashida, whose name in Arabic means "rightly guided," arrived in 1940. My older brother, Bahadur, made his entrance in 1942. The origin of his name is Persian, and means "courageous, bold, brave." My sister, Zebunissa (Zebby), was born in 1945, and her name translates to "beautiful woman." My sister, Almas, was born in 1947, and her name, from the Arabic word for "diamond," has special significance as the Diamond Jubilee of Aga Khan III occurred in 1946. Ma gave birth to my brother, Nizar, in 1948. His name in Arabic means "glance" or someone of small stature, which leads me to believe that he was a tiny baby.

Unbearable heartbreak struck my family in 1954. Khatun contracted leukemia, and died two years later. Her death devastated Bapa, and I can only imagine what it did to Ma. Khatun's tragic death occurred shortly after my birth on January 11, 1956. My name is another form of "Nazneen," and I believe it means "sensitive." Ma used to say she had me because she was bored. Given that I was an afterthought, and a late arrival into the family circle, I received immense love from my parents, and extraordinary spoiling from my siblings. At the same time, though, I was much younger than my brothers and sisters, and, in some respects, like an only child.

I was always underfoot, and thrived on the attention everyone paid me but I was mostly a "daddy's girl." As a small child, my favourite pastime in the whole world was to chat with Bapa each evening before dinner while he sat in his favourite tan leather armchair, and sipped his drink. In retrospect, I did most of the chatting, and he the listening.

Jinja was the birthplace of all us children. The midwife who delivered each one of us was Maisey de Souza, whom we called "Auntie Maisey". She was a Catholic Christian from Goa, India and was a dear family friend. She worked at the Jinja Hospital, and assisted with the births of all my brothers and sisters and me.

My Formidable Bapa

Bapa was a handsome man who stood about 1.82 metres. My brother, Bahadur, resembles him. His eyes were golden brown, and he had thick, iron grey hair. Everyone in our family went grey prematurely, including me at the untimely age of seventeen. Thank heavens for my sister, Almas, who has dyed my hair for me ever since.

Bapa was a stickler for clothing, and a dapper dresser. In Africa, he always wore dress pants and long sleeved white shirts stitched by Indian tailors. The extent of his casual wear was to roll up his sleeves to combat the heat of the day. Even in retirement, he always dressed well, usually wearing a three piece suit. He was immaculate in all his personal habits. For example, he kept an impressive collection of classic gold and silver Parker fountain pens, and wrote with nothing but them.

He smoked Benson and Hedges 555 like a trooper, and drank Johnny Walker Black Label Scotch and Dimple Whiskey. When he came home at lunch, he imbibed two fingers of Johnny Walker, and, later in the evening, four fingers. He never drank outside our house, even when he was entertaining businessmen at a club.

Bapa suffered from diabetes from the time he was in his late thirties. Until his last years, he was rigid about controlling it with oral medication. Because he often travelled to Stuttgart on business, he consulted with physicians in Germany concerning his condition.

He was his own person, and did what he wanted to do. He was born and baptized into the Ismaili faith but did not attend the Jamatkhana or observe religious rituals. My guess is that he did not like the politics of religion. Aga Khan III appointed Bapa to the local council of the Jamatkhana in 1957 but he resigned straightaway. However, he was never overbearing about his views, and did not object to Ma raising us children as devout Ismailis.

Bapa was rigidly principled and pretty blunt. I like to think I take after him in that regard. He was a man of considerable gravitas but was able to enjoy a good laugh. He sometimes unleashed a volcanic temper, and didn't suffer fools gladly. On many occasions, I heard him raise his voice in anger to one of his workers. They were not technically savvy, and seemed to have little desire to learn. Bapa became exasperated because of the need to teach them the same tasks over and over again.

On the other hand, he was particularly good to his workers, most of whom were from Kenya. As well as paying them decent wages, he housed and fed many of them. Some actually lived in his industry compound. Overall, he was much kinder to his employees than most other British and Indian employers.

Generosity was ingrained in Bapa's nature. From organized charities to ordinary people, he gave help to everyone who needed it; and, even though he did not attend the Jamatkhana, he donated liberally to various causes.

Despite his temper, Bapa was generally patient but implacable with us children. He never raised a finger to us but he could quell us with a withering look – "don't test me." His worst but still endearing habit was that he repeated himself all the time, inculcating in us children the same advice over and over and over again. And, once an idea lodged itself in his brain, an atomic blast could not have dislodged it. After my brother, Bahadur, broke off his front teeth attempting to ride his bicycle straight up a coconut tree, Bapa decided bicycles were inherently dangerous. As a result, he refused to allow any of us children to ride a bike ever again.

Ma the Mother Hen

Ma was short, plump, sturdy, and dependable. Her countenance was serene but often gave way to an infectiously cheerful smile. She was a quiet woman, at heart a mother hen. She harboured no aspirations to learn, to accomplish anything outside the house, or even to travel. She simply wanted to look after her home and her family. On that front, she was a "doer." She wanted to do everything for everybody all the time.

She was fiercely protective of her husband and her brood. By example, she let us know that we were "family," and that we must all stick together, no matter what. And, to this day, that is what we have done.

Her chief weapon was food. She felt it her divine mission to feed everybody. In Africa, many people employed cooks but Ma never did. She cooked everything herself—breakfast, lunch, high tea, and dinner.

She was a master of the "mother's look," and could squelch us children with a well-aimed glare. She also possessed some of the more unattractive universal traits of motherhood. She was too cloying, always reminding me to do this but don't do that, and always to be careful. When I was visiting my friends, she would call two or three times, during the course of my visit, to check up on me. Like all children, I desperately wanted independence. But, in hindsight, some of Ma's over-protectiveness surely stemmed from the fragile social and political environment in which we lived. In retrospect, I'm not certain, in that place, at that time, I would even have let a child of mine out of the house.

Her one extravagance was her passion for fine clothes and elegant jewellery. She was quite the clothes horse. She was an inspired seamstress, and sometimes sewed personal garments from her own designs and patterns, which she cut from newspaper. She took special pleasure in making elaborate cotton slips, with eyelet and lace, for herself and her sister, Mariam.

When Ma was at the Jamatkhana or out socially, she favoured *sarees* (garments worn primarily by Indian women) of chiffon or silk, in muted colours, but at home she wore cotton shirtwaist dresses. She never used a veil but she covered her head with her saree when attending prayers at the Jamatkhana.

Ma owned many pieces of splendid jewellery. Her own mother had passed some pieces to her, and Bapa encouraged her to buy whatever she fancied. She acquired most of her jewellery from the Jogia family of jewellers who owned a shop in Jinja. Her favourite pieces were ornate gold, silver, and diamond filigreed bracelets, necklaces, and earrings but she was always selective and tasteful in her choices. I absorbed many lessons in style by observing her.

The Parental Tag Team

The relationship between my parents was traditional. Each of them centred the family in their own way. Bapa was the provider. Because he came from nothing, he wanted to give his children everything. But, he was wise enough to let us forge our own identities, and not influence us too much. For both my parents, we children were the main focus of their lives. We always dined together. Communication in our home was open, and usually non-judgmental.

It was a testament to Bapa and Ma that, despite their backgrounds, they were forward thinkers. They never arranged marriages, they did not rush any of us children into marriage, and they never pressured Nizar, Almas, or me, even though the three of us remained single.

Both my parents were kind, empathetic, decent, and honest, and they instilled those values in my siblings and me by example.

CHAPTER FOUR

Bapa's Business Ventures and Other Pursuits

The Eastern Province Bus Company

Bapa was the quintessential self-made man. He was virtually illiterate when he arrived in Jinja. He could not speak, read, or write either English or Swahili. He had received little, if any, formal education, and he had not a shilling to his name. Yet, despite these handicaps, he possessed sufficient entrepreneurial fortitude, vision, confidence, and "smarts" to build two thriving businesses from the ground up. To aid him, he had a secret weapon on the home front. I have no doubt that Ma's unwavering support and practical assistance were critical to Bapa's business accomplishments.

Indians in Uganda had little choice but to try to make a go of it in the business sector. They found it difficult to acquire landholdings, they had virtually no political voice, and the British excluded them from many opportunities for advancement at which they might otherwise have excelled.

"Transportation" was the venture in which Bapa foresaw a prospect for success. He started by driving a taxi as an employee. He worked like a son of a gun, and saved his fares. As soon as he could, he bought his own cab, and started a mini-taxi business.

His business soon grew to include three taxis, and he pictured himself on the way to economic independence. Unfortunately, the Second World War put a spoke in the wheel of his grand design. As a result of the wartime petrol shortage, the British banned the provision of petrol to independent operators like Bapa, and required them to pool their resources into a single company. As a result, Bapa was instrumental in convincing the other taxi owners in Jinja to join with him to form the "Eastern Province Bus Company."

At its inception, the bus company, ironically, did not own any buses. The owners utilized imported second-hand British cabs. In time, the company made enough money from the taxi business to buy chassis for buses from the British. They then assembled the buses in Jinja at a four hectare compound owned by the company. As time went by, they acquired between fifty and one hundred buses in this manner. The buses ran in the eastern region of Uganda from Jinja to Mbale. The passengers were mainly Africans who had no other mode of transportation. Each trip cost a few shillings.

The Eastern Province Bus Company's founding members were Bapa, Mohamed Manek, Rajabali Rashid, Hassanali Rashid, and other small shareholders. Bapa, who owned 12% of the shares, was the largest shareholder. Because none of the owners could speak or write English, which was essential in dealing with the British who ran the country, they brought in H.K. Jaffer and Ebrahim Mitha. Neither of these gentlemen owned taxis but they both spoke, read, and wrote English. Ebrahim Mitha's secondary role was to look after the interests of the Ismaili shareholders, and he brought along his brother, Mohamed Mitha, to assist him. H.K. Jaffer, with the help of Mohamed Manek, was to safeguard the interests of the *Ithnasheri* shareholders, Ithnasheris being the largest branch of Shi'a Islam.

Unhappily, the shareholders were never able to form a cohesive business unit, or to agree upon an equitable division of duties. Bapa, for example, was the only mechanic in the group. He wore himself into the ground trying to maintain the creaky and dilapidated buses, some of which were not running at all.

By 1947, Bapa was so discouraged that he ended his active participation in the bus company business, and started a new enterprise manufacturing soft drinks. However, fate intervened in the person of Aga Khan III who was visiting Kampala during his Diamond Jubilee year.

The company shareholders all travelled to Kampala, and met with the Aga Khan to discuss their problems. The Aga Khan was vociferously in favour of encouraging and assisting the growth of small businesses in the Ismaili community, and took a hands-on interest in such matters. Thus, the Imam quizzed Bapa, in considerable detail, about the bus company operations. Bapa recounted the numerous travails they were facing, and confessed that he was ready to give up on the company. He mentioned to the Aga Khan that he had started up a small soda manufacturing and distribution business, and was anxious to concentrate all his attention on its growth.

The Aga Khan was immensely supportive of Bapa, and assured him that he would be successful at whatever he did. The Aga Khan then asked Bapa to stick it out with the bus company for two more years after which, to reward his loyal service, the Aga Khan would accord Bapa of the signal privilege of including the word "Jubilee" in the title of his soda company.

Bapa heeded the Aga Khan's request, and continued his participation in the day-to-day management of the company for another two years. After that, although he remained a shareholder and director and continued to receive dividends, he diverted his energies full-time to his soda pop business.

Over the next several years, some severe problems that led to the demise of the bus company surfaced. Among other things, Bapa's departure left no competent mechanic to service the buses. At one time, the value of the bus company was 36,000,000 shillings. However, in 1969, it fell off the precipice into bankruptcy. Bapa lost somewhere in the region of 5,000,000 shillings.

Although this loss put a significant crimp in Bapa's financial armoury, he was able to survive because of the phenomenal success of his carbon dioxide and soft drink businesses.

Jubilee Ice & Soda Works

Bapa was an exceptionally hard worker, labouring seven days a week, to make a go of his business ventures. In the late 1940s, using his salary and dividends from the bus company, Bapa began to manufacture his own soft drink formula. At the time, no major soft drink brands existed in Uganda although three local Indian manufacturers were in production. The kitchen in Ma and Bapa's home on Iganga Road doubled as a make-shift factory.

Each day, Ma prepared the soda mixture, and Bapa stayed up late at night to bottle it. They started by producing twenty-five to thirty crates per day. After a time, he rented a small warehouse across the street from their home, and began to produce the soft drink in increasing volumes.

Eventually, Bapa needed another pair of hands so Nanabapa and Nanima moved from Bujuta to Jinja to live with my parents. Nanabapa worked for Bapa, selling the soft drinks in town. Regrettably, after several years, Bapa and Nanabapa had a falling-out, and Nanabapa retired from the business. He and Nanima moved to a rental house near Jinja's Main Street.

G.S. Karim, an Ismaili, was a partner in N.P. Patel & Co., which owned several commercial enterprises including the Pontiac Auto Dealership in Jinja. Mr. Karim lent 1,000,000 shillings to Bapa to pay out Nanabapa for his efforts in promoting the soda pop. Neither Bapa nor Nanabapa ever spoke of the reason for their quarrel. As time passed, they were unfailingly polite to one another but never reconciled.

Bapa repaid the loan to Mr. Karim, and, several years later, lent him some money in order to return the earlier favour. Mr. Karim declared bankruptcy, and was unable to repay Bapa. This loss put another critical dent in Bapa's finances but, again, he managed to survive.

As demand for the soft drink increased, Bapa realized that he needed to build a modern manufacturing and bottling plant. With continuing dividends from the bus company and profits from the sale of the soft drink, he was able to do so.

Having fulfilled his promise to Aga Khan III regarding his commitment to the bus company, Bapa was thrilled when he was able to formally name his company "Jubilee Ice & Soda Works." His soft drink, which he named *Portello*, was a carbonated grape drink.

Jubilee's Portello soft drink bottles

Portello became the most popular drink in the Busoga District, especially among Africans who found it more refreshing than other drinks on the market. Because everyone knew and liked Bapa, it was a huge seller, plus it tasted delicious. It was also cheaper than other sodas as Bapa did not have to pay royalties. Pepsi and Coca-Cola had introduced their drinks to Uganda but, eventually, I believe that in the Busoga District, the sales of Portello equalled the total sales of Pepsi and Coke combined.

Jubilee Ice & Soda Works owned about a dozen Ford lorries. Bapa employed African drivers to distribute the Portello. The men, who wore company uniforms, were generally long-time employees. Bapa treated them well, and they were good, trustworthy workers.

They drove the lorries on set routes, and delivered Portello to dukas in small towns and villages. The dukas were everywhere but the larger distributors apparently did not want to bother with them.

In due course, several companies began to produce soft drinks. All of them imported the necessary carbon dioxide from Nairobi, Kenya. As a business strategy to force Jubilee out of competition, two of the largest producers convinced the Nairobi manufacturer to stop supplying Bapa and the other local companies with carbon dioxide gas. In response, in 1956, Bapa built his own plant in Jinja to manufacture the gas. It stood cheek by jowl with the soft drink plant. He bought equipment for the plant from a supplier in Stuttgart, Germany. By 1957, Jubilee Ice & Soda Works was manufacturing enough carbon dioxide gas to supply the rest of the bottling plants not just in Uganda but also in Tanganyika, Burundi, and the Congo.

Jubilee Ice & Soda Works Carbon Dioxide Plant

Jubilee Ice & Soda Works Bottling Plant

Opening of carbon dioxide plant (1956)

Opening of carbon dioxide plant (1956)
(L-R) District Governor's Wife, District Governor, Ma, Bapa, H.K. Jaffer

Opening of carbon dioxide plant (1956)

The Madhvanis were a hugely successful and influential Hindu family in Uganda. Muljibhai Prabhudas Madhvani, the founder, had thirteen children. Three of the brothers who figure in my family's story were Jayant, Manubhai, and Suru. My brother, Bahadur, and Suru were close friends.

Because of Suru's friendship with Bahadur, Jayant Madhvani convinced the President of Uganda to ban the importation of carbon dioxide as the country now had its own plant.

The President concurred, and halted the importation of Kenyan carbon dioxide. As a result, the soda pop producers had no choice but to purchase the product from Bapa. In addition, the ban resulted in Jubilee supplying the gas to all the breweries and fire extinguisher companies as well as to the Coca-Cola and Pepsi-Cola plants. The sale of Portello was always profitable but the carbon dioxide monopoly proved to be a gold mine.

Help was available from other quarters, too. Abdul Rehman (Manni) Khan, a close friend of Bahadur's, was in charge of purchasing supplies for all the army barracks in Uganda. He made sure to order Portello, thus jacking up Bapa's sales volumes significantly.

As an example of the road blocks Bapa had to overcome by virtue of his lack of education, until Bahadur returned from his studies in England, Bapa never knew he could borrow money from a bank.

When Bahadur arrived home, he was eighteen years old, and a keen cricket player. Through cricket, he got to know several Brits including Mr. Phillips, the Barclay's Bank Manager in Jinja. This connection gave Bahadur the "in" he needed to secure a 50,000 shilling overdraft facility for Jubilee. Through cricket playing, Bahadur also got to know the Pepsi people, and they gave Bahadur the exclusive distribution rights for Pepsi in the Eastern Provinces.

As Bapa's sales continued to increase in the early 1970s, he began modification to the existing plant to manufacture carbon dioxide by using crude oil. Until then, he had utilized diesel for the chemical production of carbon dioxide. At the time, the cost of diesel was almost double that of crude oil so he anticipated that the change in production would enhance profits significantly. Bapa ordered the necessary equipment from Stuttgart, and was awaiting its arrival in mid-1972.

Bapa's Other Pursuits

Truth be told, Bapa had virtually no other pursuits. He did little except work. His one indulgence was to treat himself to a new automobile each year. Like most men, he had an eye for a good vehicle. The apple of his eye, though, was a swanky 1953 green four-door Pontiac Chieftain that he bought new from the Pontiac Dealership in Jinja. The car featured an eight cylinder engine, heavily chromed grill work trim, a chrome silver streak running along each side, and two parallel lines of three-piece chrome running from the grill to the windshield, and continuing at the back over the trunk. Another highlight was the iconic Chieftain hood ornament. Bapa kept the car for all the years we lived in Jinja, and it was his proverbial pride and joy.

CHAPTER FIVE

My Home Stamping Grounds

Lake Victoria and the River Nile

Lake Victoria, adjacent to Jinja, is the source of the River Nile—its royal crown. The lake is one of the world's most magnificent wonders. As I have mentioned, it is the largest body of fresh water in Africa; and, it is the largest tropical lake on the face of the earth. It comprises almost 70,000 square kilometres.

When we lived in Jinja, the lake's water was like a living creature. It changed colour from turquoise to midnight blue to azure according to the time of day and the weather. Glorious sunrises and sunsets glistened off the water in shades of brilliant cream, orange, and red. Mornings over the lake were usually cloudy but, during the day, the sky cleared to a seamless blue.

A myriad of emerald and jade islands dotted Lake Victoria, and long narrow peninsulas penetrated from the shore. Coarse wetlands of green and brown papyrus swamps dominated the shorelines of both the lake and river. Small dilapidated fishing villages rimmed the edge of the lake. African fishermen eked out a marginal existence plying the water in precarious craft, fishing for tilapia and perch to sell at the town market.

The vegetation in the vicinity of the lake and river was varied and lush. The landscape overflowed with flowering bottlebrush, mango, papaya, plantain, acacia, mahogany, avocado, and elgin teak trees.

The abundance of foliage provided an incredibly rich habitat for a remarkable assortment of birds, reptiles, and mammals. One of my favourite sights was that of a small, furry mongoose riding on the back of a warthog while combing out parasites from the warthog's skin. Animals such as giraffes, elephants, and wildebeests did not inhabit the area around Jinja because urbanization had driven them away.

The papyrus swamps were an ideal home for the darling sitatunga antelope or marsh buck. Standing about 1.5 metres at the shoulder, the sitatunga are brown with white stripes on their bodies and white stains on their faces. They rely on their excellent swimming ability to escape predators.

Occasionally, my friends and I were fortunate enough to catch glimpses of papyrus canaries, white-winged warblers, red-chested sun-birds, and brown-throated weavers that sheltered in the wetlands.

For sheer magnificence, though, you couldn't beat the great crested crane, the national bird of Uganda, which appears on both the Ugandan national flag and coat of arms. The front of its face and its stiff, gawky legs are black. The sides of its face and wings are mainly white, the body plumage and beak grey, the eyes a piercing blue, and the tail feathers a rich reddish brown. A crimson wattle sac adorns its throat, and a splendid spray of rigid golden feathers crowns its head. Another feature setting it apart from lesser cranes is its resounding, honking voice which could be quite startling if you weren't expecting to hear it.

The Great Crested Crane

The lake and river wetlands were a haven for my personal favourite—the shoebill stork. It stands 1.5 metres tall, and looks scarily primeval. Its body is a mottled grey, its wing span gigantic, and its beak, shaped like a giant shoe but hooked on the end, a pallid orange. The shoebill is elusive, and its craftiness enables it to snare fish, frogs, snakes, and even small crocodiles with its beak.

Although catching sight of the diverse wildlife that inhabited the lake and river and their environs was always a treat, we did so from the safety of the town's streets, the Jinja pier, or the public park. Our parents never allowed us to venture to the lakeshore or river bank, both of which were fraught with natural perils.

Hippopotami and crocodiles hung about in the water and papyrus reeds. Water snakes, cobras, and black mambas, one of the world's most venomous snakes, lurked in the water and nearby vegetation. Some snakes camouflaged themselves by twisting their sinuous bodies around the thick branches of mango and other trees.

The Bujagali Falls, below Lake Victoria, near our home, were raging and treacherous. An immense volume of water surged and tumbled continuously over a series of large but low rapids.

My Home Town of Jinja

My memories of Jinja are precious to me. Endless waves of tea, sugar cane, and cotton plantations rippled across the countryside around Jinja. Low hills, garbed perpetually in orange, red, and yellow tropical flowers, rimmed the town.

The road leading into Jinja was a dual carriageway that crossed over the top of Owen Falls Dam. Completion of this massive hydroelectric dam occurred in 1954, a couple of years before my birth. One rather sad side effect of its construction was the submersion of Ripon Falls and their memorable flat rocks.

Owen Falls Dam (1993)

Overstating the dam's importance to Jinja would be impossible. It fuelled the industrial growth of the town, and provided its inhabitants with potable water and a constant electrical supply. In addition, it supplied electricity to other areas of Uganda and portions of Kenya.

Driving over the dam will remain etched in my mind always. Looking down afforded us a dramatic view of the River Nile as the noise from the turbines vibrated in our ears, and it served as an impressive entrance to the town. The dam lent considerable prestige to our backwater village as Queen Elizabeth II attended its grand opening. She actually stayed in Jinja at the Ripon Falls Hotel, the scene of many of our family gatherings.

Macadam topped the wide avenues of Jinja. Traffic lights were non-existent but, in the British tradition, we did suffer from ubiquitous round-abouts. Every morning, Africans, in their two-wheeled vehicles, crowded the roads leading into town as they wobbled their way to market bearing the fruit, vegetables, livestock, and chattels they planned to offer for sale.

Main Street, a broad, friendly and vibrant avenue, constituted the central core of the town. A meridian planted with bushes ran down the middle of the street. The town itself was fashioned as a grid. The grid encompassed a considerable area, and included a pulsating industrial sector where I often visited Bapa at his factory. The residential neighbourhoods were quiet and charming. Spacious and well-tended homes afforded panoramic views over Lake Victoria. The hotels sat in the residential areas rather than in the bustling town centre.

Jinja Main Street (1993)

The architecture of the residences, churches, schools, industrial buildings, commercial shops, and government offices embraced an enchanting and haphazard mix of art deco, colonial, Indian, and African styles. To counter the heat, builders used concrete in the construction of older buildings, and brick in the construction of the newer ones.

Notable buildings included the colonial Ripon Falls Hotel complete with an orchestral stage; the Crested Crane Hotel; the governor's residence on Circular Road; St. Andrew's church; two Hindu temples; the town hall; the post office adorned with the town clock; the low, sprawling, cream administrative offices of Jinja District, with long outdoor covered verandas supported by cream columns topped by a cheerful red tile roof; the Bank of Uganda; the Central Police Station; Nile Breweries; and, of course, Bapa's soft drink and carbon dioxide manufacturing facilities.

Ripon Falls Hotel (1993)

Jinja Town Hall (1993)

Jinja Post Office (1993)

The town's architecture reflected our mixed population of British, Muslims, Sikhs, Hindus, Chinese, Koreans, and indigenous Africans. By and large, the expatriate Brits constituted the professional and administrative classes. They ran the schools and hospitals. The Indians comprised the commercial class, and had made some forays into the professional sector. The Chinese and Koreans worked the mines and large construction projects. Africans toiled in the factories, and laboured as servants to the British and Indians.

In the 1960s, Uganda was a model for higher education, and Africans were beginning to take advantage of the educational opportunities. Some of them became professionals. They joined the teaching ranks in increasing numbers, and most of the nurses at the hospital were black. One of my teachers was black, and she was an excellent instructor.

During the 1950s and 1960s, segregation was still the order of the day, and neighbourhoods tended to consist of separate enclaves of British (Africans referred to white people as *Wazungu*), Indians, or Africans. From our Indian perspective, we found the Brits rather snobby, and perceived that they tolerated rather than liked us. In retrospect, I'm sure that the Africans felt exactly the same way about us Indians.

The British expatriates formed several clubs—the Jinja Club, Sailing Club, Nile Rugby Club, and Nile Football Club—and did their best to bar Indians and Africans from them. After Uganda achieved independence, the British, to avoid the appearance of discrimination, ostensibly opened their club doors to Indians and Africans but not many succeeded in joining the club ranks.

Although my brother, Bahadur, and his friend, Dolar Kotecha, were not really interested in joining the Jinja Club, they mischievously decided to test the new "open door" policy, and applied for membership. The Club's ten member board discussed applications, and cast their votes by throwing balls on the table. Ten white balls signalled acceptance but even one black ball signified, well, blackballing.

Not surprisingly, Bahadur and Dolar didn't make the grade. Just to stir things up a bit, they retained a lawyer, who threatened to sue the Club unless it had a good reason for barring the boys. The Club's rationale, that the boys didn't know enough white people, was not a sufficient ground for refusing entry. After some legal posturing, the Club caved and admitted them. The boys promptly paid the fees and became members. They didn't socialize with the whites at the Club but they were avid golfers so they took advantage of the perfectly maintained golf course with its magnificent views of both Lake Victoria and the River Nile. One famous but quirky rule at the course permitted a free drop of any golf ball that landed in the foot print of a hippopotamus.

A number of workers from Great Britain had migrated to Jinja to help construct the Owen Falls Dam. The British built the Amber Court Club for their recreation. After completion of the dam, the workers drifted away, and the Indians took over the Club. Because the British attitude about their own clubs ticked off the Indians, they did not encourage Brits to join Amber Court. However, some of the English people in Jinja made concerted efforts to integrate, and they were most welcome. This Club was where I spent a lot of time during my childhood.

The Indians were not lily white either when it came to segregation. Neither the British nor the Indians were keen about allowing Africans to join their clubs. Not wanting to seem discriminatory, they didn't bar Africans but were secure in the knowledge that few of them could afford the entrance fees.

Far more interesting than the petty prejudices that diminished the stature of the people of Jinja was the avian influx that routinely spilled out from the swampy wetlands of Lake Victoria and the River Nile into the trees and streets of the town. The trees were usually brim full of black headed weaver birds. Their heads were black, and their bodies chestnut blending into yellow. Their name came from the complex nests they wove. The nests were oval, and dangled from trees throughout the town. Oftentimes, weavers would heavily laden one branch with several nests. That was quite the sight.

We children found the weaver birds and their fancy nests enchanting but we were wary of the ominous marabou storks. These huge birds can reach a height of 1.5 metres, a weight of about nine kilograms, and a wing span of 3.5 metres. They are scrawny and scraggly with bald reddish-pink heads, gaunt necks, gigantic bills, black plumage on their backs and wings and white on their breasts, skinny black legs, and long pink gular pouches drooping from their throats.

Like vultures, the marabous are scavengers. Also like vultures, the evolutionary process has endowed them with bald heads so they can keep relatively clean when they dive inside corpses to eat. Their gular sacs are expandable in order to store prey until they wish to devour it. The marabous roamed everywhere in Jinja. They perched on tree branches and lamp standards. They meandered through the streets, around the pier, and on the grounds of the Amber Court Club. We gave them a wide berth. When I was a small child, a marabou who ventured too close would send me screaming into Ma's arms.

My siblings and I disliked the sometimes threatening political climate of Uganda, and the constant undercurrent of animosity from the Africans was at times unnerving. However, we loved the simple, low-key lifestyle of Jinja, uninterrupted by so many of the distractions of western society, and we thrived on our close relationships with family and friends.

CHAPTER SIX

My Kith and Kin

Nanima and Nanabapa

Nanabapa was a tall, slim man who favoured white loose cotton pants and white shirts. He never left his house without donning a black fez. Nanabapa was surpassingly kind, decent to his core, and incapable of harming a soul. I never knew his mother, Fatmabai, who was my great-grandmother, but my older siblings remember her as a tall lady. Apparently, she went to bed one night, and simply never woke up.

After years of toiling as a labourer in Bujuta, Nanabapa was content to finish out his working days selling Portello. Bapa was generous in paying commissions to him. He was able to use those commissions along with the compensation Bapa paid him, after their falling out, to buy a commercial and residential building in Jinja on Nizam Road near the *sokoni* (Swahili for "open air market"). The rent he received from the shops and premises in the building were sufficient to support him and Nanima. Because it was in the centre of town, they continued to live in the house they had rented when they moved out of my parents' home. They were able to walk to Main Street and the Jamatkhana, and friends who lived close by could drop in to visit them.

Nanima habitually wore long, colourful cotton dresses and *pacheris* (scarves). If she was shopping at the market or visiting someone whom she respected, she wrapped the pacheri around her face but, otherwise, preferred to let it flow loosely.

Nanima was a prototypical grandmother, and we all adored her. She was calm, quiet, and gentle but possessed a droll sense of humour. She was a dab hand at cooking. We children found every excuse to eat at her home. We'll forever remember her fruit pudding, concocted from a mixture of mangos, papaya, passion fruit, and custard. No one could make it like she could.

Nanima was famous for her homespun sayings. If a downpour cast doubt on an impending sports day at school, she would say, "go and tie knots in the grass and it will stop raining," and I swear that it did! When the sun blazed from the sky after one of those downpours, she would pronounce that "the lion had just had a baby."

Nanabapa and Nanima worried constantly about the poverty that mired their daughter, Mariam, and her seven children. They helped financially to the extent they could. My aunt's fourth child, Azmina, was the apple of their eye. When she was five or six years old, they brought her to live with them. She was a brilliant girl, and they saw to her education.

Nanabapa always kept a box at home stocked with pitch black chewing gum called "Black Cat." It tasted like liquorice, and my cousins and I loved it. We could blow awesome bubbles, and usually ended up with black gum sticking to our faces and hair. He cemented his reputation as our favourite grandfather, albeit our only one, by sometimes taking us to the home of a woman who manufactured candy floss from a machine in her back yard.

Religion was the mainstay of my grandparents' lives. They were rigorously observant, and attended the Jamatkhana regularly. Although unusual in our culture, Nanabapa and Nanima were ferociously independent, and were never a burden to anyone.

Nanabapa and Nanima suffered a terrible tragedy when their daughter, Malek, died. She was only about thirty years old when she suddenly began vomiting blood. Her parents rushed her to the hospital. My sister, Rashida, remembers visiting Malek in the hospital just a day or so before she expired from an undiagnosed illness. She is buried in Bombo, a small town thirty two kilometres north of Kampala.

In 1962, Nanabapa suffered a paralyzing stroke. Nanima devoted herself to caring for him until his death. They both died in their own home, Nanabapa in 1965, and Nanima, after a mercifully brief illness, in 1967.

They were super grandparents. I don't know whether or not their parents subjected them to an arranged marriage but I do know that they loved one another, and their children and grandchildren, with all their hearts. They were simply good people.

Nanabapa and Nanima

Mariam Masi and her Children

Nanabapa and Nanima's daughter, Mariam, our *Masi* (aunt from mother's side), married Noorali Karim. In the early years of their marriage, they lived some distance from Jinja where Noorali *Masa* (uncle) owned a small store. Their habitation was quite primitive. They drank well water, and used kerosene lamps because they lacked electricity. We used to visit them but I was so young, I was still drinking milk from a soother bottle, and don't remember the trips. Almas, though, doted on Mariam Masi, and has fond memories of our visits. All of Mariam Masi's seven children were born in Uganda. Their names were Yasmin, Iqubal, Mehboob, Azmina, Karim, Shelah, and Shenin.

My aunt was too proud to accept financial aid but she made do as best she could, and she was quite ingenious. For instance, she could not afford baby bottles so she attached nipples to Portello soda bottles.

Masi and Masa eventually moved to Jinja where he became the proprietor of a duka near the market, and sold basic goods and sundries to the Africans. Masa died when their children were very young. After his death, the older children kept the duka running but barely made a subsidence living.

Mariam Masi and her children lived in the middle of town in a tiny abode, constructed of corrugated iron, adjacent to a walled-in courtyard. Despite being poor, my aunt's home was always spotless, and her children scrubbed and clean. Often, on Saturday mornings, Bapa dropped me off at Mariam Masi's place on his way to work. Before I left home, Ma gave me one shilling, which bought a lot of candy, to spend on my cousins. Once Bapa and I were in the car, he habitually slipped me a few more shillings so that I could also buy treats for my cousins and their cousins who lived next door to them.

I sometimes arrived at their dwelling bearing a fresh loaf of bread Ma had acquired from the town bakery. Mariam Masi toasted the bread on her *sagri* (a small coal burning stove). We enjoyed the toast by dipping it in *masala chai* (spiced tea).

My cousins and I played in their courtyard, and their cousins often joined us. I always brought any new toys and board games I'd acquired during the previous week.

Other Kin

On Bapa's side of the family, I knew only a few of my relations as most of them lived in Tanzania. Khursa, Gulbanu, Mariam, and Ahmed were the children of Bapa's oldest brother, Ali Rahemtulla. Ali died young but his wife, Bhachibai, was excellent about keeping in touch with us. The youngsters were the same age as my older siblings, and they often visited us in Jinja. I also had the privilege of knowing Bapa's sister, Sajabai, who visited us annually from Tanzania.

Bapa's nephew, Ramzan, and his wife, Gulbanu, lived in Nairobi, Kenya. Ramzan was the son of Bapa's brother, Karmali. Although he was my first cousin, he was much older than I, and I called him Ramzanbha. "Bha" was a term of respect for an elder. He and his wife were warm and welcoming people, and I sometimes spent school holidays at their home. Their younger son, Arif, and I were the same age, and we often played together. One occasion printed indelibly in my childhood memory bank was taking a bus to Nairobi's city centre with Arif to see *Chitty Chitty Bang Bang* at the big city movie theatre. What I remember most about Nairobi were endless rows of eucalyptus trees that lined the dusty roads. Ramzanbha and Gulbanu also had a daughter, Nargis, and an older son, Amir. Amir died in a car crash on a rough patch of road between Nairobi and Mombasa when he was just a teenager. Amir's death broke his mother's heart.

Mary was a cousin of mine, a few times removed, on Ma's side. Mary and her three siblings suffered the grotesque loss of their mom at a young age. She was electrocuted while hanging laundry. Her sister-in-law tried to save her but died as well. Mary's father, Kamrudin Mohamed, subsequently married Khursa, Bapa's niece. Kamrudin (we called him *Mama* meaning uncle from mother's side of the family) was a sawmill magnate, and they lived in a mansion in Kampala where we frequently visited them.

As most of my parents' families emigrated from India to Africa, we had no contact with more distant relatives who stayed in the Gujarat. Finding any of them now would likely be close to impossible. On the other hand, given the oral traditions and tangled relationships of rural villages everywhere, I bet I could stand in the centre of Madhapur, hold up a sign, and some of my second or third cousins would appear to claim kinship. I might do that one day, just for fun.

Friends and Neighbours

My best friends growing up in Jinja were all about my age. We had known one another since we were toddlers, and we attended elementary school and played at the club together. Even though security was always tight, and our parents ever watchful, we managed to see each other a lot.

Maira Butt was my closest friend. Her family originated in the State of Kashmir in northern India. Because of an influx of Caucasians into that region thousands of years ago, the Kashmiri people tend to be fair-skinned, and Maira was no exception. Maira's father was a handsome Muslim man by the name of Anwar Butt. He was a mechanic who owned a large garage in Jinja. Anwar always possessed a souped-up car, and raced in the annual East African Safari Rally.

While Bapa had forbidden us to ride bicycles, I conned Maira into teaching me how to ride her brother's bike on her driveway which inclined downward toward their house. Her father roared into the drive-way in one of his fancy cars, and startled me. I crashed and took a flyer over the rose bushes but escaped with only scrapes and injured dignity. Maira thought it was hilarious.

Maira lived across the street from me, and Tazmina Pradhan, another friend, lived next door. I used to nip over the fence to Tazmina's house, and Maira would join us. Our favourite pastime was to swing while belting out the hits of Engelbert Humperdinck, Elvis Presley, and Tom Jones, at the top of our lungs, with no regard whatsoever for musicality.

Music was our mainstay, and my friends and I almost wore out our vinyl records. We could mimic every lyric—from Elvis Presley's *Jailhouse Rock* to Simon and Garfunkel's *Sound of Silence*. When the Beatles' *Ob-La-Di, Ob-La-Da* hit the charts, we gyrated crazily to our interpreta-tion of the *Watusi,* a popular solo dance during the 1960s.

Nasreen Adatia's parents were family friends. Her dad, Yusuf, was the architect who designed our house at 7 Nalufenya Road. In 1967, I flew to Kisumu, Kenya with Nasreen and her two sisters to visit their grand-parents who owned the Coca-Cola franchise there. Our flight took off from a tiny airstrip near my home. As our fathers watched, in horror, a descending aeroplane missed our small de Havilland prop plane by mere centimetres. Luckily, we girls were oblivious to the near tragedy.

Nasreen, Maira and Nazlin (1969)

Fatima Velji lived across the road from Nasreen. I considered Fatima my intellectual friend, perhaps because she was left-handed. I lost touch with Fatima for many years until an astounding coincidence brought us together again.

Shenaz Khimji and I were distant cousins. Some of Bapa's relatives, including Shenaz's family, were Ithnasheri. We were both the youngest children of aging parents, and we were inseparable in our younger years. Shenaz's mom used to make us matching smoking dresses by sewing separate accent frills of smoking, and then attaching them to the bodices. We considered ourselves the best dressed little girls in Jinja. When we were about ten years old, heartbreak struck us. Shenaz's family moved to Kampala, and, after that, we saw each other only rarely.

Dr. Thakkar was our family physician. He and his wife, Rama, were Hindus and close family friends. Their elder daughter, Shefali, was a good pal of mine. Her younger sister, Sukeshi, whose pet name is Chinchu, was a thalidomide baby who was born without forearms and only a few fingers attached to her upper arms. Dr. Thakkar was an unrepentant workaholic, and Rama a stunningly beautiful socialite and gracious woman. Shefali and Chinchu spent endless hours at our home. Their main claim to fame in our childhood world was their pet *kasuku* (Swahili for "parrot"). Her name was "Cuckoo," and she swore constantly in Gujarati.

Aunt Maisy de Souza, our midwife, second from left; Dr. Thakkar, centre with Chinchu

Janet Anderson was the only child of British expatriates who worked in Jinja. Her parents were lovely people. They were among the few British who made a concerted effort to integrate with the Indians. They joined the Amber Court Club, and Janet and I often played there as well. We also attended school together, and spent a lot of time playing at my house. Janet and her family returned to England in the late 1960s and unfortunately we did not keep in touch.

Tazim Pabani was a friend who lost her mom at a young age. Tazim had an unhappy life at home, and was rarely permitted to go out. However, once in awhile, on a Saturday, Tazim and I were able to go shopping together. We always dropped in at her dad's office. He was involved with government tenders, and also owned a jaggery producing facility. Jaggery is made from unrefined whole sugar cane, and has a variety of uses as a sweetener. It is popular in many areas of Africa and Asia including the Gujarat. Her dad filled her pockets with shillings when we visited, and then we were off to shop on the Main Street. Tazim and I also spent hours at my house dancing to Tom Jones, the Beatles and the Rolling Stones.

Tazim was quite disruptive at school. She giggled a lot, and incited the rest of us to giggling fits as well. Our teacher, Mr. Davies, nicknamed her "Cackles." On many occasions, he chastised her by saying, "Cackles, go and lay your eggs somewhere else." That admonishment, naturally, served to leave us prostrate with laughter. Tazim was also left-handed, was as bright as the noon day sun, and came first in the school after writing final exams. The night before the first exam, Tazim was extremely nervous, and Mr. Davies commented to her how interesting it was that the students who should not need to worry academically did so while the ones who did need to worry sailed blithely through life without a care.

Two of my more adventuresome (my parents would say troublemaking) buddies were Sabira and Rukhsana Manek, relatives of the bus company Maneks. The mother of these girls was quite liberal and lenient compared to my mother. She allowed them to throw co-ed parties, and didn't object to Sabira having a friend who drove a motorbike.

When I was about fourteen years old, I went to what was to be my last party at Sabira's home. A number of us wore hot pants, and we all danced to "*He Ain't Heavy, He's My Brother*." In the middle of the night, we bribed the Maneks' *askari* (Swahili for "night watchman") with our pocket money. The *quid pro quo* was that the askari turned a blind eye while we snuck out to meet Sabira's friend, and blast around with him on his motorbike. I was excited when it was finally my turn for a joyride on the forbidden bike. Unfortunately, the boy crashed it while I was holding on to him, and I burnt my leg on the exhaust pipe. The crash occurred outside the home of one of my teachers, and she immediately called my Bapa, and snitched on me. Suffice it to say that Bapa grounded me for life.

During my enforced incarceration, my family sent me to Coventry. They were chilly at best, and Zebby took perverse satisfaction in playing prison matron. I couldn't play with my friends or go to the Club. I spent my time reading books and crying. I was a heroine to my friends, though, and I still bear the scar on my leg as a defiant memento of my brief excursion into a life of crime.

In time, Bapa grudgingly granted me parole. My first outing was to a pyjama party at the home of my friend, Nilam Ramji. Nilam was a bit of a wild child who drowned me in a world of trouble from time to time. Her parents both ran a business, and were seldom home as they worked terribly long hours. When Nilam was a young teenager, her parents sent her to the Aga Khan boarding school in Kampala.

When my parents and I journeyed to Kampala for our audience with the Aga Khan, we ran into Nilam at the Jamatkhana. She was hysterical. The school had expelled her and other girls for sneaking out to a nightclub with some boys, and she had nowhere to stay. My parents brought her home with us to Jinja to spend the night. The next morning, though, Bapa made her confess to her parents, and face the music. Clever bunnies that we were, Nilam and I once crept out to a co-ed party at the YMCA across the street from my own home. While I was outside talking to a male friend, retribution arrived in the form of my brother, Bahadur, who happened to pass by with his wife. Bahadur forcibly removed me from the scene of my latest misdemeanour. More detention followed.

Bapa's long-time and trusted comptroller, Yasin, was a dark-skinned Pakistani and devout Sunni Muslim. Yasin's wife was a classically beautiful light-skinned Persian woman whose name I've forgotten but of whom I was very fond. When I was a small child, they often visited our home for evening tea, and the wife would confide to me that she performed magic tricks. She would then secretly remove her dentures, and pretend that her teeth had disappeared. I howled with laughter every time she gummed a toothless smile at me. (I'm still easily entertained.)

One of our neighbours was an African woman by the name of Victoria who was head of the local hospital. She was a midwife, and a staunch support to our family during later trying times. She was one of our more fascinating friends by virtue of her relationship with Milton Obote, the President of Uganda. She was, in fact, Obote's mistress, and we were unwillingly complicit in their affair. Saying "no" to Obote was not an option. When the President paid Victoria clandestine visits, his helicopter landed in our courtyard, and he snuck through our house and across the fence to rendezvous with her. Occasionally he left his briefcase, presumably full of state secrets, with Bahadur.

After Obote disembarked, the pilot took off and parked the helicopter at a nearby airstrip. Sometimes, he returned to our courtyard to retrieve the President. At other times, Bahadur drove the President to the airstrip.

As a child, I could not have fathomed how many of our kith and kin, colourful threads in the fabric of our daily existence, would disappear so abruptly from our lives, and how many I would not see for decades or ever again.

CHAPTER SEVEN

Our Home Life

The Family Homesteads

Bapa had long nursed a passion to build houses. After I was born, he contracted for the construction of our home at 39 Ripon Garden, and, several years later, in 1965, for our second home at 7 Nalufenya Road.

7 Nalufenya Road

Bapa's attention to detail in the design of both homes was painstaking. It was perhaps a genetic indicator that our ancestry traced back to one of the Mistri Hindu warrior architects who had migrated to the Gujarat in the twelfth century.

Our home at 7 Nalufenya Road was a one-storey brick and concrete rancher topped by a red tile roof. It stood on the outskirts of town, near the source of the River Nile, in the company of other estates. Meticulous landscaping, along with well-maintained macadam roads, accentuated the elegance of the neighbourhood. Even in such a settled and quiet enclave, we could never forget that we lived in Africa. Constant vigilance was second nature to us. On one horrifying occasion, a gargantuan and deadly black mamba wound its way into the middle of the road. In a courageous but sickening scene, our neighbour hacked the snake to pieces with a machete, and then burned it.

The estates were about one half of a hectare in size. Trees and bushes lined their walled frontages, broken by ornate iron gates. As municipal height restrictions did not exist, the backyard walls were generally quite high. Broken bottles to thwart the *chor* (thieves) embedded the tops of most estate walls but Bapa never employed that particular defence mechanism. He probably figured that one of us kids was sure to try scrambling over the wall.

Inside our home, the front foyer was spacious and welcoming. Its centerpiece was a large glass case which Bapa built especially to house my precious collection of dolls. Most floors in Jinja were concrete but, in our home, terrazzo tile overlaid the impersonal concrete in most of the rooms. The tiles helped to mitigate the heat, and were easy to scrub. To the right of our foyer was a formal living and dining area, the floors of which were wood parquet. In our living room hung a painting, *Elephants at Amboseli*, by David Shepherd, who many people now regard as one of the leading wildlife painters in the world.

To the left of the living and dining rooms were Ma and Bapa's bedroom, then Zebby and Almas' bedroom, followed by a large bathroom, and three more bedrooms and bathrooms, one for me, one for Nizar, and one for guests. Each bedroom featured a different colour scheme—baby blue for Almas and Zebby, light yellow for Bahadur, taupe for each of Nizar and me, and beige for Ma and Bapa. For some mysterious reason, beige was Ma's favourite colour. Padded and buttoned leather clad the headboards of the beds and doors of the roomy closets in each of the bedrooms.

Books and magazines occupied every nook and cranny of my boudoir. My magazines contained posters of my pop star idols—David Cassidy, Cliff Richard, Elvis Presley, Michael Jackson, and the *Jackson Five*. I raided the magazines for the posters, and tacked them on my walls.

A fork in the corridor led to a powder room. Behind the living and dining rooms was a huge dining table for every-day eating. Our kitchen boasted a pantry and an informal eating area on a closed-in verandah. Further down from the kitchen were Bahadur's living quarters.

The source of our domestic water supply was the River Nile. In the early days, we relied on wells but later graduated to the luxury of pipes and taps. To keep the tap water cool, we stored it in the kitchen in a *matoongi* (a muddy brown lidded clay pot.)

Although we had no need for mosquito netting in our bedrooms, we had to put up with literally millions of flies, lizards and cockroaches. Cockroaches are nefarious pests in Uganda, and they habitually invaded every room in our house. Ma waged an obsessively relentless war against them. Her weapon of choice was her slipper, and, in the middle of the night, we often heard the "tap, tap, tap" of that slipper as she inexorably squashed the yellowish-brown insects to death.

Many doors led from the house into a huge walled courtyard. The courtyard often served as the centre of family celebrations and entertainment. It also housed the servants' quarters.

The most fun we had in the courtyard was the nightly collection of proceeds from Bapa's soft drink sales. At about 8:30 p.m. each evening, after dinner, our family gathered at an outdoor table. Each driver who distributed Portello to the villages arrived, and dropped off his sale proceeds in a gunny sack. A number marked on each gunny sack corresponded to the lorry number of each driver. The system was simple but effective, and, in any case, Bapa trusted his drivers.

After the shilling notes and loose change shimmied onto the table, we all helped to count it. Then we bundled the notes by denomination, and rolled the coins in newspaper. Bapa allowed us children to keep any loose bills and change that did not fit into bundles or rolls. Zebby was infamous for secretly siphoning off money, and sliding it under her bum, to feed her extravagant spending habits. All of us, including Bapa, knew what she was up to but we never let on. After we finished counting the money, Bapa put it in his safe. Each morning, Bahadur deposited it in Barclay's Bank.

The entrance to our *shamba* (Swahili for "garden") lay through a metal door encased in the back wall of the courtyard. A luxuriant and verdant paradise of trees, shrubs, and flowers graced the garden. Almas has always possessed the green thumb in the family, and, even at a young age, she supervised the gardeners as they tended to their chores.

When we relaxed out of doors in the evening, we inhaled the delectable scents of the light rose frangipani petals, creamy white jasmine flowers, and rose bushes in a rainbow of colours. Mauve, purple, pink, and orange bougainvillea blossoms scrambled everywhere their vines could grab hold. Thorny, flat topped acacia trees spread their ancient limbs like inverted umbrella spokes.

A profusion of tropical fruits and vegetables flourished in the garden. Lush trees dripped with mangos and *paw paws* (Swahili for "papaya"); bananas grew in hanging clusters; pineapple plants were plentiful; and tuberous cassava plants thrived in the fertile soil. Sugar cane grew abundantly. We loved to suck the juice from its tough stalks. The canopies of overhanging mango trees consisted of dense dark green foliage, and gave us welcome shade.

Our garden was a stage setting for uniquely African adventures. Comical hippopotami, with round, brownish-gray, mud-spattered bodies, short legs, broad heads and pink splotched faces and bellies, lived near Lake Victoria, and roamed through our pristine neighbourhood. Sometimes, at night, they trampled the wooden fences and thick hedges, and lurched through our garden, devouring papaya, pineapple, mango, tomatoes, and rhubarb. Monkeys dangled from branches, and grabbed bananas we offered to them.

Paradoxically, our garden was also perilous. We never ventured into it unless we were wearing protective boots. Venomous snakes coiled around the limbs of trees, and slithered through the ground foliage.

Our Servants

Like the British community in Jinja, and well-to-do local African families, we employed African servants. Some of them lived in our compound, and others lived in town or in nearby villages. They commuted to our home by bus or bicycle. By and large, they were Catholic.

Masawa, who was in her twenties, was my *ayah* (nanny) until I was seven or eight years old. She was my companion and friend, and I loved her dearly. Although my childhood was idyllic in most respects, I must have absorbed the underlying taint of trepidation at a young age. I distinctly remember asking Masawa to sit outside my bathroom door to ward off intruders who might break into the house while I bathed. And, for years, Masawa slept on a mattress in my bedroom to protect me from nameless terrors.

Our principal servants were John and Jackson. Their duties included house cleaning and laundry. Our courtyard contained a small divided washing area with taps. John and Jackson washed our clothes by hand every day, and hung them out to dry in the sunlight on a clothesline. While washing machines were available, Ma preferred to have our laundry done by hand.

John and his wife, Mary, lived in the servants' quarters off the courtyard. They were with us for at least fifteen years. My recollection of Mary is that of a kind, maternal woman. She helped John and Jackson with the chores, and Ma with chopping vegetables. Ma, though, did all her own cooking.

John and Mary had one son named Ato. Although Ato was several years younger than I, we enjoyed playing together.

I can't bring to mind our gardener's name but we called him "Skinny" because he was bone thin with long spider legs. No matter what task we assigned to him, his favourite response was *hakuna matata* (Swahili for "no problem"). That was the stock answer all Africans gave, no matter how herculean or even impossible the task might be.

Two askaris rotated duties. They carried rifles and *pimbos* (Swahili for "batons"). They often fell asleep on the job but that was the least of Bapa's concerns. It was not uncommon for them to accept bribes from home invaders. Bapa, however, paid our watchmen well in both salary and benefits, and trusted them. We still endured home invasions but fewer of them than our neighbours.

Mary often invited me to eat with her family in their quarters. I was especially fond of *ugali*, Swahili for a popular staple food among Africans in Uganda. To make ugali, Mary mixed maize flour or cornmeal and water to form a dough which she cooked in a pot. To eat the ugali, we broke it into lumps, rolled the lumps into balls, and made depressions in them with our thumbs. We dipped the ugali into sauces or filled the depressions with vegetables or meat stews. They were delicious, and extremely filling.

Senene (Swahili for "grasshoppers") are a Ugandan delicacy, rich in protein and quite salty. During monsoon season, we kids shook the trees and hedges, and senene galore rained down on us. We collected them, in buckets and baskets, for Mary to cook. The servants ate the senene with ugali or fried them with onions and pepper. Senene swarmed the street lamps in Jinja as well, and the local kids harvested them. As an adult, I've learned that they are actually bush crickets or katydids but remembering them simply as "senene" is more fun.

Another subsidence food for Africans was *matooke* (Swahili for "green bananas"). Mary concocted it by boiling or steaming bunches of green bananas, mashing them until mushy, and then ladling over them a sauce with meat or fish. Poached fish from Lake Victoria was also a common staple in Mary's kitchen.

Speaking in Tongues

Our household has always resonated with a cacophonous jumble of languages—Gujarati, Kutchi, Swahili, and English. Gujarati and Kutchi are distinct but closely related languages which originated in the western region of India. Swahili is a Bantu tongue, and is quite sophisticated. It is the working language of Uganda, Kenya, and Tanzania. Bapa spoke his mother tongue Kutchi as well as Gujarati, Swahili, English, and a smattering of Hindustani. Ma was fluent in Kutchi, Gujarati, and Swahili. Growing up, we children chattered away at home in Kutchi, Swahili, and English, all at the same time. At school, we spoke English. We did not learn Gujarati until later when we needed it to communicate with some of our friends. At home today, we are not much different. People have asked me in which language I think, and I don't really know. I guess the answer is that I think in whatever lingo I happen to be speaking at the moment, and, otherwise, in English.

Puppy Love and Loss

The Madhvani family bred Pekingese dogs which everyone coveted. When I was about ten years old, I met the first love of my life. She was an Irish Cream Liqueur coloured Pekingese from a Madhvani litter. I named her "Mickey" because I thought she was a boy. Our neighbours followed suit, and acquired a Madhvani Pekingese who impregnated my poor Mickey. That's when it dawned on me that she was a girl. Mickey gave birth to two puppies, one of whom died. We gave the other one, a girl we named Susie, to Mr. and Mrs. G.S. Karim, owners of the Pontiac dealership.

Mickey travelled everywhere with us. She slept in my room at night next to my bed. Ma wouldn't allow her on the bed because, in Africa, dogs were prone to pick up exotic germs and bacteria. Mickey was the cause of the first great tragedy in my life. At the age of five, she ran into Clive Road near our house one morning. A taxi driver ran over her, and crushed her to death. Because of the heat in Jinja, we held Mickey's funeral that very afternoon. Bahadur and a servant wrapped her in white cloth, and buried her in our back yard. My whole family was in mourning, and none of us ate for days.

Our only other pets in Jinja were mud turtles captured from Lake Victoria which Zebby and Almas raced through the courtyard. Because they liked an audience for the races, Zebby and Almas enticed their friends to come and watch by promising them a free Jubilee soft drink. Such was racing, bribery, and drinking in Jinja. I don't know whether or not they placed bets on the turtles but I wouldn't be surprised.

Ma's Mortal Enemies

Although we suffered from the usual childhood maladies such as measles and chicken pox, other health concerns in Jinja were considerably different from those children faced in the western world. We were fortunate that our friend, Dr. Thakkar, was an excellent general practitioner,

Because mosquito bites were a year round nuisance, we caught malaria all the time but were able to knock it out with quinine, after which we would sleep it off. Zebby, as a teenager, came down with jaundice, and was ill for quite some time.

Whooping cough was another common ailment. I endured a bout of it when I was quite young. At St. Xavier Elementary School, each recess, we received a snack of cassava root along with a tetra pack of milk. For no known reason except that I first started whooping at school, I associated milk with my whooping cough attack, and, even now, I hate the taste.

Ma's greatest fear was trachoma, a dreadful eye infection. Flies are carriers, and children often pass it to other children. If left untreated, the disease causes the eyelid to turn inward, and the eyelashes to rub on the eyeball. In addition to intense pain and scarring, it ultimately causes irreversible blindness. Ma was ever vigilant, and I'm sure her fastidious cleanliness went a long way to ensuring that none of us kids ever contracted trachoma. The consequences of the disease were so devastating that British and Indian physicians and African nurses visited our school every few months to test us for it.

We were ever mindful of insidious insects such as beetles that burrowed in children's ears and deafened them, and of tsetse fly bites which caused trypanosomiasis, known as "African lethargy" or "sleeping sickness."

Sleeping sickness is endemic in Uganda and other African countries. It has resulted in four major epidemics since the end of the nineteenth century, including one in Uganda as recently as 2008. It begins with fever, headaches, joint pain, and itching. Without treatment, symptoms may extend to anaemia, cardiac distress, and kidney problems. In the second phase, it passes through the blood-brain barrier, and attacks the central nervous system, inevitably ending in death. Ma ensured that the doctor checked us for it all the time, and luckily we escaped its ravages.

Head lice were less harmful but darned annoying. In elementary school, nurses came by routinely to check all the kids but they couldn't hold a candle to my Nanima. Every time we visited her home, she combed through our long braided hair with her fingers or a metal pick, searching for nits.

When I turned nine, I decided that I wanted to cut my hair, which hung below my waist. I badgered Ma incessantly to take me to our family friend, Gulshan Adatia, who performed hair dressing services out of her family home. One afternoon, I spied her walking past our house, and asked her to come in as Ma wanted to see her. To Ma's surprise, I brazenly asked Gulshan when she might be available to cut my hair. At that juncture, Ma and Gulshan had a quick word, and Ma then told me that I could follow Gulshan home, and she would cut my hair. Gulshan gave me a lovely bob, and saved all my hair in a bag which she gave to Ma when she came to pick me up.

That evening, I went to the Jamatkhana. When Nanima saw me, she began to cry, and was most upset that Ma had allowed my beautiful hair to be cut and destroyed.

Almas, who also had long hair, decided to cut hers just a few weeks later. Gulshan performed the operation, and also saved Almas' shorn tresses. When Almas went to hairdressing school in London, our hair was used to create an elegant hair piece which Ma, who had short permed hair, used to put her hair in a bun.

A girl named Hamida Molu was a good friend of my older sisters. We children were wary of her mother, Sakina, as we steadfastly believed that she practised witchcraft. Looking back, it was actually herbal medicine as we know it today. I used to suffer frequently from stomach aches, and Ma would drag me to their home. Sakina would roll stones in her hands, and then rub her hands around my tummy. I despised this treatment because she yawned mightily all the time she was rubbing but I have to admit that her therapy helped.

I also suffered from severe nosebleeds so Bapa escorted me to a village witch doctor. The witch doctor instructed Bapa to bring him a clean red brick. He pounded the brick to powder, and heated it on hot coals. The witch doctor then inveigled me into snorting the powder. Its effect was to cauterize the blood vessels, and I never again suffered from nosebleeds. My healer dressed rather boringly in western clothes but some of the medicine men still wore breech cloths, necklaces, rattles, and head bands with feathers sticking out. Their reputations were well-known in East Africa.

Salemohamed Dhanji, a distant cousin of Bapa, and his wife, Noorbanu, who lived in Mombasa, had several sons, three of whom were Amir, Zul, and Sadru. When Zul was in his early twenties, a car accident left him paralyzed. We had maintained contact with the family and visited with them on our trips to Mombasa. Noorbanu heard of a palm reader near Jinja, and she and Zul came to stay with us in our Ripon Garden home. Noorbanu was adorable, and every night we played cards with them amid lots of laughter, cheating, and fun.

The palm reader was a manager at the Madhvani estate. Bahadur contacted Suru Madhvani, and set up an appointment. Disappointingly but accurately, the palm reader told Zul he would never recover. Noorbanu dragged Zul to an acupuncturist, and to some of the local healers, as well, but all to no avail. Zul was fortunate to have a loyal childhood sweetheart, Farial. After the accident, everyone thought she would abandon him but, instead, they married, moved to Toronto, and spent the rest of their lives together.

Because of Ma's constant vigilance and the rigorous rules she and Bapa imposed, I can offer no hair-raising tales about life and death encounters between me or my siblings and wild African animals. The best I can do is to relate Bahadur's fish story.

When Bahadur was about nine, he and his friend, Manni, went fishing off a cement jetty next to the John Hanning Speke monument by the source of the Nile at Lake Victoria. Manni cast his line but, because the water was shallow, and Bahadur could see tilapia swimming just under the surface, he decided to pluck the fish out of the water with his bare hands. Just as he was about to execute his plan, a baby crocodile ambushed him by chomping down on his hand. Bahadur jumped up screaming, and managed to shake off the crocodile. He and his pal ran home, with Bahadur's hand dripping blood. Ma rushed him off to Dr. Thakkar, who stitched him up.

Bahadur has never even been able to embellish this story because the scar is still evident, and it obviously didn't come from the pressure of an adult crocodile bite which would have sheared off his whole hand and probably his arm.

Vigilance First and Foremost

Rashida tells me that, when she was small, personal safety was of little concern. But, by the time I came along, Bapa and Ma worried about it much more. In fact, to the best of my recollection, caution always came first.

Uganda was a poor country so looting and other crimes, most of them committed by Africans, were common. One of their favourites was extortion. When I was a teenager, kidnapping the children of wealthy industrialists was not uncommon. Nor was it uncommon for the kidnappers to chop off a child's ear as proof of the abduction. But once kidnapped, the child never returned. Although most of the kidnap victims were Indian, I did not know any of them personally.

Our family was religious about being vigilant, and none of us, except for Ma, ever suffered an assault on the street. Ma was notorious for carrying her purse on her arm, and thieves sometimes wrestled it away from her. As she carried our house keys in her purse, Bapa had to keep a locksmith virtually on retainer. Later rather than sooner, Ma smartened up, and, when she trekked to the market, took only cash, which she hid in her bosom.

Despite Bapa's employment of askaris he trusted, some of them were corruptible or just turned a blind eye. As a result, robbers broke into our home several times. One chilling incident occurred at 39 Ripon Garden when we suffered a home invasion. Bapa heard a suspicious noise in the middle of the night. When he crept out to investigate, one of the thieves chucked a huge padlock at him but missed because Ma pulled Bapa out of harm's way.

We kept our money and jewellery in a safe so thieves just picked up whatever was lying around and caught their fancy. Sometimes, we could hear burglars breaking in but just ignored them for fear of our lives.

I could not travel by bus to visit friends, and Bapa ensured that, wherever I went, I had an escort. Because we lived on a relatively secluded property away from the centre of town, my friends, by and large, were not easily accessible. Welcome exceptions were my best friend, Maira, who lived across the street, and Tazmina who lived next door.

As a consequence, I often had to entertain myself, and one of my favourite pastimes was, and still is, reading. Nothing, though, could compare to the joy of shopping.

CHAPTER EIGHT

Life's Essentials

Weaned on Shopping

My friends often suggest to me that I need therapy to cure my shopping addiction but I have two reasons for sloughing them off. First, my compulsion has been almost fifty years in the making, and is now too deep-seated to mend. Second, like a manic-depressive on an optimism binge, I love, love, love shopping! "Retail therapy" is what works for me. Besides, I know I can quit any time I want.

As a youngster, I especially adored shopping on the Main Street of Jinja. Simply strolling along the sidewalks was magic. We mingled with Indian women in their beautifully draped sarees of vibrant fuchsias, blues, and magentas; African ladies in gay *gomezis* and *basutis* (colourful native apparel); buttoned-down British matrons in conservative English clothing; African men riding to and fro on their bicycles; and Sikh gentlemen in neatly wound turbans. What we all had in common was shopping, and we bustled cheerfully along, stopping in clusters to gossip with our countless friends and relatives. Whenever we set out to shop, we brought along a servant, usually Skinny, to carry our packages in woven baskets.

Rows of dukas nestled next to one another in old one-storey buildings of traditionally detailed Indian design. At curb side, single round columns of cobalt blue and double square pillars of turquoise and cream supported portico roofs that overhung the sidewalks in front of the dukas. Next to the porches low, flowering bougainvillea bushes lined the curbs. The buildings were cream, and, while most of the roofs were flat, some sported jaunty red tiles.

As a rule, Indians owned the buildings, and rented individual dukas to Hindus, Ismailis, Sikhs, and Bugandans. Cobblers, bicycle repairers, chemists, fabric retailers, clothing merchants, bakers, confectioners, toy vendors, produce hawkers, and book sellers all jostled cheerfully to attract customers. The wares and services they offered often overflowed from their dukas onto the porches.

As we walked and shopped, we soaked up the constant chatter of Indian, Swahili, and British tongues, listened to the whirr of sewing machines operating on storefront verandahs, and inhaled the delicious aromas of spices and fresh baked goods.

Through the years, I've shopped till I dropped in incredibly sophisticated high-end retail havens in New York, London, Paris, Rome, Mumbai, Milan, and Geneva. However, if I had to name the shops at the top of my all-time hit list, the Kenya Bakery and Uganda Argus Bookstore, from my childhood, would be one and two with a bullet.

Ma and I often stopped in at the Kenya Bakery. Ma bought all her baked goods there. The proprietors, who were Catholic Goans, sold white bread, cakes, pastries, jam tarts, and cheese. They manufactured the cheese, right on the premises, from goat milk.

When I was quite young, Bapa, who was well aware of my sweet tooth and spoiled me terribly, opened an account for me at the bakery. My ayah, Masawa, and I popped in frequently. We always emerged munching on goodies while more sweets waited in our bags. Masawa signed for my purchases, and even though Bapa knew that I couldn't possibly have eaten everything that showed up on the bill, he never confronted her. Nor did he mention the discrepancies to anyone until years later.

The Uganda Argus Bookstore was my personal paradise on earth. Tucked away though it was in a backwater town in Africa, its proprietors, who were Hindu, stocked an eclectic selection of books and magazines imported from Great Britain. The store, which sat at the intersection of Main Street and a side road, never failed to beckon to me. Its front entrance formed the base of a triangle at the corner junction. The double columns supporting the porch roof were white, and rested on turquoise blue blocks. The shop itself was quite large, and had a nicely appointed interior. It was remarkably similar to the lay-out of a Western bookstore.

Bapa had also set up an account for me at the bookstore. Accounts were necessary in Jinja because carrying cash was dangerous. I liked to drop into the Argus almost every day, and Bahadur was kind enough to escort me whenever he could.

I was a die-hard bookworm, and spent endless hours, in my bedroom, pouring over my literary treasure trove. The British children's author, Enid Blyton, was a spectacular and prolific storyteller, and I was addicted to her two most popular series—the *Famous Five* and the *Secret Seven*.

The *Famous Five*—four children and a mongrel dog—entangled themselves in remarkable adventures in ancient mansions and secret smugglers' tunnels in the English countryside. I lived and breathed their heroic exploits of derring-do. I considered myself the eighth member of the *Secret Seven Society*. In my mind's eye, I helped the six kids and their golden spaniel, Shadow, track suspected criminals, and search for clues to solve the peculiar mysteries that haunted their community.

British magazines were usually stale-dated by about three months when they arrived in Jinja but that didn't matter to me. Fashion and entertainment publications like *Mirabelle* were my lifeblood. I drank in every current clothing vogue and style tip they had to offer. I was quite the little manipulator. I often cut out a picture of the latest trendy outfit, and mailed it, along with precise instructions on where to buy it for me, to whichever of my sisters happened to be sojourning in London.

The bookstore stocked an impressive variety of Ugandan, Kenyan, and Tanzanian newspapers, in both English and Swahili, but I have to confess they were of far more interest to Bapa than to me. English was the language of choice for the *Uganda Argus*, the local newspaper.

Another of my favourite haunts was the Jinja record store, G.V. Mohamed & Sons. My friend, Sabira, and I hung out there, ever ready to pounce on the newest, bestselling LP or EP record.

On the entertainment scene, Jinja boasted three movie theatres—the Odeon Cinema, the Town Talkies, and Gill's Opera House which did not stage operas. I guess the owner just liked the grand name. They all featured movies starring the likes of Elvis Presley and Cliff Richard along with countless Indian films.

My brothers and sisters and I wore British clothes we bought from the Ann Wallace Department Store or from Deacon's, which specialized in Marks & Spencer attire. I favoured cotton frocks or stirrup pants and party dresses underlaid by fancy crinolines. Ma and various seamstresses also designed and sewed clothes for me from cotton manufactured by Nyanza Textile, also known as Nytil, a huge local textile mill. The mill, constructed in the 1950s, jointly by Manchester's Calico Printers Association and the Ugandan Development Corporation, employed about 3,000 workers; produced only Ugandan cotton; and sold its fabric across Uganda and Kenya.

Ann Wallace and Bata were the source of my British school shoes, which were leather and fitted with straps and buckles. They also stocked the black patent dress shoes which I liked to wear on high days and holidays.

Once each week, I invaded the Main Street candy store with Mariam Masi's children and their neighbouring cousins in tow, and spent a few shillings buying us British chocolate and toffee. I was always thrilled at how far my few shillings seemed to stretch. I didn't realize that Bapa had instructed the shopkeeper to let me buy as much candy as I wanted for the kids, and to put the balance on his account.

Another of my much-loved Main Street shops was the magical Good Hopes Toy Store where I stocked up on metal jacks, Ludo, Chinese Checkers, and Monopoly. My friends and I carried our jacks in our school uniform pockets, and played all the time. I was forever arriving home in tears, having lost my ball. Bahadur always knew what was wrong, and would run over to the shop to pick up a replacement for me. Believe it or not, I still have a set of my original metal jacks.

I remember vividly my trips, on Saturday mornings, to the sokoni with Ma and various of my brothers and sisters. The market was close to the centre of town about eight kilometres from our home. Decrepit wooden stalls pinched against one another higgledy-piggledy. Narrow, dirt lanes meandered around and through the grounds. Acacia and mango trees rimmed the perimeter, and often overhung the stalls, offering a welcome bit of shade. The bazaar-like atmosphere was intoxicating, a pulsing cacophony of sights and sounds. The air was redolent with a muddle of delectable, pungent, and sometimes revolting odours.

Entering the market was always heart-wrenching. *Maskinis* (Swahili for "beggars") clustered around the entrance in a sorry state, missing limbs and eyes. They had no wheelchairs so they scurried about on horizontal dollies. I became friendly with some of them, and made it my practice to collect change for them. On Friday mornings, they turned out in great numbers, seeking *baksheesh* (offerings of money) because they knew that our religion mandates generosity on Muslim prayer days.

Inside the square, the hustle and bustle of Indians, Africans, and Caucasians rivalled that of Main Street. I especially loved to watch the African women. They wove their way up and down the aisles in gaudy gomezis, gracefully balancing colourfully woven baskets of fruit and vegetables on their heads, sometimes with a baby strapped to their back.

Vendors at the market flogged a bewildering jumble of produce and merchandise from goat intestines to nails. Heaps of reddish-yellow mangoes, ripe amber papayas, pineapples with brownish-yellow rinds and spiked leaves, luscious red tomatoes, and other fresh fruits and vegetables overflowed baskets or lay on brown paper on the ground. Huge clusters of bananas hung from pillar to post. Masses of sisal, a fibre used to make products like twine, cloth and carpets spilled out of baskets. Waist-high white gunny sacks full of peanuts, flour, rice, and other grains lined the lanes in front of the stalls.

Fish from Lake Victoria and the River Nile were abundant. Slabs of yellowish-grey meat coated in flies hung from huge hooks, and vendors hacked pieces from them with machetes for sale to African customers. Ramshackle clothing racks swayed precariously as customers jostled against them. We bought some goods such as vegetables in bunches but hawkers employed large, pan-shaped scales to weigh others. We always had a great time wandering around the stalls to check on who was displaying the best produce, and stopping to socialize with our friends and neighbours.

Our major shopping excursions took us to Kampala. At least once a month, my con artist sister, Zebby, sweet-talked Bapa into allowing Almas and her to spend the day there. The price Baba exacted was that they had to take me with them.

The road to Kampala passed by Mabira Forest, a stretch that was noto-
riously dangerous and sometimes deadly. It was infamous for car crashes,
bandits, looting, and muggings. Everyone feared this portion of the road,
and considered it jinxed. Therefore, Bapa never let us go alone. For each
trip, he seconded one of his African employees to drive us as the criminals
who trolled the road for victims did not generally attack other Africans.

The Main Street of Kampala was similar to the Main Street of Jinja but
bigger and more cosmopolitan. On each occasion, as soon as we arrived,
Zebby and Almas ditched me at the hair salon where they abandoned me
for hours. My hairdresser, Molly, was a family friend. After my haircut, I
happily immersed myself in one of the books I was never without while
Molly plied me with cakes and chocolates.

Near the end of the day, my sisters came to my rescue, and, in case
Bapa questioned them, took me shopping for an hour or so before our
return home. Bapa always gave them money for me to spend but they
adroitly managed to squander most of it on themselves. When Zebby
added to it the money she routinely pilfered from the soft drink proceeds,
she accumulated quite a bundle which she spent on gobs of material for
herself and later for her design store.

The material came from a store called A.S. Jaffer which imported a
divine collection of fabrics from all over the world. The store owners,
Abdul and Roshan Jaffer, were family friends. The shop I liked best was
the Sudan Store. It was the Ugandan equivalent of a Canadian five and
dime. The odd time my sisters didn't expropriate all my spending money,
I bought little purses, dolls, and hair clips there.

A Cornucopia of Foodstuff

Ma was an all-powerful kitchen diva. For her, life was simple. Food
equalled love. She was fiercely possessive of her kitchen, and, as I've
mentioned, prepared all our meals. She allowed one helper, usually
Mary, to chop vegetables and help clean up but she cooked everything
herself. Ma was utterly fastidious about the cleanliness of her kitchen, her
cooking implements, and the food. But, we often laughed at her because
she whirled around the kitchen like a tornado, leaving a path of culinary
destruction in her wake. Once her always sublime meal was ready to
serve, she gusted away, leaving others to set the wreckage to rights.

Ma, Mariam Masi, and Nanima began cooking, in the early days, on
small *sagris* (coal burning stoves). They later cooked on primus stoves
that operated on kerosene fuel, and needed pumping to start. In time, Ma
graduated to a fancy electric stove, complete with an oven, but we often
found her still cooking on the primus, which she never discarded.

Bapa was exceedingly proud of Ma's cooking and hosting skills. He
liked to entertain business associates at home, often springing them on

Ma at the last moment. She was accustomed, though, to his habits, and always equal to the occasion.

Ma recognized early on that I was a lily of the field, and never bothered to teach me to cook. But, when Bahadur's wife, Zubeda, joined our family circle, Ma was thrilled to pass on her cooking prowess, and even to share her kitchen with Zubeda.

Kindness was perhaps Ma's best attribute. She seldom arrived home from the market without an extra kilo of meat for John and Mary, and she always cooked extra portions for the servants. Her food-inspired kindness even extended to the beggars who hovered outside the market gates in town. On their way home, some of them developed the habit, almost every evening, of knocking on our gate. Bapa allowed the askari to open the gate, and escort them to the courtyard. We kept an extra refrigerator in the courtyard which we called the "beggars' fridge" (different place, different time). We and our servants kept it stocked with bread, leftovers, water, and Portello. Although they were supplicants, the beggars were proud and polite, and never ever raided the fridge. They always waited until someone offered them food or drink, and they always offered profuse thanks along with blessings and prayers.

Our main courses at dinnertime usually consisted of various vegetable and rice concoctions topped with chicken, beef, or fish. Those of us who were vegetarian, including myself, simply picked off the non-vegetarian ingredients. Needless to say, anything curried, including lentils, potatoes, lima beans, and cauliflower, were staples in Ma's kitchen. Her "go-to" dish was tandoori chicken but she used a light hand with its spices.

Acquiring the chicken, beef, and fish was a far different process from going to the local supermarket to pick up a bland styrofoam and cellophane package. Our primary obstacle was that we lacked refrigeration so we had to buy everything fresh.

We ate a lot of chicken which we purchased from Africans who rode by our house daily, balancing large crates of live poultry on their bicycles. Our servants were Catholic but Muslim servants were abundant on the street, and we paid them to slaughter the chickens for us according to the strict dictates of Islamic law.

Halal is an Islamic term meaning food that is permissible to eat. Chicken fell under this category so long as we followed strict rules. The executioner was obliged to offer a prayer, in the name of Allah, before proceeding with the ritual slaughter. Then he slashed the jugular veins and carotid arteries on both sides of the chicken's neck but stopped short of the spinal cord. This method cut off the blood supply to the brain thus causing the least amount of pain to the bird. In addition, it drained most of the blood from the body, which Muslims consider a ripe breeding ground for germs. The executions took place in a slaughter pit in our courtyard.

We bought beef and goat from a slaughterhouse in town, the fresh meat still hot and pulsating. I'm primarily a vegetarian, and I'm sure it's partly because of these experiences.

Lake Victoria teemed with fish, and we ate large quantities of tilapia and perch. Ma baked, boiled, and fried it but her favourite method was to curry the fish. Curried goat meat was another delicacy she sometimes served for our dining pleasure.

Ma bought all her spices from a local shop on Main Street. The shop-keeper imported an aromatic selection of spices from India, and kept them in gunny sacks. Sometimes, Ma bought spices such as tumeric already ground but usually asked the clerk to grind them for her.

Uganda was a paradise of riches for fruit lovers, and our kitchen was always full of the juiciest fruits imaginable. We gobbled papaya, pine-apple, mango, guava, and pomegranate from our garden. Mango was a particular family favourite, and we puckered up to eat it, unripened and tart, sprinkled with salt and cayenne pepper.

We bought imported oranges, along with apples and grapes, from fruit stores. We purchased tangerines, lemons, and jack fruit, all of which grew in the villages, from the town market. My personal favourite was jack fruit, which grew on trees. The fruit could reach enormous proportions. It was prickly or spiky on the outside but inside were yellow pods with a fleshy covering (this was the part we ate) around the seed, which looked like a chestnut.

Avocado trees were rampant around Jinja but, oddly, we never ate the avocado. We have long since remedied that sin of omission.

Ma was quite liberal in her culinary choices, and did not hesitate to cook British food. Two of our family favourites were apple pie with hot custard and authentic British trifle made with cake and sherry. I'm drool-ing now just thinking about their sublime flavours.

Because we ate dinner so late in Jinja, the British tradition of high tea was popular. Many of our friends dropped by the house to partake of Ma's baked cakes and biscuits along with British cookies and Indian sweets. Other tea time staples included *bhajia*, fried *mogo, ondhwo, chevro*, and *ganthia*. We consumed these goodies along with masala chai, a strong tea which Ma diluted with milk and sugar, and spiced with cinnamon, carda-mom, cloves, pepper, and ginger.

Some of our tea came from Ugandan tea estates but we had an affin-ity for tea from a Kenya operation of Brooke Bond Great Britain. It was my particular favourite because the packets contained illustrated tea cards depicting wild animals, birds, flowers, motor cars, and historical costumes. Like so much else, I was forced to leave my tea card collec-tion behind in Uganda which still ticks me off because they're now emi-nently collectible.

Mogo (Swahili for "cassava root") was our all-time favourite snack. It's a root vegetable that Ma deep-fried, and we dipped in tamarind sauce. Zubeda still cooks cassava root treats for us.

Junk food knows no boundaries, and, in Jinja, mogo was the junk food of choice. Our Jamatkhana's maintenance man and his wife rented a tiny hovel across the road from the Jamatkhana. There, the wife made and sold deep-fried mogo each evening, to practically everyone in Jinja in search of fattening, finger-licking snacks. The mogo was redolent with salt and red pepper, and so oily it caused the print in the newspaper in which it was wrapped to run. For a few cents, we could buy two fairly good sized pieces, and because mogo is so dense, two pieces made a meal.

CHAPTER NINE
My Childhood World

Pastimes and Play

My childhood pleasures in Jinja were simple. My favourite pastime was to hang out with Bapa. I adored and revered him but found him a bit exasperating and intimidating—in other words, a typical father.

What I liked best, beginning when I was around seven, was to accompany Bapa to his soda pop and carbon dioxide compound on Saturday or Sunday. The Portello factory included a large open office area where I drew, painted, and practised multiplication tables.

I observed Bapa walk the assembly line, oversee the soft drink process, and deal with his employees. I asked him an endless litany of questions, and he always took the time to give me serious answers. I absorbed the whole production atmosphere like a sponge. I'm sure that was how I developed my aptitude for both business and employee relations.

I loved playing with the dolls Rashida, Zebby, and Almas brought me from England. Zebby and Almas must have felt guilty about the way they mistreated me on our shopping expeditions to Kampala because the dolls were works of art, and I got a huge amount of enjoyment from them. Bapa's sister, Sajabai, was another good source for dolls. On her annual visit from Tanzania, we'd collect material for her, and she made us beautiful dolls. Another one of our simplistic pleasures was to create things like miniature tables and chairs out of Eddy match boxes.

Most days after school and sometimes on Sunday, when I was a bit older, I enjoyed recreational activities at the Amber Court Club. My parents considered it a safe haven. Most of my friends went there as well. We swam to beat the heat, played ping pong and badminton, and gobbled refreshments. Even though Bapa supplied soft drinks to the Club, I had to pay for them like everyone else.

On October 31st each year, we celebrated Guy Fawkes Day at the Club. After dusk, we set off fireworks, and lit a massive bonfire to burn Guy Fawkes in effigy. The night was always pitch black and eerie, and my friends and I quivered with anticipation and more than a little fear.

We celebrated Christmas at the Club with a lighted Christmas tree and a Santa Claus, played by a white man. Each of the parents used to put one gift for the kids in the Santa Claus bin, and Santa would hand them out. My friends and I weren't Christian but we had no intention of missing out on the presents.

Like me, Bahadur spent a great deal of time at the Club. Promptly, though, at 7:45 p.m., we left to go home for dinner.

We dined at 8 p.m. each evening. At the table, no one discussed business or politics. We talked about what we had done during the day. Ma always had telephone news from friends and relatives in Kenya, Tanzania, and Kampala. Telephone calls back then were a big deal. We had to pay a toll charge for each minute of conversation. We had a big, fat rotary telephone that sat on top of a ledge in our foyer. I was the family chatterbox at dinner, and Mom would often have to interrupt me to say, "eat your dinner, it's going to get cold."

Later in the evening, my parents allowed me one hour of television. Our set was black and white, and our reception was by way of rabbit ears. My favourite shows were *Sesame Street, The Monkeys, Leave it to Beaver, Hazel, The Fugitive, I Love Lucy*, and *Bill and Ben the Flower Pot Men*. I lived for this last show. It was British, and related the adventures of two little men made of flower pots who lived at the back of an English garden behind a potting shed.

I belonged to Brownies and Girl Guides. After school, we changed into our uniforms, and met in the gym or outside on the school grounds. For some reason, I was especially fond of my whistle lanyard. We did lots of singing, and made crafts. My favourite craft was a humpty-dumpty I sewed with a pocket in the back for my little pyjamas. It sat on my bed for years. Ma and Bapa each gave me a shilling to contribute to what we called "taking subs." It was a weekly collection for Brownie expenses.

We collected badges, and to qualify for one of them, we had to go camping and work in the "boonies" for a weekend. At the appointed time on a Friday, Maira and I and five or six other friends travelled, with some trepidation, to a village for a two-night stay.

On Friday afternoon, we planted and laid bricks. It was hard labour. We took our own bedding but had to sleep in a grass hut on the ground. The food was awful. I was quite miffed to be subjected to such discomfort, and barely made it through the night.

On Saturday morning, I spied one of Bapa's Portello lorries passing by. It was a heavenly sight. I flagged down the driver, and told him we needed a ride home immediately. The driver was more than a little suspicious. He wanted to know why Bapa wasn't picking us up. I snowed him, though, and, after he dropped off the pop, he returned to pick us up, and drove us back to town.

On the way, we passed Auntie Joyce's Montessori School. Joyce was a Catholic Goan who had been a school teacher in Goa. Her school was like a kindergarten, and she was exceedingly strict. It was on the ground floor of her house, and she and her family lived upstairs. Joyce doubled as a hair stylist, and did Ma's hair. As we went by, I saw Ma's car and chauffeur, and jumped out of the lorry. I ran into the shop to tell her about my horrid experience, and found her trussed in perm rods. I was stunned not to receive any sympathy from her. In fact, she was furious with me over my failure to stick it out in the boonies. It goes without saying that I never received my Brownie badge for meritorious camping conduct.

Local Entertainment and Outings

Jinja being a small community, Bapa knew everybody but he and Ma were not, by any means, social gadflies. Most of their entertainment was business-oriented. Businessmen from England and Germany usually stayed at the Crested Crane Hotel or Ripon Falls Hotel but they loved to come to our home for Ma's lip-smacking home-cooked meals.

Whenever we had guests, Bapa made sure that all of us came to the dinner table so our guests received the full force of the Rahemtulla "charm." Listening to the intriguing commercial talk was another way that, even as a child, I honed my business skills.

Every Christmas, Bapa distributed dozens of cakes, imported Dimple Scotch, and Johnny Walker Scotch to his business associates as well as to shopkeepers and retailers who bought his Portello pop. The Kenya Bakery made the cakes exclusively for Bapa. They were scrumptious fruit concoctions with a thick marzipan coating and rose decorations that were pure sugar.

Evenings often saw families meandering along the street across from the town hall, chatting leisurely with one another. Although I was only about seven at the time, I knew who President Kennedy was, and I distinctly remember Bahadur swinging by the town hall in his car to deliver the dreadful news about JFK's assassination.

Swimming in Lake Victoria or even picnicking by the lakeshore was too dangerous to even contemplate. Oftentimes, though, on evenings and weekends, our family and friends gathered on a grassy knoll above the Jinja Pier that jutted out into the River Nile. The pier sat across the road from the Ripon Falls Hotel, just above the Jinja Club, and next to the golf course.

The pier hummed with activity. Boats docked, parents visited, children played, and local African vendors sold us roasted peanuts and roasted corn. Our favourite hawker was a tall, African gentleman we nicknamed *Marefu* (Swahili for "tall"). He sold *karanga* (Swahili for "roasted peanuts") in homemade paper cones. One evening, I not so cleverly shoved a peanut so far up my nose it blocked my breathing. Ma was hysterical. Fortunately, Dr. and Mrs. Thakkar were strolling on the pier. Mrs. Thakkar found some tweezers in her purse which the doctor used to extract the obstruction from my nasal cavity thus saving me from death by peanut suffocation.

About 7 p.m., we watched from the pier as the sun set rapidly over Lake Victoria, and then headed home in the dark. Occasionally, after dinner, we returned to town to meet our friends at the local *paanwalla* (a vendor selling *paan.*) There, we stuffed our mouths with sweet *paan,* an Asian tradition of chewing betel leaf with *supari* (betel nut) lathered with lime paste, sugar, *katha* (brown powder), *mukhwas* or tobacco and fennel seeds, all neatly packaged within the beetle leaf and held together with a clove. Chewing paan is said to cleanse the palate, freshen one's breath, and aid with digestion.

We occasionally picnicked with family and friends at the precise spot where John Hanning Speke first discovered the source of the Nile. The site boasted a spectacular vista over Lake Victoria, and was chock-full of palm trees in which roosted eagles, other native birds, and mischievous monkeys.

Another of our favourite family outings was to drive, for the day, to Kakira for a picnic and swim. Kakira referred to both the town and the estate of the Madhvani family. The park site, called "Chico," was on the periphery of the estate, and included a natural swimming hole. The Madhvanis were most generous in allowing the use of sites like Chico by anyone who wanted to enjoy them.

Other day trip destinations included picnicking at Entebbe, and visiting our cousins in Kampala and Masaka. We always drove. We never took trains anywhere because they weren't safe.

We often received invitations from African friends, servants, workers, and shopkeepers to attend weddings, christenings, and other celebrations in the villages. The invitations arrived on bark cloth on which the host handwrote details of the event and the name of the village along with "RSVP" which meant "Rice and Stew Very Plenty!"

Fashioning bark cloth was a prehistoric craft practised by the Bugandan people. Almost every village had a workshop and chief craftsman. Workers harvested bark from fig trees during the wet season, spread it out in open sheds to prevent it from drying too rapidly, and pounded it with wooden mallets to create the cloth.

As well as invitations, the Bugandan villagers used bark cloth to make dinner mats, purses, coffee holders, fancy hats, mats, curtains, bedding, dresses or robes worn like togas, and anything else they could imagine. Most bark cloth was a terra cotta colour but members of the Bugandan royal family wore robes dyed white or black as a symbol of prestige. My own modern, and probably sacrilegious, version of bark cloth clothing was a mini-skirt and vest dyed burnt sienna.

African women used to garb themselves in bark cloth but, in more modern times, switched to a wrapped floor-length gomezi or basuti. The dresses were generally made of *kitenge* (printed cotton fabric) in vibrant hues of emerald green, blue, bronze, and magenta with peaked shoulders and a sash. Subtle differences in the wearing of the basuti or gomezi signi-fied differences between tribes. The women accented their costumes with colourful beads made from wood or metal. They also wore western style shift dresses.

The Busoga tribe, with which I was most familiar, were polite and hospitable people, generally tall and slim. They seized any opportunity to celebrate, even in the streets. They absolutely loved to sing, chant, and whoop, and their repertoire included intriguing tongue noises. They danced with abandon, wielding spears and shields, and pounded on drums made of wood and animal skin such as zebra. I adored listening to the big drums and lyrical Swahili songs. They consumed beer which gen-erally came from Nile Breweries, and *waragi* (Swahili for "a drink made from sugar cane").

Family Travels

While I was in grade school, I did nothing by way of international travel but my family and I embarked on lots of local overnight and extended trips. We journeyed to Kenya for safaris, but I was too young to remem-ber much about these adventures. Back then, safaris weren't a big deal.

We often travelled to Kenya to visit members of Bapa's family in Nairobi and Mombasa. Our drive was along a scary highway. Sudden downpours could turn the pavement treacherously slick, and we often ran into unpaved patches of mud. Many times, we careened out of control but Bapa was a super driver, and always managed to right the ship.

We occasionally trekked to Murchison Falls National Park in western Uganda. When we arrived at the park, we found the River Nile cascading violently down Murchison Falls, a dramatic and awe-inspiring sight. At the park, we were able, if we were lucky, to catch glimpses of elephants, buffaloes, giraffes, antelopes, and lions.

That was about the extent of our travels through Uganda as other areas were not safe.

School

All the kids, except for Bahadur and me, received both their primary and secondary schooling in Jinja. I received my primary schooling and a year or so of my secondary education there but finished my secondary schooling in London and Vancouver.

Bapa, who valued education greatly and was a forward thinker, sent Bahadur to school in Great Britain at the age of thirteen. India was not educationally competitive at the time. In common with other Indian families, Bapa expected Bahadur to complete his schooling in England, and then return to enter the family business.

I attended Auntie Joyce's Montessori School for the equivalent of kindergarten. I started my regular school years at a private school called St. Xavier established by the Goans. The students were predominantly Indian but some African children attended as well. St. Xavier School was across the street from Victoria Nile Primary School.

Almost all the kids at Victoria Nile were expatriates from Great Britain but eventually the Brits realized that they needed more money to maintain the school. And, the only way to get the money was to open their doors to Indians. Thus, the British and Indians amalgamated the two schools, and I began attending Victoria Nile in Grade 3.

The school sat on the banks of Lake Victoria. It was a handsome building, run mostly by British teachers, for students from grades one to seven. The students were mainly British and Indian but a handful of Chinese, Korean, and African children attended as well.

Victoria Nile School (1993)

My best subjects were English and history, especially Roman history. Spelling, though, was not my greatest strength. When Rashida was home, she quizzed me on my spelling, and, much to my annoyance, tweaked my ear whenever I made a mistake. I had a blind spot when it came to spelling "tomato," and received many ear plucks as a result.

Regimentation was the order of the day at our school, and English was the mandatory language. My uniform consisted of a sleeveless dress of bottle green checks, and a bottle green cardigan for cooler days. Brown leather shoes and white socks completed the uniform. Nytil manufactured the fabric for the uniforms.

The teachers were strict. Talking was the worst sin. If we chattered too much, our punishment was detention to write lines, a ruler on the knuckles, or cello tape over the mouth. "Little Miss Talkative" suffered all of these cruel penalties many times.

My pal, Sabira, also landed me in trouble at school. Her sister, Rukhsana, fancied a guy who drove a red car. She and I once tried to stop him as he drove by our school, and he nearly had an accident. We were reported to the headmaster who gave us each twenty tackies (wallops with a cane), and we were unable to sit down for some time.

The British teachers could be quite condescending and mean in small ways. Their attitude was sufficiently bad that our parents noticed and complained about it among themselves. However, I don't think they ever made a formal protest. Mr. Eccles taught math, and Mrs. Eccles taught piano. They were both cold fishes, and I didn't like either of them. Nor did I like the math or piano lessons. On the other hand, some of the British teachers were excellent. I adored Mr. and Mrs. Davies who both taught at the school.

One of my best teachers was Miss Middleton. When I was about twelve years old, Miss Middleton crashed her motor scooter, and died instantly. Her death devastated me and the other students.

Each morning at assembly, the school required us to recite the *Lord's Prayer*, and sing Christian hymns. Mrs. Eccles played the piano, and we kids dutifully belted out *Morning Has Broken* and *All Things Bright and Beautiful*. Bapa and Ma were always surprisingly liberal in their attitudes. They encouraged all us children to learn about different cultures and religions, so they took no issue with this Christian indoctrination.

The teachers set aside reading time for us in the afternoon, and Maira and I often sat outside under the shade of giant avocado trees. If you can imagine, while we read, avocadoes constantly fell from the trees, bombarding us.

We participated in physical education classes three times each week. We played rounders and basketball in the school gym, and grass hockey outside. The tall African girls could smash our feet and knock us out of the game in no time flat so I tried to play on their team as often as I could. Elizabeth was my particular nemesis. She was an Amazon, and was wickedly competitive. She thrived on whacking the legs of anyone who got in her way with her hockey stick.

After I graduated from Victoria Nile, I attended the Parvatiban Muljibhai Madhvani Girls School in Jinja for a year of secondary education. The Madhvanis built and funded this school. School fees were affordable, and while the majority of the students were Asian, a large number of African students also attended.

I recall that the principal was a tall, stout, strict Indian woman who looked like an army major. We called her "GT" short for "German Tank." Her saving grace was that she had two lusciously good-looking sons, one of whom taught at our school for a semester. I still remember the first day he arrived in class. He wore bell-bottoms and a tight shirt—the "John Travolta" look. He was a welcome sight at an all-girls' school. My friends and I drooled over him.

My secondary school teachers were a mixture of Indian, African, British, American, and French. My favourite instructor was an African American woman named Sarah. She had moved to Jinja from the State of Washington when she married an educated Ugandan African. Sarah was my math teacher, and, although math was not my favourite subject, I scored well because Sarah's teaching method totally engaged me. My friends and I used to chat frequently with Sarah, and we learned a lot from her about the American way of life, the American school system, and the slogan, "Say it Loud, I'm Black and I'm Proud!"

Our French teacher was French to her core. I can't remember her name but we nicknamed her "Bushy" as she was fond of wearing sleeveless dresses but never shaved her armpits. This was rather novel to us young teenagers because we were fastidious about shaving our legs and armpits.

Our English teacher was terrific, and her classes were enthralling. She was an Indian woman who had married a man of Indian and African ancestry. He was known as a *chotaro* (a derogatory term used to describe a mixed race child). Mixed marriages were not common, and both Indians and Africans frowned upon them. We children, however, didn't judge her for her choice of husband. We just appreciated the way she made the study of English come alive for us.

Several of the teachers from India were brilliant, especially in subjects such as chemistry, physics, and math, and their English grammar was excellent. However, we sometimes burst into rude fits of laughter at their English pronunciations.

Hindu Celebrations

We had many Hindu friends, and took every opportunity to celebrate their religious festivities with them. My personal favourite was *Diwali* (the festival of lights). Diwali occurs between October and November each year, and lasts for five days.

Hindus, Jains, and Sikhs celebrate this festival for different reasons. Hindus in Jinja conducted traditional activities in their homes. They lit *diyas* (small clay lamps) filled with oil to signify the victory of good over evil, and they distributed sweets to family and friends. They wore new clothes, and the Hindu women, especially, put on colourful sarees imported from India for this special occasion. I was not into wearing sarees but Rashida, Zebby, and Almas took full advantage to purchase new ones to wear to the festivities to which they received invitations.

Another celebration was *Holi* which occurred at the end of the winter season on the last full moon day of the lunar month, and entailed people throwing coloured powder and coloured water at one another. Most people wore white clothes for this occasion though knowing full well that the stains would not wash off.

A third Hindu celebration was *Raksha Bandhan* or *Rakhi* whereby sisters declared their undying love for their brothers or anyone they perceived to be their brothers including cousins, friends, and relatives, by tying fancy, glittering bracelets made of fabric on the wrists of their brothers. The brothers, in turn, gave their sisters money, and promised to be good brothers throughout the year. My friends and I used to race from store to store checking out all the fancy bracelets. My sisters and their friends used to giggle over the fact that they could tie a bracelet on the wrist of any boy who was wooing them, and whom they did not necessarily want as a suitor—the message being that he was considered to be a "brother", and should shelve any romantic notions.

These Hindu celebrations did not, of course, detract from our Ismaili observances and festivities which were as essential to us as breathing.

CHAPTER TEN

Our Ismaili Religion

Our Religious Tenets and Practices

Religion is the central and continuous thread that weaves its way through the tapestry of my family history. Muslims worship Allah as the divine and omnipotent creator of the universe. Our faith embraces many prophets, including Jesus and Moses, but we believe Allah entrusted Prophet Muhammad with the sacred mission of interpreting His word to the world. All Muslims regard the *Qur'an* (Koran) as the Word of God, the sacred text of which Allah revealed to Prophet Muhammad through Angel Gabriel during the course of twenty-three years.

We Ismailis believe, though, that a literal interpretation of the language of the Qur'an is not sufficient to discern the spiritual intent of Allah. Rather, we must seek the meaning of His words in the circumstances of the times.

Our religion is not something that we bring out and dust off once a week. It is an integral part of our everyday lives. Aga Khan IV has said that "faith, intellect, and achievement go hand in hand." They are the building blocks for how we put our beliefs into practice.

My practical understanding of the tenets of Ismailism is that they enjoin us both to be good and to do good. We must be empathetic, generous, helpful, and respectful of other peoples' choices, and we must pray daily to achieve these goals.

I think the most serious misperception about Ismailis is that we are radical and fanatic fundamentalists. *Sharia* (Islamic) law has no place in our religion. Because of the persecution Nizari Khojas have suffered for so many centuries, most recently by the Taliban, we tend to keep our religious practices and our community low-profile but the truth is that the discrimination we have endured has taught us to be tolerant of diversity.

The Aga Khan is the religious and administrative leader of our community. He guides us in both our spiritual and worldly lives. Our faith tells us that he is the expression of Allah's grace to humanity. Aga Khan IV has said that the role of the Imam is to be responsible for the security of the Ismaili people, for the interpretation of their faith, and for their quality of life.

The Aga Khan directs us by means of *firmans* (written edicts) concerning issues as diverse as religious practices, education, commercial affairs, and social conduct. For example, various directives from Aga Khan III dealt with the emancipation and education of Ismaili women along with the need to abolish the mandatory veil.

Ismailism is unlike other religions which ordain or appoint ministers or priests to head local parishes, or which have a central base of religious authority such as the Papacy. Rather, each community has a local council, appointed by the Aga Khan, to deal with administrative and social issues. The council reports to the Aga Khan.

The *Mukhi* (guardian), along with the *Kamadia* (assistant or accountant), administers the affairs of the Jamatkhana. They are lay officials who preside over the daily rituals in the Jamatkhana, including the conduct of marriage ceremonies and other services. The preference is for married men to perform these duties so that their wives can assist them. Their appointments are usually for a term of one to three years.

Interestingly, the institution of marriage, in the Ismaili faith, does not carry any religious connotations. It is solely a matter of civil contract.

Aga Khan III

As I've mentioned, Sir Sultan Muhammad Shah Aga Khan III, the forty-eighth Imam, was our religious and secular guide for seventy-two years. In keeping with his position, he received extensive religious and oriental training from an early age but also studied with British tutors, and attended Eton and Cambridge.

Aga Khan III spent a great deal of time in England, and enjoyed a close relationship with the British Royal Family. He exhibited both affection and admiration for the British. Aga Khans have always instructed their adherents to be loyal citizens of their state. Thus, in British-dominated Uganda, Aga Khan III advised us Ismailis to adopt the British way of life, and to make English our primary language.

These ties, together with the overwhelming influence exercised by the British in the course of their imperial reign over India and Uganda, were material factors in the choices made by many parents in our community, including my own, to send their children to study in England.

Perhaps the greatest accomplishment of Aga Khan III was to modernize Ismaili society. He travelled extensively to many different countries in order to nourish and maintain close personal contacts with the scattered Nizari communities. In return, he enjoyed the unqualified loyalty of his followers.

Aga Khan III championed many causes. He was most passionate about the supreme importance of education and the concept of equality for women. To further his various goals, he established financial institutions such as insurance and investment trust companies in East Africa in connection with the provision of financial assistance for many of his social projects. He was instrumental in the construction of many Jamatkhanas, schools, hospitals, libraries, and clubs, and he created housing societies to ensure the construction of adequate housing for Nizaris. One of his many projects was the building of the Aga Khan School in Kampala.

The death of Aga Khan III in 1957 impacted us as though we had suffered a death in our own family. Our entire community mourned his loss. The Aga Khan had an abiding love for Egypt, so his family held his funeral in Cairo, and buried him in the Aswan.

The Last Will and Testament of Sir Sultan Muhammad Shah Aga Khan III was remarkable. In it, he reiterated the tradition that, for 1300 years, the Imam had enjoyed the absolute prerogative of choosing his successor from among any of his male descendants. He then stated that because of fundamental changes in the world including the advent of atomic science, he believed that the best interests of the Shia Muslim Ismaili Community dictated that his successor should be a young man raised in the new age who would bring a new outlook on life to the office. With those words, he bypassed his son, Aly, and appointed his grandson, Karim, to succeed him.

Aga Khan IV

Thus, on July 11, 1957, at the age of twenty, Prince Karim ascended to the seat of the Imamate as the forty-ninth Imam, and assumed the title of Aga Khan IV. Karim was born in Geneva in 1936. His mother was English. He spent his childhood in Nairobi. He began his education under private tutelage, and later attended a Swiss boarding school. At the time of Aga Khan III's death, Karim was studying oriental history at Harvard University. He graduated from Harvard in 1959 with a Bachelor of Arts (Honours) in Islamic History.

Three separate ceremonies celebrated Prince Karim's accession. The third one took place in Kampala. My parents undertook the perilous drive from Jinja to Kampala through a thunder storm to participate in the celebration. The Ismaili Jamatkhana was the site of the ceremony. My parents liked to recall that brilliant sunshine broke through the clouds just in time to herald the pageantry of the day.

Kampala Jamatkhana (1993)

Aga Khan IV wasted no time in carrying on the legacy of his grandfather. He travelled extensively through India, Pakistan, Afghanistan, Iran, China, Central Asia, and East Africa visiting Khoja communities. He was indefatigable.

His goals were similar to his grandfather's in many respects but he skirted public displays. Rather, he focused on meeting with his Nizari followers, and viewing first-hand their business, educational, medical, and other enterprises, facilities, and needs.

The Aga Khan's overriding concern was the elimination of poverty which he has always considered the first line of attack in defeating extremism. The Aga Khan Foundation, a non-profit organization, was in full swing by the mid-1960s. Funded by the Aga Khan and by donations from the Ismaili community, its aims, among other things, were to promote businesses compatible with local resources; to advance the economic, social and housing prospects of the impoverished; and to provide a higher quality of medical and educational institutions and facilities.

On two occasions, my family and I, along with other devotees, travelled to Kampala to see Aga Khan IV. On one memorable occasion, I proceeded to the front of the Jamatkhana with my parents and my brother, Nizar, and received an individual blessing from the Aga Khan. He bent down, and touched my shoulder as he gave his benediction. That was an honour I shall never forget, and one that I was able to enjoy again, many years later, in Canada.

Jinja's Jamatkhana

Our local Jamatkhana in Jinja was far more humble than the ornate Kampala mosque. It was an unobtrusive building barren of the minarets with which Muslims identify as a call to prayer. It looked not unlike the commercial buildings on the Main Street of Jinja.

Our Jamatkhana was sandy in colour with turquoise posts supporting the overhanging porch roof, turquoise trim surrounding the reddish-orange tile roof, and a turquoise cap at the roof peak. The front entrance stood out from the building's facade, and crested in a triangular arch. A white wavy topped fence surrounded the Jamatkhana. The manicured grounds housed a social hall where religious festivities, including wedding ceremonies, were held.

Jinja Jamatkana (1993)

Ma and I, and whichever of my sisters were not studying in London, attended the Jamatkhana every Friday evening, that being the traditional Muslim prayer day. Ma always attended the Jamatkhana on at least one other day during the week. I usually accompanied her unless more enticing secular activities beckoned.

At the Jamatkhana, men and women sat separately but no wall divided them. At our services, we recited *dw'as* (prayers), meditated and sang *ginans* (devotional hymns), and listened, in both Gujarati and English, to revered writings from the Aga Khans. At home, our Ismaili custom was, and still is, to recite a dw'a each morning and each evening. The prayer has seven parts, and each part begins with *bismillah al-rahman al-rahim* (in the name of Allah the most beneficent and the most merciful).

I attended religious education classes in the Jamatkhana compound every Thursday evening, and occasionally on Saturdays. Our teacher was a stern missionary lady who frowned on my mini-skirts. She taught us *dw'a* (both meaning and pronunciation), made sure that we recited firmans and ginans properly, and gave us instruction in reading and writing Arabic. All my little Ismaili girlfriends attended with me, and, like children everywhere, we giggled and misbehaved our way through the classes.

Religious Observances and Celebrations

Ismaili religious and social celebrations were my favourite days of the year in Jinja. March 21 on the lunar calendar marks our *Navroz* (New Year). Navroz is a festival that Ismailis have celebrated for many centuries. It observes an age-old agrarian custom, adopted by various cultures and religions, and signifies the beginning of the new year and the first day of spring.

In the *Surah Ya-Sin* (a portion of the text of the Holy Qur'an), Allah says:

> Let the once dead earth be a sign to them. We gave it life, and from it produced grain for their sustenance. We planted it with palm and the vine and watered it with gushing springs, so that men might feed on its fruit. It was not their hands that made all this. Should they not give thanks?

> — Surah 36, Verses 33–35

On Navroz, we give thanks and praise to Allah for our blessings, recite devotional poetry, look forward to the future with buoyancy and confidence, and gather with family and friends to rejuvenate the bonds that strengthen us both individually and communally. In accordance with our rituals, we hand out dried fruits, nuts, and grains which represent blessings of abundance and sustenance.

In Jinja, we prayed in thanksgiving at the Jamatkhana, greeted one another afterward with the traditional salutation—*Navroz Mubarak* (congratulations on the auspicious occasion of Navroz), and then rejoiced in merriment, eating, and dancing.

Ramadan (the ninth month of the year in the Islamic calendar) is the Islamic holy month of dawn to sunset fasting. The purpose of Ramadan is to remind us of the virtues of patience and humility, to give us time for self-reflection, to pray more often, and to perform charitable acts.

Eid ul-Fitr (festivity at the conclusion of the fast) is a three day holiday that marks the end of Ramadan. We sometimes call it the "Smaller Eid."

Eid ul-Adha (the four-day festival to mark the homecoming that follows the annual pilgrimage to Mecca) is the "Greater Eid." Traditionally, the welcome home included slaughtering and eating a goat. In Jinja, we always hired a butcher to carry out the slaughter. In the early days, before we had refrigeration, we would eat what we could at our celebratory meal, and then give the rest of the meat away to the needy.

The traditional greeting for Eid is *Eid Mubārak* (Blessed Eid). On each Eid, we attended Jamatkhana for *Eid Namaz* (Islamic prayers) at 10 a.m., and then travelled from house to house greeting our family members and friends. One of the Eid customs in our town was for people to hand out sweets or a couple of shillings to the children who came by to visit. I always made a killing.

Ma loved to cook for every Eid. Along with goat curry, she served us a traditional meal that included *sav* (a sweet vermicelli dish) as a starter, *samosa* (pastry stuffed with beef, chicken or vegetables), and *biryani* (curried chicken or beef served on a bed of saffron rice with sauces). I set aside the poultry or meat, and just ate the rice and sauces.

During Eid, we always sent a tray of Indian sweets to the homes of relatives and friends. Most people bought their sweets from the Indian shops on Main Street for these occasions but Ma insisted on making her own. Because she was such a superb cook, everyone coveted her delicacies. The Indian names for the sweets she prepared are *laddu, paak, paara, halwo, jalebi,* and *ghanthia.* Ghanthia is actually savoury but we eat sweet and savoury at the same time.

Ismailis also rejoice, each year, on the occasion of *Khushyali* (celebration) to commemorate the December 13 birthday of Aga Khan IV, and on Imamat Day to honour the July 11 accession of Aga Khan IV.

As there have been forty-nine Imams, celebrating the birth and accession of each of them was not practical. We did, however, commemorate, by quiet prayer and reflection in the Jamatkhana, *Milad-un-Nabi,* the birth of Prophet Muhammad; *Yawm-e Ali,* the birth of Hazrat Ali; and *Idd e-Ghadir,* the choice by Prophet Muhammad to anoint Hazrat Ali, his cousin and son-in-law, as his immediate successor. Shiite Muslims revere Hazrat Ali as the most important and spiritual and intellectual authority in Islam after the Holy Prophet.

Ismaili Funeral Traditions

Funerals in Jinja were sombre ceremonies. They began at the Jamatkhana where everyone was welcome for prayers and chanting. Only the men, though, attended at the cemetery for the burial.

In accordance with Muslim tradition, we bury the body of our deceased right away. We do not cremate it. Nor do we employ a casket. We simply wrap the naked body in white muslin, a finely woven cotton fabric. Our rationale is that a person arrives on earth with nothing, and thus should leave with nothing. Likewise, our tombstones are not fancy, and display no embellishments. They show only the name and the dates of the deceased's birth and death. The mourners must be careful to position the body facing Mecca.

In Jinja, the lack of storage facilities for corpses was an added incentive for immediate burial. My Nanima died in the late afternoon, and we really had to hustle, despite our grief, to bury her before sundown, and then attend services at the Jamatkhana. Nanima, Nanabapa, my great grandmother, and my sister, Khatun, all rest in the Muslim cemetery on Nalufenya Road at the junction with Baxi Road. Unhappily, a plan is afoot today for the hospital, which owns the land, to sell it for real estate development.

CHAPTER ELEVEN

My Brothers and Sisters

My Big Brother

My older brother, Bahadur, was a privileged child but was always responsible. He and Bapa were close friends as well as father and son, and he valued Bapa's guidance. Like many other children of affluent families, Bahadur attended Hillsea College, in Basingstoke, Hampshire, about eighty kilometres southwest of London. When Aga Khan IV assumed his title in 1957, he mentioned that there were only about one hundred Ismailis in England. At the time, Bahadur was one of them.

On his return to Jinja in 1960, Bahadur joined Bapa in running the family business but he had a wild side, too—at least by Jinja standards. He was a sports enthusiast who played tennis, badminton, table tennis, snooker, and cricket. In fact, he was a table tennis champion of Jinja, and won many trophies.

Bahadur, even in Africa, was a keen bettor on British football pools. One time, he won a mess of money. I remember him sitting in our dining room deciding what to do with his winnings. He was a generous man, and shared with those closest to him which, of course, included me. I received my first board game of Chinese Checkers as a result of his bounty.

Like young men the world over, Bahadur was passionate about cars. When word reached Jinja that the Isuzu dealership in Kampala had imported three new vehicles from Japan, Bahadur and his friend, Dolar, convinced their respective fathers that each of them needed a vehicle so off they went to Kampala to purchase them. They managed the drive back to Jinja in their fancy new automobiles without incident but, once home, Bahadur promptly crashed his burgundy Isuzu in front of the post office. Luckily for Bahadur, his doting Bapa allowed him to return to the Kampala dealership to purchase a chocolate brown Isuzu.

Bahadur was a huge fan of the East African Safari Rally, one of the most arduous long distance car rallies in the world. The Rally, first named the East African Coronation Safari, to celebrate the coronation of Queen Elizabeth II, began in 1953, and wended its way through Kenya, Uganda and Tanganyika. Each year, when it roared through Jinja, the entire town turned out to spectate. Quite a few of Bahadur's friends participated. One of them was Shekhar Mehta, whose grandfather, Nanji Kalidas Mehta, was one of the legendary business pioneers from the Gujarat. He eventually established a sugar cane plantation in Lugazi, and expanded into other businesses as well. Shekhar won the East African Safari Rally a record five times in 1973, 1979, 1980, and 1981 while driving a Datsun, and in 1982 while driving a Nissan Violet (GT).

Bahadur first met Suru Madhvani a short time after he moved home from England. They clicked immediately, and they've been friends ever since. Not long after they met, Suru bought a house on Wilson Road just behind our Nalufenya Road home. Bahadur and Suru were quite the young rascals. They squandered a fair amount of time carousing and chasing the ladies. All these years later, Bahadur still closely guards the details of their philandering.

Bahadur crashed and burned when Zubeda Karmali captured his heart. Zubeda's sister, Malek, who owned the Ann Wallace Department Store, and her husband, Madat Hemani, were family friends. When I was about twelve, Madat mentioned to Bahadur that he would like to introduce him to Zubeda.

Zubeda was born in 1941 in Kisumu, Kenya, and lived there with her parents, Fatma and Abdulla Karmali. Zubeda had six brothers and sisters, and she and her family were devout adherents of our Ismaili faith. Zubeda worked at the family owned and operated Ann & Agnes Department Store in Kisumu, and was intensely fashion conscious—my kind of gal.

At her sister and brother-in-law's instigation, she came to Jinja, and she and Bahadur began dating in both Jinja and Kisumu, which were quite some distance apart. After a short courtship, Bahadur asked Zubeda to marry him. Zubeda was a beautiful young woman, with intense dark brown eyes and a gentle personality. We all adored her.

On September 21, 1969, Bahadur and Zubeda married at a grand wedding and luncheon in Kisumu. We all drove there from Jinja, a distance of about 240 kilometres. The wedding took place at the Aga Khan Social Hall where Zubeda's family and mine welcomed about 300 guests. Zubeda's sister-in-law, Laila Karamali, was the Matron of Honour and the best man was Badrudin Charania, a close friend of our family.

Zubeda and Bahadur arriving at the Aga Khan Hall

(L – R) Malek Hemani, Bahadur, Zubeda, Madat Hemani

(L – R) Rashida, Zebby, Bapa, Nazlin, Bahadur, Zubeda, Ma, Almas

(L – R) Badrudin Charania, Bahadur, Zubeda,
Laila, Abdulla and Fatma Karmali

The bride and groom arrived together in the best man's 1968 Mercedes-Benz which Bahadur's pals had decked out in colourful crepe paper streamers. Zubeda looked radiant, but Bahadur simply looked scared.

Zubeda was petite but enhanced her height with a fancy beehive hairdo, which was all the rage at the time. She wore a short white dress of silk and lace, three strands of white pearls, and low-heeled white shoes as she was never comfortable in high heels. In keeping with tradition, she adorned the palms of her hands and feet with henna. Bahadur wore a conservative dark blue suit, white shirt, and dark tie.

I was thirteen years old at the time, and, if I do say, a miniature fashion plate. I poured over my magazines to find the perfect pink lace frock for the wedding, and Ma engaged a famous seamstress in Kampala to re-create it for me. Ma bought the material at the A.S. Jaffer store in Kampala. On my dress, I wore a stylish brooch which belonged to Almas. My hair was short, almost like a pixie cut, with bangs. Actually, my hair style has changed little over the years.

After the ceremony, we all drove back to Jinja in a caravan of cars with horns honking. Ma greeted Bahadur and Zubeda at our front door, and welcomed them home with sweets which she placed on their tongues— an Ismaili tradition, a huge hug, and her trademark welcoming smile.

Bapa, Bahadur, Zebby, and Almas organized a lively reception back in Jinja at our picturesque Town Hall. We managed to festoon the bride and groom's bedroom with streamers hanging from the ceiling.

Bahadur and Zubeda lived with us at our family home on Nalufenya Road but had their own quarters and separate entrance. Bahadur loved the plush blond, amber, and brown tones of elgin teak wood from trees that grew in the vicinity of Lake Victoria, and had furniture specially handcrafted for their suite by our friend, Balbir Sagoo, whose family owned and operated sawmills.

Zubeda, who we call *bhabhi* (sister-in-law), is the heart of our family. She is quiet but self-possessed and full of love. Because her mother was an expert cook, Zubeda never mastered the art while she was growing up but Ma gave her lessons, her mom handed down recipes to her, and she became a versatile and creative chef. She still does most of the cooking for our family, and we might starve without her. Whenever she leaves home for a vacation, I rely on Zebby, Rashida, and Almas for my meals. I have no shame.

Free-Spirited Rashida

Rashida was sixteen years older than I. When I was a youngster, I didn't see too much of her. After graduating from Jinja Secondary School, Rashida moved to London. She attended St. Godrick's College in Hampstead Heath which offered secretarial and business courses. Like Bapa, she had a brain for business.

To the horror of both Ma and me, Rashida had no interest in carrying on the family "clothes horse" tradition. For years, whenever she arrived home for a visit, Ma summoned a tailor from town to come to our house and take her measurements. Ma then ordered a selection of fashionable dresses for Rashida in the vain hope that she would wear them when she returned to London.

After graduating from St. Godrick's, Rashida came back to Jinja, and worked at The Standard Bank Limited for about five years as secretary to the Managing Director. After the glitter and glamour of London, she felt as though she was suffocating in Jinja, both literally and figuratively.

From about the age of ten, Rashida suffered from serious allergies. In Uganda, she was sick all the time, couldn't sleep, and reamed her way through boxes of Kleenex. Bapa took her to dozens of medical practitioners but none of them were able to diagnose her problem. One terrible experience she endured was from a physician who gave her injections through her nose. That was a whole new strata of pain.

Bapa and Ma banned all flowers from the house for a time, and bought new mattresses and pillows. Nothing helped. Each time Rashida returned to Jinja from London, the problem surfaced, and was worse than before. She found each homecoming dreadfully depressing. Once, as she approached Entebbe by aeroplane, she said fatalistically, "my country's coming for me."

Rashida found social life in Jinja stifling, too. In addition to their natural strictness, Bapa and Ma worried about both safety and social propriety. Jinja was a small town, and, like small towns everywhere, the residents delighted in malicious gossip about the behaviour—or misbehaviour—of their young folk.

Rashida was an independent soul. Finally, she screwed up her courage, and told Bapa and Ma that she wished to return to London to live and work. Because she possessed a Ugandan passport, she needed a visa to enter Great Britain. Balbir Sagoo drove her to Kampala, in his new Mercedes, to obtain one. On the way back home, Balbir skidded on a treacherous patch of road by the notorious Mabira Forest, and totalled the car.

After their shock subsided, they checked themselves for injuries. They both sustained bad bruising but no serious harm, except that Rashida suffered a deep gash on the inside of her forearm. Terror of an attack by thieves or murderers beset them but, fortunately, some friends stopped to pick them up before any worse fate befell them. They rushed back to Jinja, and headed straight to the hospital as Rashida's arm urgently needed stitching. She then had to delay her departure until her arm healed. The gash was quite serious, and, in Africa, people did not trifle with wounds as they easily became infected. Ma felt badly about the accident but revelled in the chance to fuss over Rashida for a few more days.

Once Rashida reached London, a "help wanted" ad in the newspaper for a publishing company called Blandford Press caught her eye. She applied, and the personnel manager asked her to start the next day as a secretary to a senior executive. She faced one stumbling block in that she needed a work permit but the company wrote a letter for her, and she was able to obtain the permit without any hassle.

The corporate offices of Blandford Press sat nearby Shaftesbury Theatre. A few years later, when I was living with Rashida in London, we had a standing date to shop in Oxford Street on Thursday evenings. The staff at the theatre came to know me, and, while I was waiting for my sister, they let me sit at the back of the theatre to keep warm so I was able to watch the matinees for free.

Both as a student and as a secretary in London, Rashida was a free spirit. She developed a like-minded circle of friends, and, both before and after her marriage, she loved to explore different restaurants, attend all the plays and musicals, and travel endlessly.

Rashida had a good friend from Africa whose husband was Pakistani. One day, her friend invited Rashida along on a day trip to Battersea Park. She didn't feel like going but decided to exert herself. The husband invited a friend of his, Mansur Ali, along as well. Mansur wanted to go on the roller coaster. Nobody was interested until Rashida stepped up, and said she'd give it a try.

They chatted like old friends, and Mansur ferreted out information about where Rashida lived, and that she attended Jamatkhana every Friday. Mansur said that he drove by her home, and would be happy to pick her up and take her to the services. That was well over forty years ago, and they're still riding life's roller coaster together.

Mansur, a tall and handsome young man, was an Ismaili who hailed from Karachi, Pakistan. His parents were Mariambanu, born in 1912, and Gulamhussein Ali, born in 1918, both in Karachi. He had seven brothers and sisters. He immigrated to London, in his early twenties, without a shilling in his pocket, to look for better opportunities. He worked at all kinds of odd jobs. At the time Mansur came to London, it was the most common thing to do. People from his region were not yet thinking of heading for Canada or the United States. Except for his younger brother, Ashik, who joined Mansur in London, all of his family remained in Pakistan.

Rashida and Mansur dated for about a year, became engaged in England, and then travelled to Jinja to meet the family and marry. I was agog with excitement. When they arrived, we all loved Mansur at once but had great difficulty understanding him. His native tongue was Sindhi, and his accent British. Sindhi bears little similarity to Kutchi, my family's language of origin, but somehow we worked it out. The language snag amused all the guests who deluged our home to meet him.

Mansur's baggage disappeared on the way to Jinja, and we were unable to trace it. The marriage ceremony was to take place only two or three days hence so Bapa sent out an SOS for some Indian tailors. Overnight, they sewed a new wardrobe for Mansur that included his wedding suit along with some other western suits and pants. Zubeda's sister, Malek, ordered shirts for him from her family's Ann & Agnes Department Store in Kisumu.

Fortunately, Rashida's luggage, which contained her wedding dress, arrived in Jinja without incident. Rashida herself was not so fortunate. For two days before the wedding, she suffered, predictably, from her allergy affliction, and wasn't sure she'd even be able to stand up at the ceremony. Dr. Thakkar, though, paid her a house call, and either patched her up or drugged her enough to make it through her wedding day.

During the few days before the wedding, Mansur stayed in a guest room at our home. Because he had a passionate love affair with food, he found it no trouble at all to charm Ma. She was at her best planning menus, and positively twittered while she prepared his favourite dishes. Mansur's meal of choice from Ma's repertoire was biryani, a bed of rice topped with spices and dried curried chicken or tilapia which he gobbled down as fast as she whipped it up.

At the wedding, I was resplendent (or so I thought) in a pink flowery printed mini dress Rashida had purchased for me at Selfridges in London, and funky white lace boots. Rashida had told Mansur of my shoe fetish, and he had actually made the boots for me before they left London.

Rashida and Mansur wed at the Jamatkhana on April 21, 1971. We were slightly downcast that none of Mansur's family or friends from Pakistan were able to attend but we invited about 300 guests from Jinja and Kampala. Our family tradition was to hold our wedding ceremonies in the social section of the Jamatkhana so our non-Ismaili friends could attend. The elegant reception Bapa and Ma arranged consisted of a dinner at the Crested Crane Hotel on Nalufenya Road, only a few blocks from our home.

Rashida and Mansur

(L – R) Nazlin, Almas (with baby Shalina), Mansur, Rashida and Zebby

They honeymooned in Kenya because Rashida didn't want Mansur to miss the opportunity to see that spectacular country. I don't know if other families are like ours but Bahadur and Zubeda accompanied them!

After their honeymoon, Rashida and Mansur returned immediately to England.

Bapa encouraged them to buy a large house, likely with a view to family members having a place to stay when they visited London. Accordingly, they bought a run-down three level home in Stoke Newington, in the London borough of Hackney, that was in urgent need of renovation. Bapa flew to England to see the house, and the condition of the plumbing and electrical works horrified him. He immediately commissioned some trades people to fix it all.

When Rashida and Mansur met, he was working as a salesman obtaining contracts for a shoe design and manufacturing business owned by a Greek gentleman and his son. Mansur endeared himself to me forever by ensuring that his shoe samples, which he was entitled to keep, were all in my size.

After their marriage, Blandford Press relocated to the countryside to be closer to its printing presses. Rashida did not wish to move, and she received a generous severance package from her company.

Rashida and Mansur decided to strike out as proprietors of their own firm. Rashida asked Bapa for a loan but, in his typical generous fashion, he gave the money to them as a gift. They combined that gift with her severance pay to acquire a shoe business. They set up in two locations. The first was a huge stall at the indoor bohemian Kensington Market, where Freddie Mercury and Roger Taylor, before the legendary rock band, *Queen*, took off, manned a stall selling artwork and later clothes. The second location was in their own neighbourhood of Stoke Newington.

Mansur was able to purchase designer shoes wholesale from his former boss's factory under a different label. It was a common practice. He sold the shoes at cheaper prices than those bearing the original designer label, and was phenomenally successful.

Rashida and Mansur often visited his family in Karachi. The first time they went, Rashida was fortunate to meet his mother who was elderly and in poor health. She also came to know Mansur's two older spinster sisters.

Headstrong Zebby and Artistic Almas

Because Zebby and Almas were close in age and their lives so intertwined, I must write about them together.

How do I best diplomatically describe my darling sister, Zebby, as a young adult? I would say that she was a headstrong, charming, carousing social butterfly. Although that sounds alarming, our lives were pretty simple, and her worst "carousing" was probably driving her car too fast—which she did frequently—careening through the streets of Jinja as though she were on the Indianapolis Motor Speedway. Almas was a quieter soul but implacably stubborn.

Zebby, following in Ma's footsteps, was a talented and creative dress designer and seamstress. In 1965, she moved to the London Borough of Hammersmith and Fulham to study dress design at Paris Academy in quirky Shepherd's Bush.

Almas followed Zebby to London a year or so later. Like Zebby, Almas was an artistic child. Through Zebby, she developed an interest in hairdressing, and she studied at the Alan School of Hairdressing.

Zebby boarded for about three years in Shepherd's Bush at the home of the formidable Mrs. Hookway, recommended to Bapa by a friend. Almas joined her there. Mrs. Hookway's house rules were stringent, and she was a strict landlady, but, at the same time, she loved and spoiled her boarders. She cooked them delectable meals, and took care of their laundry. She was an interesting soul, not a learned person, but well-read.

Bapa adored Mrs. Hookway, and spoiled her incessantly. When he was in London, he wined and dined her, and showered her with jewellery and other gifts. Bapa was exhibiting more than a little method in his madness as he wanted the best possible care for his girls.

Mrs. Hookway has another claim to fame in our family annals. The name "Zebunissa" was a mouthful, and, in Jinja, we had shortened it to "Zebun" which was not too attractive. Mrs. Hookway came up with the diminutive "Zebby." It suited my sister perfectly, and we have all called her "Zebby" ever since. Zebby arrived in England with her buddy, Rozina Shariff, whose family and ours were friends. Rozina worked as a secretary, and was also a Mrs. Hookway protégé.

With regard to Mrs. Hookway's infamous house rules, she may have been utilizing the old adage that the best defence is a good offence. Almas was walking down the street one day when she spied Mrs. Hookway arm in arm with Albert, another of the boarders. Clandestine snooping then revealed to the girls that Mrs. Hookway and Albert were secret lovers which titillated Zebby, Almas, and Rozina no end. Zebby and Almas still giggle about that surreptitious romance.

Foreign exchange restrictions in Uganda were tight. So, in order to pay school tuition, to reimburse Mrs. Hookway for room and board, and to give Zebby, and later Almas, a small spending allowance, Bapa was obliged to siphon off money to England via the black market in currency, exchanging Ugandan shillings for British currency.

The scheme, which was common, worked this way. British expatriates returned from visits to England with pounds sterling. They did not declare the money because they knew they could sell it on the black market, and realize a profit. Bapa acquired the pounds, and gave them to Ma. She then crammed care packages bound for England with all manner of personal items and spices, including Johnson's baby powder tins containing the contraband loot.

Upholding the extravagant traditions of the females in our family, Zebby was an extreme fashionista and shopaholic. On one occasion, she and her friends decided they wanted a shopping vacation in Europe but they needed spending money so Zebby telephoned Bapa. Unbelievably to me, she conned him into flying to London, and escorting her and her friends to Europe. For such a hard-headed businessman, he was a push-over when it came to Zebby.

Zebby's friend, Rozina Shariff, who was rather short, adored high heels, and wore them all the time, partly to be fashionable but mostly to add to her height. Bapa wanted her to buy sensible shoes but she refused. In a department store in Paris, she tripped and fell down the escalator but didn't break any bones. Bapa, nonetheless, was horrified, and angry with Rozina.

On her return to Jinja from her studies in England, Zebby first worked, as a teller, at the Standard Bank with Rashida.

After Almas returned, Bapa rented a shop for them on Iganga Road close to the Argus Bookstore. It was a combined hair-dressing salon and dress-making establishment. Zebby designed the clothes, and, in the back of the store, they divided an area off for the seamstresses. Nanima could see the shop from her home, and used to keep an eye on them.

As well as being a business establishment, the shop was the social conversation pit of the town. At 10 a.m. each morning, Nanima sent goodies over, and their friends of all persuasions, including British, Indians, and some professional Africans, dropped by to catch up on the town gossip. Zebby and Almas did a brisk business as they pretty much enjoyed a monopoly.

Ultimately, though, they closed the shop because Zebby wanted to work at Nytil, the giant textile mill. She made a dear friend there, Mrs. Brennan, who was the salt of the earth. Almas, meanwhile, carved out a hair salon at our house. Zebby was the antithesis of our practical, grounded Rashida. For instance, when Bahadur's friend, Bahadur Alibhai, who owned the Toyota dealership in Kampala, imported a Celica for his family, Zebby convinced Bapa she wanted that vehicle, and Bahadur, in turn, convinced his friend to sell the car to Bapa. Zebby had great fun slewing around Jinja in her one of a kind, light grey Celica while Rashida, on the other hand, drove sedately in an old, blue Ford Prefect.

Rustam Jeraj's first meeting with Zebby was the result of a conspiracy between his brother-in-law, Noorali Mohamed, and my ready, willing, and able Ma. Noorali was a cousin of ours, and his wife, Noorjahan, was Rustam's sister. Noorali and Noorjahan, along with Rustam and his family, lived in Fort Portal near the Ruwenzori Mountains in western Uganda close to the border with the Congo. The Ruwenzori Mountains, with their permanently snow-capped peaks, often shrouded by mist, are a designated World Heritage Site.

Rustam was born in 1942 in Fort Portal. His parents were Shirinbai Jeraj and Abdulrasul Jeraj, both born in Kutch, India. He had six brothers and sisters. His parents owned a tea plantation.

Rustam obtained a degree in chemical engineering from Loughborough University in Leicestershire, England. He financed part of his education with a grant from the Ugandan government. As a result, on his return to Uganda, he had to work for the state. His assignment was to participate in the United Nations Industrial Development Project, staffed by four engineers and economists, of whom two were Ismaili and two African. They travelled every nook and cranny of Uganda together, surveying industries, and interviewing mayors and district commissioners.

The goal of the project was to lay the groundwork for a plan to develop small-scale local industries. One of the schemes was to establish a brewery to distil alcohol using green bananas but it failed to come to fruition.

Rustam's first project was in Jinja, and he stayed at the Crested Crane Hotel. Noorali was in Jinja at the same time, and was staying in the guest bedroom next to my room. I was in bed but heard Ma and Noorali whispering in the corridor. I eavesdropped shamelessly. Noorali suggested to Ma that he introduce Zebby to Rustam. Ma was a keen participant in their little conspiracy. She replied that the first birthday of Bahadur and Zubeda's daughter, Shalina, was coming up shortly, and that Noorali and his wife should bring Rustam to the party.

Thus, Noorali and Noorjahan arrived in the evening with Rustam in tow. Zebby and Almas were in the courtyard organizing everything. When Rustam first saw them, he thought Almas was Zebby but they quickly righted the confusion. Zebby had decked herself out in a gold Twiggy pant suit with a tunic top, and had done up her hair. Rustam was smitten.

Rustam and Zebby began dating. At the time, he worked for the government in Kampala but he came to Jinja every weekend, and stayed with us. He drove a beat-up Volkswagen which Zebby abhorred so she made him hide it in the garage, and they drove her dashing Celica.

Rustam was an intellectual, and every weekend, he conquered the crossword puzzle in a newspaper called *The Nation*. He endeared himself to me by helping me with my homework.

Zebby and Rustam dated for about a year before their marriage. Almas didn't enjoy the same good fortune as Zebby. While she was boarding at Mrs. Hookway's, she and another boarder, Michael, fell in love. Mrs. Hookway was suspicious but they managed to thwart her. Michael was the great love of Almas' life but she left him to return to Jinja as she did not think our parents would accept him.

Almas was devastated, and lost so much weight she was skin and bones. Years later, Ma told Almas she should not have rejected Michael but, at the time, Almas thought it was the right thing to do.

Dependable Nizar

Nizar has always kept a low profile in our boisterous family. He is quiet, kind, and dependable. Nizar treasured his solitude in Jinja but also loved hanging out with Mariam Masi and her children. He possesses a wicked sense of humour; is an excellent artist, working in water colours; and, like Ma and Zebby, he has a flair for designing clothes.

When Nizar finished school in Jinja, he went to work for Bapa. By that time, Bapa had opened a depot to distribute Pepsi and Schweppes. Nizar managed the depot, and impressed Bapa with his acumen and attention to detail.

I rarely missed my brothers and sisters while they lived in London because they were always coming and going to and from Jinja. Then, my turn came.

CHAPTER TWELVE

My London Sojourn

Black Despair and Purple Passion

The first cataclysmic shifting of the earth under my feet occurred in August of 1971 when I was fifteen years old. We were at the family dinner table, and Ma had served my favourite foods. That, coupled with my parents, in the weeks before, engaging in secretive conversations that ceased whenever I joined them gave me an inkling that something was up involving me.

Once we finished dinner, my parents got right to it. They told me that I was to leave Jinja to live in London with Rashida and Mansur, and attend school there. At first, I was excited, and surprisingly mature about their decision. My parents said they were anxious that I obtain the best secondary education possible, and that all my sisters loved living in London so they were comfortable that I would, too.

However, reality set in when I told my best friend, Maira, that my parents were sending me away. Her reaction was disbelief, and then despair. She infected me. The two of us were so close that leaving Maira was as difficult as leaving my family for what I now thought of as my banishment. For weeks, we wallowed in that black void of despair of which only teenagers are capable.

We said our goodbyes the day before, and shed enough tears in Maira's bedroom to flood the River Nile. Maira was working on her homework at the time, and cried so much she smeared the pages until they were indecipherable.

Although I knew that life under the political regime in Uganda was menacing, I didn't realize the extent of my parents' concern for my personal safety. Idi Amin had overthrown Obote, the environment was unsettling, and the Africans were growing increasingly resentful toward

Indians. Soldiers began patrolling the streets. They were arrogant, abusive, and puffed up with their own power. My parents were apprehensive about kidnappings, and even more vigilant than usual.

Ma was devastated about my leaving but resolute in backing Bapa's plan for me. On the day of my departure, she was so upset she refused to drive to the airport with us. We said our farewells at the front door. I wasn't sure Ma would ever stop hugging me—and I didn't want her to let go.

Bapa and Bahadur drove Almas and me to the Entebbe airport. Almas was taking a vacation from her hairdressing job to escort me to England. Things went from bad to worse at the airport. I was sitting in the lounge, and had placed my purse at my feet when a disgusting felon stole my leopard skin wallet, one of my most treasured possessions. I never recovered it.

Except for short trips to Kenya, I had never flown internationally. The immense Lufthansa aeroplane and the flight scared me silly. When we arrived in Frankfurt, the massive and confusing hubbub of an expanded airport confounded Almas. By the time we stumbled across our gate, we had missed our flight.

Meanwhile, in London, Rashida and Mansur were waiting patiently at Heathrow Airport to meet us. Those days preceded the instant communication of cell phones and the like so we had no way to advise them of our delay. When the last passengers trickled through customs, Rashida and Mansur were alarmed but had no option other than to return home, and await news about what had befallen us.

Almas and I managed to catch a later flight but when we arrived at Heathrow, no one was there to welcome us. I was wearing only a thin cotton dress and cardigan. London, that evening, was almost a caricature of itself—cold, rainy, dismal, and dreary. I had never experienced such inclement weather.

Almas had enough smarts that we were able to hail a cab which delivered us to my new home at 34 Manse Road, Stoke Newington in Hackney. The streetscape was charming. Old-fashioned lamp standards punctuated the sidewalks. Reddish-brown brick walls, two feet high and embedded with black wrought-iron fences, separated the sidewalks from small front courtyards. Bushes and trees planted in the courtyards overhung the street. The facade of the house was reddish-brown brick adorned with white trim edging tall narrow windows. To my young eye, though, it resembled a drab prison.

Rashida and Mansur had just recently bought the house, and, when I arrived, were in the throes of renovating and re-decorating. They were relocating the living room and dining room to the second floor, and converting the first floor to two bedrooms. The second floor was to house a living room, dining room, and small kitchen. On the third floor were another two bedrooms.

The only saving grace in my tortuous day was that they had finished my bedroom, and carpeted it in dark purple. Rashida knew that my favourite colours since childhood had been purple and mauve. And, bless her heart, she had even bought me a waste paper basket with David Cassidy's face on it.

When I awoke the next morning, miserable grey clouds still overcast the sky. Being wrenched from my home, parents and friends; flying internationally for the first time; missing our flight; arriving with no one to meet us; freezing in my thin tropical clothes; and finding the house in chaos were almost too much for me to bear. To top it off, I was so homesick that, even today, when I think about it, my stomach cramps.

Rashida and Almas, though, knew me well. After a tear-drenched breakfast, they asked if I would like to indulge in some retail shopping therapy on Oxford Street. "Oxford Street!" It was the epicentre of my fashion magazine fantasies. I cheered up instantly.

And, as I cheered up, so did the day. Our bus ride was splendid. I was able to identify many of the sights since I knew a great deal about London from my sisters' endless descriptions and from my Argus Bookstore books and magazines. I even knew the history of Oxford Street. Originally a Roman road, and located in the City of Westminster in Central London, it runs from the Marble Arch to Hyde Park, and houses major chain department stores, flagship stores, traditional British shops, and "mod" boutiques.

Even at that age, I lived and breathed fashion, and here, on Oxford Street, was my ticket to fashion heaven. My favourite stores were Selfridges, a high end department store which had one-of-a-kind Christmas decorations; John Lewis, the world's oldest department store, an iconic building highlighted by the statue *Winged Figure*, and known for its slogan "Never Knowingly Undersold"; the celebrated Marks & Spencer flagship store, the largest clothing retailer in Great Britain; Dickens & Jones on Regent Street opposite Liberty's, a department store famous for its fabrics; and an infinite array of other shops including two of my personal favourites, Dorothy Perkins and C & A, a large retailer of ladies clothing.

I wasted no time buying myself some warm clothing including a handsome black wool coat with yellow rickrack, numerous sweaters in a rainbow of colours, and bellbottom pants. The retail highlight of the day, though, was at Marks & Spencer where Rashida bought me a bedspread and drapes, in shades of mauve and purple, for my new bedroom.

In the course of the morning, I rebounded from the abyss of teenage desolation to the peak of teenage ecstasy. And, then, the day got even better as Rashida and Almas introduced me to Wimpy's in London.

I have always been a junk food aficionado, and loved to indulge myself at Wimpy's in Kampala. I almost always ordered a horrible hamburger consisting of a dry, overcooked meat patty skimpily garnished with a smidgeon of cheese and mustard, and topped by a pickle. It was worth the price of admission, though, for my favourite dessert in the entire world—a Knickerbocker Glory, an ice cream sundae served in a tall glass with elaborate layers of ice cream, jelly, and fruit topped by an enormous maraschino cherry. And there, on the menu, at Wimpy's in London was the self-same Knickerbocker Glory!

When we arrived home at 34 Manse Road, I called Ma right away. She had expected a sobbing and reproachful call from me begging to return to Jinja. Instead, I babbled blissfully about the wonders of London shopping, my divine purple bedroom, and Knickerbocker Glories. Ma was certainly relieved, but I think perhaps a bit miffed that I didn't seem to miss her at all.

Harambe, Harambe!

For a few days, Almas and I visited with friends, and attended Jamatkhana. But, inevitably, I had to face school registration. Rashida and Almas accompanied me.

To my eyes, the Hackney & Stoke Newington Polytechnic was huge, grey, ugly, and cold. Exposed central heating pipes on the walls ran through the corridors. It was the antithesis of the Parvatiban Muljibhai Madhvani Girls School which, in hindsight, I viewed as perfect.

As the school was within walking distance from my new home, I registered as a day student. As a foreigner, I was obliged to pay tuition which Bapa gladly shelled out.

The next day, I trudged off, absent the protection of my sisters, to face my first day at school. I was scared and forlorn. Surrounded by a crowd of strange faces, I sidled into the maths classroom, and huddled at a desk, desperately seeking invisibility.

Oftentimes, the twists and turns of my life have convinced me that a guardian angel perches on my shoulder, and, on that day in that classroom, my angel shapeshifted, before my eyes, into the glorious Gita Gosai.

Before the lesson even began, Gita rushed to my desk, and joyously introduced herself. Until my arrival, she had been the only brown kid in the whole school. Born and raised in Kenya, she and her family had relocated to London five years previously.

In the original Sanskrit, Gita's name means "song," a moniker which suited her perfectly. She was an incessant chatterbox, possessed a bubbly personality, and was terrifically popular. Gita befriended me immediately, took me to the lunchroom, introduced me to other students, and, after school, walked me home. We were the same age, and became inseparable.

As a result of Gita's intervention, I quickly developed a comfortable circle of friends, settled easily into the rhythm of school life, and, by and large, thoroughly enjoyed my time at the Polytechnic. An international potpourri of Jamaican, Greek, Turkish, Jewish, and English kids attended the school.

With a couple of exceptions, I don't remember too much about my teachers. The maths instructor was a nice enough man but was old, dithery, and nondescript, and droned ceaselessly. I did encounter some prejudice from British culture, and one teacher, in particular, looked down her nose at me disdainfully.

On the other hand, I recall my English teacher, whose name now escapes me, with fondness. I loved English literature, and she taught us the classics including Shakespeare, Charles Dickens, and the Brontë sisters. I had a knack for recapping the stories, which endeared me to my teacher, and she and I had some enthusiastic debates.

When I was out and about, shopping and so on, I sometimes received derisive looks from passersby while others, especially shopkeepers, just ignored me. Generally, though, the kindness of people far outweighed the bigotry.

Despite Gita's gregariousness, she was a lonely child. She had only her parents and one older brother, Girish, and she was frequently alone at home. As a result, she hung out at my house all the time, and we did everything together. A few of our special pastimes stand out in my memory. At recess and lunch, we used to aim ourselves, like missiles, at a Woolworth's near the school grounds. We continually bought licorice all-sorts, chocolates, and junk food, and stuffed ourselves to oblivion. I don't know how we made it through the afternoons without upchucking.

When cherries came into season, we bought bags of them from nearby confectionaries. Row houses surrounded the school, and, for some reason known only to young teenage girls, the highlight of our day was to park ourselves illicitly on the cement stoops, eat the cherries, and spit out the pits. The neighbours complained to the school, and the principal busted us. He gave us quite a verbal raking.

To celebrate our extraordinary friendship, Gita used to sing *Harambe, Harambe* all the time. It's a Swahili phrase meaning "all pull together" or "pulling together." Then we would both break into flamboyant song, and dissolve into fits of laughter. We used to sneak into a cemetery at the end of Manse Road where we sat on a bench, engaged in endless conversations, sometimes serious and sometimes inane, and sang *Harambe, Harambe* to the dead.

We wrote our O-levels at a facility close by the British Museum. We made a pact that as soon as either of us finished an exam, we would meet at the entrance to the Museum. Because we were school children, the Museum staff allowed us free entry. Our favourite hang-out in the museum was the floor that housed the Egyptian mummies in their tombs. Guess what we sang to them.

My first boyfriend, although we were so young I could scarcely call him that, was Bill. He was Anglican, and his father a vicar. One of the flip teenage comments at the time was "Oh, knickers" which meant "Oh, shit." Don't ask me why. One day, Bill voiced the slang in front of Bapa, and was horribly embarrassed but the significance flew over my upright Bapa's head.

Purveyor of Shoes in Petticoat Lane and Sundry Other Jobs

During my first Christmas break in London, Rashida encouraged me to seek part-time employment so I wouldn't feel homesick. My first paying job was at Bourne & Hollingsworth, a department store on Oxford Street near Selfridges. I worked for about a month in their haberdashery or notions department selling what seemed like a zillion varieties of buttons.

Then I moved over to Marks & Spencer in our neighbourhood simply because most of my friends worked there. At the start, I worked only on Saturdays but later added shifts after school on Thursdays and Fridays from 4 p.m. to 9 p.m. I rotated through every department doing a variety of jobs including my favourite—working the till. Each Saturday evening, I received a small see-through envelope containing my wages of two pounds fifty.

Marks & Spencer had a large grocery department. The law banned stores from selling food about a week before the "sell by" date so management flogged the food to staff for a fraction of the retail price. I spent about fifty pence each week buying all kinds of goodies. The store had a lunch room where staff, for about ten pence, could get a fullblown meal. There was even an in-house hairdresser. I loved Marks & Spencer.

Two of the girls with whom I clerked were Sarah and Jane Marks. Their claim to fame was that they were Rod Stewart's cousins. He was in the midst of becoming famous, and they brought us autographed posters of him.

On Sundays, I worked, in Petticoat Lane, as a purveyor of shoes. I found the history of Petticoat Lane captivating and colourful. Its original name, in the sixteenth century, was "Hogs Lane," and it was likely a drovers' trail used to herd cattle and pigs to market. By the early seventeenth century, it had shed its rural coat, and had become a commercial area called "Peticote Lane." In the seventeenth century, many Spaniards settled there but the Great Plague of 1665 decimated the district, to say nothing of the rest of London, which lost a good 20% of its population to the plague.

Later in that century, many Huguenots, French Protestants who had fled from persecution in France, took up residence in Petticoat Lane. Some of them were master weavers, and the district, in the eighteenth century, became a clothing manufacturing centre noted for ladies' underwear and Huguenot lace.

During that period, the austere Queen Victoria changed the lane's official name to Middlesex Street as the prudish Victorians deemed the reference to a lady's undergarment unseemly. I've wondered why they found a direct reference to "sex" less titillating than alluding to an underskirt. In popular parlance, though, even today, everyone knows it as "Petticoat Lane."

Jewish settlers made their home in the lane from the 1880s until the Second World War, and continued the garment industry. The 1970s saw the emergence in the district of Indian immigrants.

I was in my element in Petticoat Lane. Brick buildings lining either side of the street housed a variety of shops. The street itself was a vibrant jumble of stalls, some open and some covered by multi-hued umbrellas and canvas awnings. The proprietors ranged from high-end vendors to mongers. The goods and wares, displayed on racks, tables and pavement, included a mishmash of crockery, clothing, underwear, leather, fabrics, jewellery, spices, antiques, both real and fake, and everything else imaginable. The hullabaloo of shouting vendors, raucous music, customers of every race and colour, and enticing odours from fish and chips to curry was intoxicating.

Each Sunday, Rashida and Mansur rented a table at curb side in Petticoat Lane, and Mansur dropped off hundreds of pairs of shoes early in the morning. His brother, Ashik, and I began setting up at 7 a.m. prior to the market opening. Ashik had recently moved from Pakistan to London to live with Rashida, Mansur, and me.

Once we had finished setting up, and before opening, we filled our stomachs with exotic culinary treats. I, knowing all the vendors, scoured their tables, and asked them to set aside for me, until the end of the day, merchandise I wanted to buy.

When the market opened at 10 a.m., we sold the shoes, cash in pocket, for five or six pounds each, which was much cheaper than the shoe stores. Sometimes, we sold all our shoes within a couple of hours, and other times, it took us until 4 p.m.

The shoes were so popular that we had to be vigilant against pilferage. Scurrilous thieves tried on new shoes, put their old ones in the box, and walked away wearing the new ones. I took my duties seriously, and when our volume increased to two tables, I had no choice but to hire friends as security guards.

As soon as the customers emptied our tables, I foraged around Petticoat Lane, my apron bulging with money, and bought anything and everything I desired including suede coats, suede purses complete with fringes, change purses, watches, hippy clothes, psychedelic skirts, bohemian blouses, and belts. It was here that I honed the formidable bargaining skills that are the envy of all my friends.

At the end of the day, we came home and washed up. Then, as a treat, Mansur would take Rashida, Ashik, and me to dinner at an authentic Pakistani restaurant.

Schoolgirl Travels

While I lived in London, I travelled around England and Europe several times on school trips, sometimes accompanying British friends and their parents.

Like my sisters, I returned to Jinja for holidays and special occasions. On our last visit, in the summer of 1972 for the wedding of Zebby and Rustam, we ran smack-dab into the seething cauldron of Ugandan politics and the ceaselessly violent Ugandan power struggle.

CHAPTER THIRTEEN

Uganda's Growing Pains

Ugandan Prosperity and Underlying Discontent

During the latter part of the nineteenth and early part of the twentieth century, Great Britain focused, with single-minded determination, on completing the British East African Railroad. By 1901, the railway ran from Mombasa to Kisumu, the Kenyan town on the eastern shore of Lake Victoria where Zubeda was born. By 1931, the British had stretched the railway as far as Kampala in Uganda.

The purpose the British had in mind was profit—immense profit. They wanted to establish a reliable means of transportation to haul raw materials from Uganda to the Indian Ocean for shipment overseas, and to import manufactured commodities from Great Britain to East Africa.

The success of the British in achieving these goals created a double-edged sword. On the one hand, the ever-mounting exports of cotton, sugar, tea, and coffee elevated Uganda to the status of a self-sustaining and affluent dependency.

On the other hand, the increasing prosperity of the protectorate strained the already tense relations between the Indian entrepreneurial class and indigenous African population. The British governors kept an extremely tight rein on the production, pricing, and export of the lucrative cash crops. They considered the Indians more reliable, efficient, and compliant than the Africans. As a result, the British allowed the Indians to act as middlemen and to own plantations to the exclusion of Africans.

Many members of the Indian population thrived. They became the heart and soul of the economy, and comprised a good percentage of the professional class. They achieved their success through boundless hard work. Whole families pitched in to grow small businesses. They often lived where they worked, and put in long, tedious hours.

That is not to say the Indians were blameless in their own treatment of Africans. The Indians were the product of a caste system, and, in Uganda, a similar rigid hierarchy existed. The British constituted the upper-class, and often treated the Indian middle class and African lower class with disdain. Many Indians, in turn, exhibited arrogance and disrespect toward the Africans.

Meanwhile, the majority of Africans continued, as they had done for centuries, to subsist by farming and herding. Others supported their families by becoming servants to the richer British and Indian families. Most Africans lived bleak and impoverished lives. They lacked both education and opportunity for advancement. Their escalating bitterness and rage toward the British and Indian communities smouldered through the 1930s and '40s.

Fanning the embers of their disgruntlement was the practice of Indian plantation owners, encouraged by the British, to import itinerant workers from distant regions of Uganda, and from outside Uganda, to toil in the fields for minimal wages.

To complicate these volatile strands of discontent, the many African tribes that inhabited Uganda had never found ways to live in harmony, except that they were united in their envy of the Bugandan tribe. Many members of the Bugandan upper crust were achieving financial success. They focused their agricultural endeavours on supplying the Indians with meats and vegetables. They harvested flowers for sale to Indian women. And, they began to acquire the education that permitted them to advance in careers within the British and Indian administrative and financial hierarchies. One consequence was that the ambitious Bugandans and the Indians became more accepting of one another, and began, ever so slowly, to integrate.

The Advent of Ugandan Independence

The Africans of Uganda, with the Bugandans in the forefront of the nationalist movement, lobbied for independence for decades. However, the British, who exercised ironclad rule over the territory, were masters at dividing and conquering by exciting rivalries between the various tribes who had historically battled one another.

In 1949, angry Bugandans attempted to strike a signal blow for independence. They rioted in the streets; burned down buildings; demanded a representative voice in government; called for an exemption from the British regulation of cotton export prices; and insisted on the right to participate in cotton ginning which was the exclusive province of the Indians. The British governor blamed the upheaval on communist activists. Consequently, he rebuffed the agitators, and squelched all demands for change.

After a few years, the Bugandans' overt push toward independence fizzled but, in an odd twist, the British themselves began to propel the impetus for self-government. The British had pulled out of India after World War II, and were changing their political perspective from colonial rule over their protectorates to self-rule. The British, no doubt, recognized the inevitability of the need for reform, and decided to sail ahead of the winds of change.

The British government, in the person of a new governor by the name of Sir Andrew Cohen, began, in 1952, to establish the groundwork to allow Uganda to emerge as an independent, self-governing state. The protectorate's administration opened the door to permit Africans to participate in the cotton ginning industry; removed certain price controls; created the Uganda Development Corporation to assist with industrial and economic development; and paved the way for the inclusion of elected African representatives on the governing Legislative Council.

The Ascension of Milton Obote

The measured steps the British were taking toward Ugandan independence dovetailed neatly with the political ascendance of Apollo Milton Obote. The village of Akokoro in northern Uganda was the birthplace, in 1924, of Obote. His father was a local chief of the Lango tribe and a farmer. Milton was one of nine children.

Despite an impoverished background, Obote was an intelligent boy, and must have harboured, within himself, a thirst for learning and a font of ambition. He attended the Protestant Missionary School in Lira and Gulu Junior Secondary School, both in his northern home territory. He then made his way south, and studied at Busoga College, a boarding school in Jinja District.

The next and last stop on his educational journey was Makerere University in Kampala. Apparently, he had hoped to study law but the school did not offer legal courses. So, he enrolled in a general arts programme which included English instruction. For reasons that are unclear, he apparently left university before graduating. One possible reason was that the school expelled him for joining in a student strike.

Obote worked in southern Uganda for a time but, because Bugandans constituted the majority of the populace, job opportunities for a northern Lango tribesman were scarce. So, he moved to Kenya where he found employment as a construction worker. In Kenya, Obote developed an avid interest in politics. During his sojourn in that country, he participated in the Kenyan movement for independence.

When Obote, in 1956, went back to Uganda, the stars were aligning in his favour. He returned to the Lango District, his home stamping grounds. He joined the political party known as the Uganda National

Congress, whose goal was independence, and took the place, in the party, of a local functionary who had been incarcerated.

In 1958, a Lango representative on the reformed Legislative Council resigned unexpectedly. Obote, by appointment, replaced him. Later that same year, Uganda held its first direct elections, and Obote won his seat on the Council by a wide majority of votes.

Soon, Obote ascended to the presidency of the Uganda National Congress. In 1959, a split occurred between two opposing groups within the party. One faction, spearheaded by Obote, merged with another party known as the Uganda People's Union. The merger culminated in the formation of the Uganda People's Congress with Obote as its president.

Benedicto Kiwanuka was a Ugandan who studied law at University College London, and became a member of the British bar at Gray's Inn in 1956. He returned to Uganda, and practised law for a few years. He then ascended to the leadership of the Democratic Party, the majority of whom were Catholics. Kiwanuka became the first prime minister when Uganda, in 1961, became internally self-ruling.

In 1961, in anticipation of a pre-independence election, Obote skilfully aligned the Uganda People's Congress with the Buganda political party under the aegis of the Bugandan *Kabaka* (Swahili for "king"), Sir Edward Frederick William David Walugembe Mutebi Luwangula Mutesa II. This expedient alliance won the election, and ousted Kiwanuka and the majority Democratic party. Obote assumed the office of prime minister of Uganda.

In October, 1962, Uganda achieved the goal of full independence from Great Britain. Prime Minister Obote officiated over the British withdrawal, and, in a formal ceremony, received the instruments of power, thus formalizing Uganda's status as a self-governing sovereign state.

When Obote began his governance, as the leader of a coalition party, he made an effort to appease the historically fractious tribes and ethnicities that were now, in name at least, united under the Ugandan flag.

Uganda's newly minted constitution mandated that the central government would exercise strong and effective federal control but that the time-honoured Bugandan tribal kingdom would continue to enjoy a degree of autonomy and maintain its royal customs.

Obote promised to honour the dictates of the constitution. And, in 1963, as evidence of his good intentions, he backed the appointment of the Kabaka as president of the virgin nation albeit that the presidential post was mainly ceremonial.

The Tumultuous Reign of Milton Obote

Milton Obote assumed office as the first prime minister of an independent Uganda when he was only about thirty-eight years old. He exhibited classic African facial features, accentuated by a charming, gap-toothed smile. His lanky and unassuming appearance was reminiscent of a slightly rumpled professor. His personality was appealing, and his command of the English language excellent. Another attribute that appealed to many of us Ugandans was that he was a civilian, and apparently not beholden to the military.

To give him his due, I believe that, at the beginning of his tenure, Obote was genuinely concerned about the common good of the country and its people. His confidence was doubtless buoyed by the fact that, in the first blush of independence, Uganda blossomed economically, aided by escalating levels of coffee, cotton, and tea exports.

But, underlying the optimism fuelled by the realization of self-determination and burgeoning economic prosperity, the hoary problems of tribal jealousies, ethnic clashes, disgruntlement toward Indians, and the military wild card continued to fester. Added to those concerns was Obote's paranoia that a coup might depose him.

In 1964, the military provoked the first major crisis for the fledgling government when Ugandan army units staged an insurrection. Their demands included salary increases and more frequent opportunities for promotion.

When Obote's Minister of Defence ventured out to negotiate with the army rebels, they detained him, and held him hostage. Obote felt he had no choice but to humbly request the British army to quash the rebellion, and restore the status quo. The army did so but, in the end, Obote caved in to the insurrectionists, and complied with their demands. This defeat seriously undermined Obote's authority, and humiliated him personally.

The year 1964 witnessed the arrival of a new player on the Ugandan national stage. A soldier by the name of Idi Amin had risen through the ranks of the King's African Rifles, an African division in the British colonial army, known after independence as the Ugandan Rifles. Amin became one of the first African commissioned officers. He continued his ascension, and achieved the heady status of deputy commander of the army. Obote trusted Amin's loyalty, and welcomed him into Obote's tightly knit coterie of advisors and confidantes.

The Prime Minister managed to briefly tamp down the increasing friction in the country when Princess Margaret and Lord Snowdon arrived on a Royal Tour in 1965. Obote greeted the royals on the tarmac at Entebbe when they disembarked from their plane, and escorted Princess Margaret across the airfield to inspect the waiting troops. Kampala was gussied up for the royal appearance with flags flying, decorations mounted on buildings, and women in the streets wearing their traditional and colourful gomezis and basutis.

Behind the scenes, though, despite Obote's efforts to extinguish the flames, dissension and dissatisfaction raked the coals of discontent. Chief among his problems were the prosperous and better educated Bugandans. Although the ancient kingdom of Buganda was entitled to special autonomous status within the nation, the Bugandans thought they deserved more control and influence within the central government.

On the other side of the ledger, Obote was becoming increasingly despotic. In response to the political and tribal dissension and to feed his own ambition, he began to pursue the notion of single party rule. His rationale was that a one-party state was essential for the nation's sense of unity to flourish.

Obote's adversaries, both outside and inside his own party, were seeking avenues to force him out of office. An ill-advised bank deposit made by Amin provided the fuel that allowed them to accuse Obote and his cronies of corruption.

Obote vociferously denied the accusation but the charge was too good an opportunity for his opponents to pass up. In February, 1966, while Obote was visiting the northern region of the country, members of Parliament from Obote's own Uganda People's Congress Party organized and lobbied for a "no confidence" motion against Obote's leadership. The vote passed almost unanimously.

People naively thought that Obote, once he learned of this crushing condemnation, would turn tail and resign. But, they could not have been more off the mark. Shored up by his cohort, Amin, and the Ugandan army, Obote retaliated with blinding speed and raging fury, overthrowing his own government.

He ordered armed police to storm the cabinet room, arrest five of his ministers, and incarcerate them. He abrogated Uganda's constitution; declared a state of emergency; shelved the National Assembly; assumed dictatorial control over the government; anointed Idi Amin commander-in-chief of the army; and sacked the Bugandan Kabaka from the presidency.

Within a couple of months, Obote ramrodded a new constitution through Parliament, failing to bother with the democratic niceties of either a reading or a quorum. The thrust of this constitution was to abolish the powers of the tribal kingdoms, roll all powers into the prime minister's arsenal, and vastly extend his authority and control over the whole of the nation.

The recalcitrant Bugandans and their Kabaka refused to bow in the face of Obote's *de facto* coup, and prepared a legal challenge to his authority. Obote's response was to order Idi Amin and his soldiers to storm the Kabaka's palace in Kampala, and kill the king. In the ensuing day-long battle between Amin's forces, armed with tanks and heavy artillery, and the king's bodyguards, bearing only small arms, several hundred Bugandans lost their lives. The Kabaka, meanwhile, climbed over a high wall that surrounded the palace, flagged down a passing taxicab, and fled the country. He died in exile in London in 1969. Alcohol poisoning was the presumed cause of "King Freddie's" death but some people believed that Obote's henchmen had tracked him down, and assassinated him by forcing liquor down his throat.

In the aftermath of this rout, Obote granted Amin and his troops the run of the palace; imposed martial law in Buganda; banned Bugandan political parties; and imprisoned several hundred Bugandans without the benefit of a trial. In 1967, Obote put the finishing touches to his *coup d'état* by imposing a new republican constitution which totally eradicated the tribal kingdoms.

Obote had succeeded in concentrating absolute power in his own hands. But, he was only too aware that the continued existence of his government depended upon the oppressive tactics employed by the armed forces and police, and by their continued loyalty to him.

His strategy to maintain power was two-fold. First, he created a secret police department known as the General Service Unit, appointed a relative to head it, and stacked it with members from his own Langi ethnic group. He then endowed the new department with a sweeping mandate to arrest anyone suspected of opposing or attempting to subvert or derail his regime. Second, he wooed and befriended senior commissioned officers in the army, and campaigned for the backing of Langi and Acholi soldiers from his northern territory.

Amin, meanwhile, was busy bolstering his own loyalists within the army by recruiting tribesmen from his West Nile district and other allied tribes.

The trust the people of Uganda had placed in Obote by electing him the first prime minister dissipated in the aftermath of his seizure of absolute power. The hallmarks of his dictatorial rule were the incarceration, torture, and murder of anyone he or his secret police perceived as a threat; a severe scarcity of food; skyrocketing prices; and blatant corruption.

Obote's mistrust of Amin was growing apace, and he was concerned about how much longer he could rely on the loyalty of his military forces. In 1969, Obote was wounded in an attempted assassination, and narrowly escaped death when a grenade thrown at him proved to be a dud.

During this period, Amin faced accusations of selling his own army's munitions to Congolese rebels in order to line his pockets, and of misappropriating funds earmarked for the army for his personal gain. In 1970, Obote felt he had no choice but to place Amin under temporary house arrest during an investigation of his alleged crimes. However, for no discernible reason, Obote never carried through to charge and arrest Amin formally.

The Ugandan president's suspicions of Amin peaked with the murder of the deputy commander of the army, an Acholi tribesman who was Amin's principal rival and an Obote loyalist. Then Obote escaped assassination a second time when bullets tore into his motorcade but missed his vehicle.

By early 1971, Obote concluded that he needed to rid himself of the spectre of Amin. Before leaving for a Commonwealth conference in Singapore, he ordered some of his steadfast Langi army officers to arrest Amin and his adherents.

Amin, though, caught wind of the threat, and struck first. He ordered troops who were faithful to him to stage strategic attacks in Kampala and at the Entebbe airport. They met little opposition, and Amin's coup, in January of 1971, was immediately successful. Obote fled to Tanzania, and Amin quickly established a military regime.

The Indian Experience

In the 1920s, the British government created a Legislative Council for Uganda. The governor at the time thought that permitting three *ex officio* members to sit at the Council table would be a good idea, and appointed two Europeans and one Indian.

The Indians subsequently agitated for more equal representation. By the late 1920s, they succeeded in gaining equal representation on the municipal councils of Kampala and Jinja but not on the national front.

Through the Great Depression, the struggle for independence in India, and the Second World War, Indians in Uganda put most of their energy into conserving and developing their businesses. Because of their economic success, Indians contributed substantially more by way of taxation than other ethnic groups but the benefits they received were dis-proportionately fewer. Through these times of depression, turmoil, and conflict, Indians continued to push for political reform by way of more representation in government for the Indian community.

In the aftermath of the war, though, Africans were becoming more politically conscious, their progress toward independence was picking up steam, and Indians became somewhat lost in the shuffle. The government re-constituted the Legislative Council, and, in doing so, allocated three seats to Africans but only two to Indians. In 1948, the number of African seats increased to four, and the Indian participation to three. By 1950, the Africans held eight seats, and the Indians four.

As the 1950s progressed, the Indians gave up on pursuing their politi-cal agenda. They concentrated, instead, on solidifying their economic and social toehold in the changing Ugandan society. Thus, their concerns shifted to job security, betterment of their schools, and involvement in the protectorate's decisions relating to trade and commerce.

This period saw a fundamental change in the political make-up of the protectorate. While Indian political traditionalists were anxious to maintain seats in government allocated specifically to the Indian minor-ity, Jayant Madhvani, the industrial entrepreneur, thought that Indians should throw their whole-hearted support to the Africans in their quest for independence and political unity. As a result, he favoured a unified legislature rather than one distinguished by racial components. Jayant himself became a member of the Legislative Assembly in 1954.

Madhvani's point of view prevailed, and by the time independence was about to become a reality, the three major political parties included Indian members, albeit not many. When Uganda achieved sovereign status, the constitution did not provide for the allocation of parliamentary seats on the basis of race. A few Indians actually became members of Parliament but too many others chose not to participate in the establishment of the new democracy. One who did was Sherali Bandali Jaffer, Ma's second cousin, who became the Member of Parliament for Kampala West.

In the eyes of the Indians, a much more significant issue that arose from the creation of a self-governing state was that of citizenship. Under the *Uganda Independence Act, 1962*, Indians could become Ugandan citizens automatically but only if they applied for such status within two years, and only if they renounced their United Kingdom citizenship.

Each alternative carried the possibility of momentous consequences. Indians who chose to retain their British citizenship would have the right to carry British passports, and to enter the United Kingdom without being subject to immigration restrictions under the United Kingdom's *Commonwealth Immigrants Act, 1962*.

On the other hand, if they did opt for the benefits of UK citizenship, they would remain foreigners in Uganda with no legal right to stay there, even though many of them, including all the children in my family, were Ugandan born.

Another layer of complexity was the fear of many Indians that even if they chose to renounce their UK rights, and become citizens of Uganda, the African majority would still treat them as foreigners, and perhaps even strip them of their citizenship. And, in that eventuality, they might have nowhere to turn for sanctuary.

As a result, the great majority of Indians elected to rely upon British rather than Ugandan protection. Many Ismailis, though, under the Aga Khan's aegis, chose to become full participating citizens of Uganda. Bapa thought that our allegiance should lie with the country in which we had lived and prospered for so many years, and all of us acquired Ugandan citizenship. Still other Indians found themselves paralyzed by indecision, and did nothing.

Of the Indians who applied to become citizens of Uganda, thousands of them claimed that the Obote government purposely failed to process their applications. As a result, even though they had renounced their right to British protection, they never acquired citizenship status.

Although some Indians participated in quilting the political fabric of the new nation, the majority—be they Sikh, Goan, Hindu, or Ismaili— kept their heads down, and carried on with their own family and social lives and business ventures in a closed sub-society. In some respects, the Africans did not welcome Indians into a national melting pot but, in other respects, Indians chose not to assimilate.

Whether or not greater efforts by Indians to do so or by Africans to accept them would have changed the subsequent course of events is, of course, a moot point. The fact remains that it did not happen, and, as the push toward Ugandan nationalism surged, its African proponents found a handy scapegoat in the thriving and easily identifiable Indian minority community. "Indophobia" took on a life of its own, and the substantial contributions Indians had made over the years to Uganda and its economy began to pale into insignificance.

By 1967, many Indians from Uganda, fearing the upsurge in prejudice, began to relocate to Great Britain. As early as 1968, many of their fears came to fruition. The 1968 Committee on "Africanization in Commerce and Industry" in Uganda came up with a series of broad proposals whose effect was to discriminate against Indians in all aspects of their lives.

For example, the Obote government initiated a scheme of work permits and trade licences designed to hobble Indians from freely carrying on their business and professional endeavours. One devastatingly cruel twist of fate was that many people in the Indian community had heralded the coup by Idi Amin as an encouraging new beginning.

Had the coup not happened, my personal belief is that President Obote would ultimately have nationalized Indian businesses and perhaps expelled us. But, I think that he would have employed a longer time frame to do so, thus ensuring that Africans would be better educated and better trained to run the businesses and industries they took over.

Thankfully, the increasing levels of national rhetoric and discrimination, the intermittent violence, and the political machinations did not directly affect my family or our friends. Jinja was off the track of the power struggle, and, during the sixties, we did not experience a military presence in Jinja. All the adults, though, were concerned about the issues, and talked about them incessantly amongst themselves in Kutchi and Gujarati.

We children sort of understood the undertones without anyone really telling us. We knew that safety was paramount, and that we needed to be cautious at all times. But that was just a way of life. We didn't stop to analyze it.

We realized, too, that any criticism of the government or of President Obote was absolutely out of the question. When the President landed his helicopter in our compound in order to liaise with his mistress no one in our family was going to say "no."

CHAPTER FOURTEEN

The Advent of Evil

Lest We Forget

I would prefer not to sully these pages by writing about Idi Amin. However, I think the importance of people remembering, or learning for the first time, about his malignance far outweighs my personal repugnance.

Recorded history has spewed forth an untold number of psychotic dictators, not the least of whom was Idi Amin. His reign of terror and its malevolent tentacles strangled far more than just the Indian community. He perpetrated perhaps irreparable harm to African Ugandans and the nation of Uganda from which, almost four decades later, they are still struggling to recover.

I believe that Amin was incapable of respect for any legal, moral, or ethical boundaries because his reptilian brain was devoid of any comprehension of law, morals, or ethics.

Half-truths and outright lies, likely generated by Amin to demonstrate commonality with his Ugandan subjects, shroud his actual origins. The story goes that he was a member of the Kakwa tribe, a tiny ethnic group that lived in the extreme northwestern corner of Uganda. The year of his birth was 1924 or 1925. He either didn't know, or barely knew, his father; his family was desperately poor; in his early years, he and his family survived through primitive farming and goat herding; and, he attended a missionary school sporadically but his formal education was almost non-existent.

In 1946, when Amin was about twenty-one years old, recruiters from the King's African Rifles appeared in Kakwa territory to enlist tribal members. The lure of soldiering and of drawing a steady salary enticed uneducated, young men who otherwise foresaw no hope for their future.

Amin was one of those young men, and he joined the unit as a cook in training.

As he began his climb through the ranks, his reputation as a vicious, vindictive, and cruel man, who carried out orders with ruthless fierceness, and took disgusting pleasure in torture, grew apace. When he attained the rank of corporal, the army posted him to Kenya where it was attempting to stifle the Mau Mau uprising. The interrogation techniques Amin employed against suspects were so horrific that the British came close to booting him out of the military. But, he somehow emerged from this early crisis, and, in due course, rose to the rank of sergeant-major. And, as I said earlier, he later became one of the first African commissioned officers.

After Amin overthrew Obote, his self-styled sobriquet was "Idi Amin Dada: His Excellency President for Life Field Marshal Al Hadji Dr. Idi Amin Dada, VC, DSO, MC, Lord of All the Beasts of the Earth and Fishes of the Sea and Conqueror of the British Empire in Africa in General and Uganda in Particular." This moniker, in and of itself, paints a lurid self-portrait of the man.

Amin was a massive, physically imposing figure. He was the light heavyweight boxing champion of Uganda for nine years. His skin was ebony, and his facial features broad. He leaned forward, to dominate and intimidate people, when he spoke. He used his hands expressively, and often pounded a fist into his palm to emphasize his point. He was a bully. He could appear to be affable and amusing but his smile was predatory, and his eyes bleak and soulless.

Amin was not intellectually clever, and his English was poor, but his personality was magnetic, and he was viscerally shrewd and crafty. His speeches reflected his animal aggressiveness. He often used boxing analogies. For example, he said, "when you tackle me, I can harm you. I think you should know this," and then laughed with hearty pleasure when his audience predictably applauded.

He dressed with sartorial elegance. His wardrobe included an abundance of military uniforms from bush fatigues to full regalia which he decorated with an ostentatious display of insignias, medals, badges, bars, epaulets, and lanyards. As well, he delighted in the British look, wearing impeccably tailored dark blue suits with starched white shirts, red and navy blue striped and patterned ties, and expensive gold watches. His obsession with all things Scottish led him, incongruously, to sport Highland kilts, and to entertain guests with Scottish music.

But behind his geniality and what some considered his buffoonery was a rapacious, appallingly corrupt, and loathsome sadist. He violated human rights with abandon. He degraded, abused, tortured, mutilated, and murdered people indiscriminately. He was a sexual marauder who ploughed through several wives, and an endless procession of mistresses. Rumours abounded among Ugandans, and one of his former ministers claimed, that he was a cannibal.

Some dismissed him as insane but I think he was simply evil. Islam does not profess a belief in Satan but, were I a Christian, I would have no difficulty believing that Idi Amin Dada was a spawn of the devil.

Idi Amin's Barbaric Rule

When Idi Amin, commander of the Ugandan army, ousted Milton Obote, and implemented military rule, the Africans responded with jubilation. In Kampala, colossal crowds of people poured into the streets. They rejoiced in a frenzy of singing, dancing and drum beating. Elation and euphoria ruled. The Bugandans, who had been so hostile to Obote, were especially thrilled. Seemingly forgotten was the fact that Amin had been a close crony of Obote, a willing soldier in shoring up Obote's repressive regime, and the commander of the brutal attack on the Kabaka's palace.

In the early days after the coup, the African people cloaked Amin with the mantle of the nation's saviour, and he revelled in the role. He swooped from one area of the country to another, visiting with tribal chieftains and giving speeches to his ecstatic acolytes.

Like all psychopaths, Amin was a manipulator *par excellence*. He promised that his military government was provisional, and that free elections waited just around the corner. He selected for his Cabinet educated and successful civil servants, lawyers, and Makerere University professors. He freed political prisoners. He even organized the homecoming of the Kabaka's corpse for a proper funeral.

On the international stage, Amin renounced Obote's foreign policy of nonalignment with major power blocks. The United States, Great Britain, and Israel officially recognized his government. By contrast, the leaders of Kenya, Tanzania, and the Organization of African Unity at first refused to recognize the legitimacy of Amin's regime. Indeed, the President of Tanzania offered a safe haven to Milton Obote.

However, the good will Amin initially engendered dissipated rapidly, and his popularity shrank. He possessed absolutely no notion of how to govern, and evinced absolutely no interest in learning. His reading, writing, and English language skills were rudimentary, and in no way equal to the task of administering a country.

He had a simple mind. If he wanted to issue an order, he announced it on the radio, over the telephone, or in a speech. If he needed money, and he always did, he scooped it from the government treasury. He displaced the supremacy of civil law with the dictates of military tribunals. He placed members of the army in charge of government departments and state-owned agencies. He notified his newly appointed, elite cadre of civilian Cabinet ministers that they must submit to military discipline.

Amin's need for money was limitless. He was wildly profligate in his personal spending habits, and he desperately needed to divert endless funds to maintain his control of the army which constituted the source and backbone of his power. Many commentators on Amin's enormously preferential treatment of the military have quoted an African proverb which says, "A dog with a bone in its mouth can't bite."

Amin had no choice but to rely on the military to maintain his regime, and he vastly increased its size. The army itself, though, was a wriggling mass of lethal ethnic, regional, and tribal discord and rivalries. Amin's solution was to elevate to command status soldiers from his own West Nile district; Nubians, originally from southern Sudan; and even ill-qualified civilians. His promotions sometimes verged on the ludicrous. The senior officer of the Uganda Air Force was a former telephone operator. A night watchman became a feared executioner. Amin gave these men, who were faithful only to him, an unconditional mandate to hunt down and punish (which usually meant murder) soldiers they suspected of disloyalty, mutinous plots, or even untoward ambitions.

To buoy his coffers, Amin did a capricious about-face on his foreign policy. In order to woo financial and military assistance from Muammar Abu Minyar al-Gaddafi, the Libyan dictator, he reversed Uganda's pro-Israel stance, and banished all Israeli advisors from the country. To obtain financial assistance from Saudi Arabia, he resurrected his Islamic roots. He also accepted a substantial supply of weaponry from the Soviet Union. He had no compunction about prostrating himself before any nation or group that would slake his unquenchable thirst for money and military armaments.

Amin deep-sixed the Ugandan General Service Unit formed by Obote, and instituted, in its place, the Ugandan State Research Bureau, aka the secret police. At their zenith, the State Research Bureau, Public Safety Unit, and military police boasted about 18,000 members.

The main function of the secret police force, which East Germany had helped Amin to create, was to search out enemies of the state, meaning anyone who opposed Idi Amin, and to suppress political dissent. Like secret police forces everywhere, the tools of their trade included clandestine investigation and surveillance, intimidation, terror, kidnapping, torture, disappearances, and murder.

Affairs in Uganda went from bad to worse. Milton Obote instigated a bungled attack from Tanzania. Amin was desperate to maintain his regime, fearful about a further thrust by Obote, and enraged by people he suspected of supporting Obote.

His response was potent and predictable—state-sanctioned terrorism. No one was immune from his wrath. The death toll included Cabinet ministers, university professors, tribal chiefs, judges, Christian clergy, physicians, journalists, diplomats, storekeepers, farmers, and fisher folk. He decimated whole villages. Perhaps even more devastating for Uganda than the economic collapse and physical ruination wrought by Amin was the loss of so many of its best and brightest citizens.

The state controlled radio sometimes announced the names of people, even as they listened, who were on the "wanted" list, and about to "vanish." The Anglican archbishop spoke out in opposition to Amin. A short time later, his assailants offloaded his body, garbed in his religious vestments, at a mortuary in Kampala.

Benedicto Kiwanuka, the first prime minister, fared no better. In 1969, Obote had imprisoned Kiwanuka. Amin later freed him, and appointed him Chief Justice of the High Court. Amin, however, soon saw Kiwanuka as a threat to his rule. He accused Kiwanuka, who was a steadfast Catholic, of promoting national disunity through a religious schism.

The truth, though, was that, in his role as Chief Justice, Kiwanuka issued judgments based on the law rather than the dictates of Amin. For example, he had bravely ruled that the armed forces had no power to arrest and detain citizens.

Retaliation was merciless. Amin's savage henchmen hijacked Kiwanuka from his own court. The kidnappers forced him to take off his shoes, and then dumped him into the trunk of a vehicle. That was his last appearance on earth. Many reports indicated that Kiwanuka suffered unspeakable torture before his release into death. Empty shoes abandoned by the roadside became a symbol of the campaign of terror that was smothering Uganda.

Thomas Melady, the American ambassador to Uganda at that time, who had met Kiwanuka some years before, in America, indicated in his book, *Idi Amin Dada: Hitler in Africa*, that he considered Kiwanuka committed to the construction of a just society. Kiwanuka himself had declared that he was a crusader for good governance and the democratic ideal for Uganda. History is full of "what if's," and one of the big questions for Ugandans is "what if Kiwanuka, rather than Obote, had governed Uganda during its formative years of independence?"

An interesting footnote to Kiwanuka's tragic story is that his grandson, Mathias Kiwanuka, who was born in the United States, played defensive end for the New York Giants, and won a Super Bowl with them.

During this brutal time, Joseph Mubiru, a governor of the Bank of Uganda, also disappeared. Rumours persisted for years that Amin personally shot and killed both Kiwanuka and Mubiru. Mohamed Hassan, head of the Criminal Investigations Division, and Anil Clerk, a former Member of Parliament and prominent lawyer, were two other well-known citizens who died at the hands of Amin or his underlings.

Civilians were not the only casualties. Amin employed his secret police apparatus and death squads to eliminate an enormous number of soldiers and policemen he suspected of disloyalty. They included hundreds of Langi and Acholi tribesmen who were or may have been loyal to Obote. Reputedly, Amin mustered the military, and issued ammunition to all of them except the Langi and Acholi soldiers who were then cut down by a hail of bullets.

Fortunate victims were simply shot. Amin's death squads subjected those less fortunate to mutilation, beheading, throat slitting, burning, disembowelment, or bashing to death by sledgehammer. Bashing saved bullets. Decomposing corpses rotted in forests, fields, and wetlands. The death toll was impossible to estimate accurately, but thousands of Ugandans disappeared.

Soldiers drove trucks filled with bodies to the River Nile and Lake Victoria near Jinja, and chucked them in the water. Their theory was that the crocodiles would eat them but the crocodiles couldn't keep up. Many of the decaying bodies just floated on the waves or washed up on shore. Lake Victoria was the recipient of so many cadavers that they clogged up the hydroelectric intake channels at the Owen Falls dam.

One day, Bapa was driving Bahadur, Zebby, and me over the dam when we spied a couple of men in a small canoe trying to fish a blob out of the reservoir. We were curious, and stopped to watch. To our horror, the men were trying to secure a decomposing corpse with a rope in order to haul it into the canoe. But, each time they tied the rope around an extremity, the arm or leg would just dissolve away from the body. That picture will be seared in my brain forever.

Lynching was another popular form of execution. Before we children left the house each morning, Bapa or a servant or askari would peer out the front door to make sure no dead bodies were hanging from trees.

Because of the poverty that plagued the country, the fear of looting was ever present. Requesting protection from the police or army wasn't an option. As often as not, policemen or soldiers were themselves the *kondos* (Swahili for "armed thieves"), stealing cash, vehicles, jewellery, and any other belongings of value. As the lawlessness and despair escalated, the looters escalated as well, destroying businesses and massacring families caught in home invasions. Yet another pastime of soldiers and police was to arrest businessmen on trumped up charges, and then release them on payment of a ransom.

Targetting Indians as Scapegoats

From the moment Amin seized power, his economic woes threatened to overwhelm him. His voracious personal excesses and his dependence on a loyal army were much like boats—bottomless holes into which he constantly needed to sink money. Prices skyrocketed. The availability of consumer goods and services plummeted. Incarcerations, torture, disappearances, and vicious murders escalated. Ugandans were becoming rapidly disenchanted with Amin's disorganized, capricious, and cruel regime.

So, like tin-pot dictators throughout history, Amin fell back on the tried and true ruse of targeting a visible minority, namely the Indians, as scapegoats. He manipulated the black Africans by whipping up their long-held antipathy and envy toward the successful and tightly-knit Indian community. He incited bigotry and racial violence. His aim was to distract attention from the economic and political morass he had created by unifying and rallying black Africans and the armed forces to the cause of eradicating Indians from Uganda.

The theme of his hateful rhetoric against the Indians was that, "They milked the cow, but never fed it." Amin jump-started his campaign against the Indian community with a series of discriminatory measures. First, he singled Indians out by requiring them to comply with a special census. I remember the census day well. We had to register at a YMCA building in our neighbourhood. The process took most of the day but I didn't mind because we passed the time visiting with friends. The sinister significance of the government-imposed registration of Indians went right over my teenage head.

Amin's next discriminatory foray was his refusal to approve the citizenship requests of several thousand Indians. Then, he imposed a variety of restrictions on us including an admonishment about holding political meetings. He violated our human rights with impunity, and stirred a frenzy of hatred by blaming the Indians for sabotaging the economy. He denigrated us as "bloodsuckers."

The local Africans responded predictably. Many of them verbally abused Indians, shouting at us in Swahili *"Wahindi Tokka!"* meaning "Indians, Get Out!" Soldiers and others committed acts of violence against Asians, stole from us, and looted our homes. The atmosphere was scary and nasty.

On the plus side of the ledger, some Africans who were friends or servants of Indian families displayed loyalty and courage on our behalf. They understood that the departure of the Asians would result in the loss of their livelihoods, and force them to return to their villages to eke out a meagre existence.

CHAPTER FIFTEEN

Life Goes On

Two Hair-Raising Births

Despite the political and social upheaval, we had no choice but to continue on with our lives as normally as we could in the impossibly abnormal circumstances.

January 26, 1971 is emblazoned in our family's collective memory in colours of both terror and joy.

Despite our uncertainty and anxiety about Amin's regime, Zubeda and Bahadur were ecstatic about the imminent birth of their first child. On January 25, Zubeda went into labour. Idi Amin had imposed an evening curfew of 6 p.m. so Bahadur was unable to drive Zubeda to the local hospital. Our friend and neighbour, the midwife, Victoria, hustled through the fence to our house to help out.

She decided that Zubeda had no option but to get to the hospital. So, just after midnight, Victoria called an army officer to inform him of Zubeda's plight. The officer replied that he would send a military escort to Nalufenya Road but that we must turn on all the lights in the compound, and gather everyone out front. His concern was that the phone call was a ploy to lure soldiers to our home for the purpose of blowing them up.

In the early hours of the morning, four army jeeps bearing a dozen soldiers, dressed menacingly in fatigues and wielding machine guns, arrived and surrounded the compound. The soldiers used the rescue mission as an excuse to systematically and exhaustively search the entire courtyard, garden, and house. Words cannot describe the paralyzing fear that enveloped us as we clustered together, shivering in the sickly yellow glare of the jeeps' headlamps, while guards circled us with weapons at the ready.

After what seemed time without end, an officer ordered Bahadur and Zubeda into one of the jeeps. Bahadur defiantly refused because he feared the army would "disappear" them. He had the gift of the gab, and somehow convinced the officer to let them travel in their own vehicle. The convoy set off with two jeeps in front of Bahadur's car, and two behind. My family and I watched the procession until it disappeared from sight, not knowing if we would ever see our beloved Bahadur and Zubeda again.

Blessedly, they made it safely to the hospital. Zubeda's labour was interminable. She did not give birth until five o'clock in the afternoon. With the 6 p.m. curfew in the back of our minds, we all dashed pell-mell to the hospital ward to check out the baby.

The nurse had not yet cleaned the baby up, and her grey eyes mystified us. However, it turned out to be just a film, and the next day her eyes were glowing black. Bahadur and Zubeda had allowed me, beforehand, to choose the baby's name. I called her "Selina" after the moon goddess from Greek mythology. Unfortunately, the official who filled out her birth certificate misspelled her name as "Shalina."

Narmin's birth at the Jinja Hospital, on June 28, 1972, was far less dramatic. I was home for my summer break at the time. The only noteworthy fact was that she emerged from the womb crowned with a full head of horrible black hair that I swear stood straight on end.

Shalina and Narmin were the last of the Rahemtulla babies born in Uganda. After their births, we enjoyed one last celebration in Jinja—the marriage of Zebby and Rustam.

Zebby and Rustam Tie the Knot

Zebby and Rustam's wedding was the social event of the summer season. We invited about 350 guests. Relatives and friends from out of town, mainly from Kampala, Tanzania and Kenya, turned up in droves. I was home for my summer vacation, and Rashida arrived from London. Rustam's parents, Shirin and Abdulrasul Jeraj, his brothers and sisters, along with their respective families, all rolled in from Fort Portal, Kampala, and London. Noorjahan and Noorali were beaming from ear to ear, their hard work of introducing Zebby and Rustam was about to pay off.

For several days before the wedding, joyful pandemonium ruled our household. Even though Bapa had reserved sufficient hotel rooms at the Ripon Falls Hotel, scads of guests converged at our house each day. Ostensibly, they came to help Ma prepare for the traditional ceremonies but, in truth, they wanted to be at the centre of the action, to catch up with family members and friends, and to gossip.

Some of the guests were actually staying with us. One of them was Noorbanu, the mother of Zul who had brought him to Jinja, when he was paralyzed, to seek out a palm reader. Noorbanu possessed a wonderful sense of humour, and her jovial disposition helped to diffuse the usual tensions when two families get together for a wedding.

The couple of days preceding the ceremony, and the wedding morning, were a hubbub of activity at 7 Nalufenya Road. Ma and Zubeda lived in the kitchen, preparing mountains of food. Our servants, who were as excited as everyone else, and other helpers that we hired, buzzed around the house. They assisted Ma and Zubeda, cleaned constantly, ironed wedding clothes, and helped people dress. One servant had the sole chore of making and serving masala chai.

We delegated to Rama Thakkar and two other Hindu ladies the task of helping the women don their sarees. That isn't as easy as the finished product may make it look. They had to tuck and wrap seven yards of fabric around a skirt and short blouse in such a way that most of the draping was visible. The secret lies in the folding.

Almas worked her fingers to the bone. She had to create perfect hairdos for Zebby for the wedding and the reception; and, most of her regular customers, including a lot of British expatriates who worked at Nytil, came to her to have their hair done as well.

Bahadur and Nizar also did their share, helping Bapa with all the arrangements. Rashida arrived just before the wedding so she was not pressed into service. For my part, I was in my best lily of the field mode although, looking back, I prefer to think of myself as the social coordinator. I flitted around like a butterfly, catching up with old friends and acquaintances, and talking their ears off.

On Friday evening, before the Saturday wedding, we held the *mandwo* (similar to a shower) at our home. Our close friends and relatives attended. Most of them were women although a few men were brave enough to show up. As much as possible, we shunted the men off to another room.

We began the evening's festivities by ceremoniously placing pineapples and sugar cane stalks in the four corners of the formal living room. They signified sweetness and well wishes for the bride's family, and also served to ward off evil spirits.

At the start of the mandwo ceremony, Ma and Zebby entered the room together. Zebby was glowing in a red saree. They held a red and black silk saree, inlaid with gold thread, over their heads to ward off evil spirits. The saree had belonged to Nanima. Once Zebby sat down, Ma took the saree, and draped it over her own head.

One of the children stood next to Zebby's chair, holding a platter. On it were four betel nuts which Ma took, and threw into the four corners of the room, again to ward off evil spirits. The platter also held raw rice, rose petals, a bowl of Smarties, and a bowl of orange saffron water. Sugar cubes were more traditional than candy but I, being a chocoholic, insisted on the use of pure British Smarties from London.

Each guest, in turn, dipped her index finger in the saffron water; dabbed an orange droplet on Zebby's forehead; stuck a pinch of rice on the saffron water; placed a candy on her tongue; scattered some rose petals on her head; and sprinkled a handful of rice over her. At the same time, each guest dropped a few shillings into Zebby's hand or lap. Her Matron of Honour, Habiba Fatehali, then dropped the money into a cloth pouch. Zebby was able to discreetly spit the candy into a handkerchief.

The saffron water symbolized good fortune, the raw rice and rose petals represented the promise of prosperity and love, and the sweet ensured that Zebby and Rustam would have a joyful life together. Interestingly, many of our wedding traditions came originally from the Hindu culture.

After this ceremony, we treated our guests to a lavish dinner outdoors in our walled courtyard. Ma and Zubeda had slaved for days preparing it. Ma grudgingly allowed some of the guests to help in the kitchen but she watched over them like an eagle guarding its nest.

After dinner, amid music, chattering, and lots of merriment, we engaged in yet another ceremony which we called *mehndi* (henna). Zebby watched the festivities while henna, a dye extracted from a plant, was applied, in intricate designs, on her palms and feet. Some of the other women and a few brave men underwent the temporary "mehndi-izing" as well.

At both the mandwo and wedding, we served a traditional drink called a *sherbat* (similar to a milkshake). It included, among other ingredients, cold milk, vanilla essence, rose syrup, and *tukmaria* (basil seeds) which swelled up beforehand in water, and turned black.

The mandwo lasted far into the night so we were all exhausted when morning arrived, and we had to prepare for the wedding itself.

Almas and Zebby chose Zebby's wedding dress. It came from a shop in Hackney owned by a Turkish lady. Almas was in London visiting Rashida and me, and she was the same size as Zebby, so she did the fittings. We brought it to Jinja in a suitcase.

The dress was gorgeous, and Zebby looked slender and elegant in it. It was floor length white satin, overlaid by chiffon, with a high neck and long sleeves. The sleeves were form-fitting from shoulder to elbow, and puffy to the wrist. The bodice and upper sleeves were lace and pearl trimmed. Zebby's necklace and matching earrings were heavy and ornate gold. Ma commissioned the Jogia family to create them, and they were Ma and Baba's gift to Zebby. Almas created an upswept hairdo with ringlets for Zebby's radiant jet black hair.

Rustam, at the time, was impossibly skinny, wore Buddy Holly eyeglasses, and sported a curly head of hair with long sideburns. For the wedding, he wore a greyish-brown suit, and a funky tie, that was almost psychedelic, in a rainbow of mauve, gold, and turquoise hues. We all thought he looked so suave.

I looked positively stunning (in my mind's eye) in a yellow mini-dress which I had purchased at the Dorothy Perkins store on Oxford Street. I carried a yellow purse, and wore wooden platform shoes in a red, yellow, green, and black pattern. Mansur had them specially manufactured for me.

Except for a brief downpour, the weather on the wedding day was picture perfect. The sky was a glorious blue, and the sun was dazzling. Colourful tropical flowers were in full bloom in all the gardens of Jinja, and on the hillsides surrounding the town.

We held the wedding, on August 5, 1972, at our Jamatkhana. Zebby's Matron of Honour was Habiba Fatehali, and Rustam's best man was Zul Devji. As we had done with previous family weddings, the ceremony was in the Social Hall in the grounds of the Jamatkhana so that our non-Ismaili friends could join in the celebration. Afterward, Zebby and Rustam signed the wedding book. The camera caught Rustam looking at Zebby as she affixed her signature, with a sly, little grin, as if to say "gotcha."

Zebby and Rustam removed their shoes before entering the mosque to say a private prayer. I immediately absconded with one of Rustam's shoes, another tradition, and made him pay me a couple of hundred shillings before I returned it to him.

Nazlin absconding with Rustam's shoe

Nazlin negotiating for the return of Rustam's shoe

After the ceremony, we returned home to dress for the reception. Zebby wore a white chiffon saree gilded with gold embroidery. Almas pulled back Zebby's long hair, and styled it in petal curls. Rustam was dapper in a navy blue pinstripe suit with a gold tie and gold pocket puff to match the gold in Zebby's dress. I myself was resplendent in a turquoise blue coat dress from the John Lewis Department Store on Oxford Street.

While we were dressing for the reception, the local news station broadcast a message from the President of Uganda. We were so busy, though, that none of us were paying attention to the local news.

The wedding reception took place at the Crested Crane Hotel which was about five minutes from our home. We decorated the hall with festive turquoise, blue, gold, and white streamers.

The Rahemtulla family and relatives (Mariam Masi at far left)

Zebby's friends and co-workers

(L – R) Ma, Shirin Jeraj, Zebby, Rustam, Bapa and Abdulrasul Jeraj

Noorjahan and Noorali Mohamad with Zebby and Rustam

The hotel manager, who was a good family friend, allowed us to hire some Indian caterers to work with the hotel chefs. We were serving a huge dinner, and, by the time the caterers and chefs finished their preparations, gargantuan aluminum vats of food filled the kitchen with enticing aromas.

Rustam's sister-in-law, Parin, concocted a three tiered wedding cake. It was a traditional fruit cake with white icing and gold and yellow icing sugar flower blossoms. We didn't serve any alcohol because, traditionally, it is forbidden at Muslim weddings.

About 7 p.m., our friends and relatives began to arrive at the reception. Among their number were Ismailis, Goans, Hindus, Sikhs, British, and a not inconsiderable number of Africans. The fact that our melting pot of guests were happily mingling and having a high old time seemed sadly ironic in retrospect.

For, it was about this time that the whispered buzz began. People reported that goofy Idi Amin had announced on the radio that he was going to expel all Asians from Uganda within ninety days. However, his announcement did not create any undercurrent of uneasiness at the reception. Everyone laughed about it, and nobody took him seriously. Little did we know that Amin's proclamation was to alter our lives and our destinies forever.

So, we continued with our festivities. People traditionally brought gifts of silverware, jewellery, and money to the reception, and engaged in a ceremony where they bestowed their gifts on the bride.

After the reception ended, Zebby and Rustam spent their wedding night at the Crested Crane Hotel. Rose petals were sprinkled on their bed, and for them, it was the perfect ending to a perfect day.

The next day, Rustam's parents hosted a luncheon for Zebby and Rustam at the home of a friend. One of the ceremonies at the luncheon was the *khobo*. Rustam's father offered a large tray of coins to Zebby. Her part was to cup as many coins as possible in her hands after which the father gave her the rest of them. The coins symbolized the blessings of the groom's family including the blessing of many children. Rustam's mother also presented Zebby with gold jewellery as part of our tradition was to give a trousseau in gold to the bride.

Yet another tradition, my personal favourite, was that the youngest member of the family, namely me, could grab hold of the groom's tie, and not let go until the groom offered some graft. I was quite vicious. I tugged on Rustam's tie until I extorted 500 shillings from him. I wanted to hold out for more but everyone yelled at me to let go.

Once the luncheon ended, we all returned to 7 Nalufenya Road for the going-away ceremony. As Zebby and Rustam crossed the threshold of our home, Ma dotted their foreheads with a *chandlo* (yellow mark) and showered them with rice as further symbols of prosperity and love.

In the house, we all sat down, and presented Zebby with her trousseau, neatly packaged in cellophane. She received sarees and jewellery, and Almas and I gave her a rose, pink, and cream silk quilt we had bought at Selfridge's in London.

Finally, we loaded all their loot into their car, which Bahadur's friends had decorated outrageously, and Rustam and Zebby, amid a flood of tears from everyone, left for their honeymoon in Rustam's hometown of Fort Portal. They quickly realized that they should probably not have attempted the trip, as Amin's expulsion order had resulted in the army taking liberties to harrass people. The highway was dangerous, and the military roadblocks, where soldiers lewdly frisked their bodies, humiliating. However, they continued on, and, once they reached Fort Portal, managed a brief excursion to Queen Elizabeth National Park, where the spectacular savannah, rain forest, swamps and lakes, eye-catching views of Mount Rwenzori, and assortment of wildlife dazzled them. But, their concern about the expulsion order far overshadowed their pleasure, and obliged them, after only a few days, to return to Kampala. Their car trip back from Fort Portal was nerve-wracking. The road was strewn with even more military roadblocks. Luckily, their African driver was able to assuage the soldiers at each checkpoint, and they reached the city without serious incident.

CHAPTER SIXTEEN

Surely, It Can't Be True

The Expulsion Proclamation

Idi Amin's August 5th announcement that he intended to expel 75,000 Asians (people of Indian descent were referred to as Asians by Idi Amin) within ninety days turned out, of course, to be tragically true. He claimed that he was acting upon a dream, he had experienced the day before, in which God had instructed him to expel the Asians. His goal was to seize all the commercial, industrial, residential, and personal property owned by Asians.

Predictably, Amin issued his proclamation with neither consultation nor consideration. He did not realize that not all Asians could claim British citizenship. In short order, he was obliged to amend his original declaration to state that Asians who were Ugandan citizens did not have to leave but, he added, woe betide anyone who had acquired a Ugandan passport through corruption or forgery. Between 50,000 and 60,000 Asians could not claim Ugandan citizenship, and they remained at the mercy of the original order.

A second exception applied to essential personnel. Some of Amin's ministers and bureaucrats found the courage to point out to him that, in many cases, Africans did not possess either the knowledge or skill to manage the Indian-owned businesses and industries. Thus Amin amended his order again to state that "non-citizen Asians whom the government will specifically invite to stay will be welcome." We Indians understood that this reprieve, which was an order in disguise, was a temporary measure to allow us time to train Africans to take over our enterprises. Amin's instructions seemed to change on a daily basis.

Amin propagandized his expulsion proclamation as a triumph for Uganda's "little man," and claimed that the people would benefit immensely from the seizure of the Asian wealth. As a result, his ruling was hugely popular among the African population.

In truth, though, the African people saw virtually nothing of the massive windfall. The confiscated booty fell into the hands of Idi Amin, his partners in crime, and the army. They plundered and stole businesses, homes, vehicles, and personal belongings. Nothing was safe.

The miscalculation by Amin and his sycophants was beyond reckoning. They either did not appreciate or chose to ignore the fact that the Indian businesses and industries were the foundation of Uganda's economic well-being. They employed a huge number of black Africans who would otherwise have lived close to the starvation level, and they were the backbone of the nation's tax base.

Within months, trade took a nose-dive, commercial enterprises were without products, machinery broke down, and factories fell into disrepair and closed. The Ugandan economy, which was in freefall before the expulsion order, was experiencing death throes.

In addition to the decimation of the physical plant that fuelled the economy, the ranks of Uganda's professional elite thinned immeasurably as Indian physicians, dentists, teachers, engineers, lawyers, and civil servants fell prey to the proclamation, and had no choice but to flee.

A question often asked, and never definitively answered, is why Idi Amin did not simply massacre the Asians he so hated. Some commentators suggest that Amin was not immune to the threat of international censure or that, for reasons advantageous to him, he did not want to risk such censure. My view was that he simply had more fun watching the Indians suffer the humiliations he heaped upon us, and the terror he instilled in us.

Simple denial was the first reaction of the Asians to Idi Amin's expulsion proclamation. Although scores of Asians held British passports, they were Ugandan to their core. Their families had lived in Uganda since the preceding century. Most of them were Ugandan born. They were shopkeepers, factory owners, plantation holders, industry leaders, and professionals. Uganda was their home.

The Asians thought privately that Idi Amin was, at best, a buffoon, and, at worst, insane. They reassured one another that his expulsion order was nothing but a capricious whim. They were quite sure that Great Britain would put Amin in his place, and convince him to reverse his order.

After a few days, though, denial morphed into exasperation, then anxiety, then apprehension. As the days turned into weeks, the gut-wrenching certainty of expulsion finally hit home. But, even then, some Asians clung to the hope that Amin would realize that Africans could not manage the economy, and invite them back.

Still, most Asians took no immediate action. Fear and uncertainty paralyzed them. They agonized over whether they should leave right away or hold on until the cutoff date, and whether they should leave as a family unit or send the women and children out first.

Meanwhile, Amin's heavily armed soldiers continued to rove through towns in jeeps and tanks, ransacking Indian homes, pillaging personal property, and beating and incarcerating Asians for a host of reasons and, often, for no reason at all. Seizure of Indian business and industrial undertakings was underway.

Asians gave no thought to armed confrontation or rebellion. The army was a constant, visible, and threatening presence, and the Asians possessed no armaments, no trained militia, and no hope of support from the local populace.

Finally facing up to the inevitable, Asians concentrated on salvaging and safeguarding their finances and possessions. Their initial strategy was to sell, at a fraction of their value, all material goods, such as vehicles and furniture, that they could not take with them to they knew not where. They used the money they garnered to invest in transportable personal chattels, like kitchenware and clothing, that they then exported to Great Britain in the hope that they would be able to follow. This strategy succeeded for a time until stricter regulations concerning such exports and supposedly inexplicable delays in shipping obstructed their efforts.

Many Ugandan Asians adhered to a centuries old tradition of collecting gold ingots or bricks, jewellery, and cash because of their portability in case of human or natural calamity. One of the many absurd restrictions imposed upon the departing Asians was that they could carry with them only two suitcases of personal possessions along with fifty pounds. As a result, they attempted to smuggle gold, jewellery, and cash in turbans, beehive or braided hairdos, and suitcase linings. Because the Africans tended to be disorganized in their searches, and because bribing soldiers and airport officials was ridiculously easy, many Asians succeeded in spiriting their caches out of the country.

Other Asians turned to European and African friends to carry money out on their behalf, and deposit it in foreign bank accounts. Ultimately, though, further government-imposed restraints choked off these channels as well. Another common avenue was to buy a world-wide open British Airways ticket for later use. Bapa bought these tickets for all of us.

As Asians geared up for evacuation or tried to prove their status as Ugandan citizens, a vortex of chaos, fear, rage, panic, frustration, turmoil, and humiliation engulfed their lives. About 50,000 of them held British passports while others were still Indian or Pakistani citizens. Those Asians who believed they were citizens of Uganda often learned that their documents were invalid; that no evidence of their citizenship existed; that they had supposedly applied for Ugandan citizenship beyond the deadline; or that Amin had simply quashed their passports, claiming that they were forgeries. Not infrequently, Amin's officials seized and destroyed passports just for the fun of it. Those luckless claimants became utterly stateless.

But, whatever their status, Asians, young and old, were obliged to queue endlessly in the merciless sun, often for days, from early morning until late in the evening; to fill out a myriad of applications and other forms; to obtain inoculations and medical records; to register their business and property holdings; to find a country that would take them and their families; and somehow to latch onto airline tickets.

Asians who lived in rural areas had seldom set foot in Kampala. The ruination of their lives, and the terror they faced was even more frightening for them. The line-ups and arrangements were gruelling and grim, and the Asians exhausted. Yet, they had absolutely no choice but to endure and persist. Their lives, and those of their parents, spouses, siblings, and children, hung in the balance.

To add to the frantic confusion, the United Nations and various countries opened offices in Kampala to process applications. Asians, including those with Ugandan citizenship, hustled from line-up to line-up, applying to every country available in the desperate hope that one of them would accept their application.

Once an Indian family navigated all the obstacles to their exodus, and found a country that would receive them, they still had to face a final massive hurdle. They were forced to run a gauntlet of brutality to reach the train station or the Entebbe airport. Roadblocks often blocked their path. They were subject to repeated random strip searches, harassment, humiliation, beatings, theft of their few remaining belongings, and, for the women, occasionally rape.

At the airport, families sometimes had to face Idi Amin who often showed up, in full military regalia, to beat his breast and laugh jubilantly at the cowering Asians. Then, as they scurried across the tarmac to reach their aeroplanes, they were forced to dodge lumbering army tanks with gun turrets pivoting threateningly. Even in the aeroplanes or on the trains, so long as they remained within the Ugandan borders, they were not safe.

The Indian Diaspora

The 50,000 or so Ugandan Asians who were *bona fide* British citizens should have been the most secure about their future but, given the legal, political, and social climate prevalent in the United Kingdom, they were in danger of being the least secure.

In 1967, the upsurge of prejudice in Kenya and Uganda, and a fear that the United Kingdom might tighten immigration controls, caused the number of Indian emigrants from East Africa to the United Kingdom to swell exponentially.

This influx caused the conservative and reactionary firebrand, Enoch Powell, to lead an explosive, effective, and highly popular campaign to impose tighter restrictions on Asians who wished to enter the United Kingdom. In concluding an emotive and rabble-rousing oration, later titled the "Rivers of Blood" speech, he compared the increasing Indian population in England with the black population in America, stating:

> As I look ahead, I am filled with foreboding. Like the Roman, I seem to see 'the River Tiber foaming with much blood'.

> That tragic and intractable phenomenon which we watch with horror on the other side of the Atlantic but which there is interwoven with the history and existence of the States itself, is coming upon us here by our own volition and our own neglect. Indeed, it has all but come. In numerical terms, it will be of American proportions long before the end of the century.

> Only resolute and urgent action will avert it even now. Whether there will be the public will to demand and obtain that action, I do not know. All I know is that to see, and not to speak, would be the great betrayal.

In a kneejerk response to the growing dissension, Prime Minister Harold Wilson's Labour government rammed a shameful piece of emergency legislation through Parliament in only three days and nights. The *Commonwealth Immigrants Act, 1968*, provided that a person could enter the United Kingdom, without being subject to immigration restrictions, only if he, or at least one of his parents or grandparents, was born, naturalised, or adopted in the United Kingdom, or had become a citizen within the United Kingdom.

The tussle over this inflammatory bill created a cavernous fissure within the Cabinet. Member of Parliament and Commonwealth Secretary, George Thomson, courageously opposed its passage, declaring that "to pass such legislation would be wrong in principle, clearly discrimination on the grounds of colour, and contrary to everything we stand for." However, his protest was futile in light of the majority opinion which deemed the new law essential to prevent "a large influx from the Asian Community in East Africa to this country."

The legal effect of this repugnant Act was to discriminate against legitimate British citizens, primarily from East Africa, who happened to be people of colour. And, in the United Kingdom, Parliament was supreme. Recourse to the courts was not possible. The practical effect was to catapult most Asians from Kenya and Uganda into stateless limbo.

The only remedy open to the affected Asians was to seek redress from the European Commission of Human Rights. They did so in 1970, claiming that enactment of the Commonwealth Immigrants Act breached their rights under the *European Convention on Human Rights*.

In December 1973, the European Commission issued a report in which it judged "that the 1968 Act had racial motives and that it covered a racial group. When it was introduced into Parliament as a Bill, it was made clear that it was directed against the Asian citizens of the United Kingdom and Colonies in East Africa and especially those in Kenya." The Commission's final judgment was that the Commonwealth Immigrants Act "discriminated against this group of people on grounds of their colour or race."

In 2003, Lord Anthony Lester spoke about the Commonwealth Immigrants Act and the decision of the European Commission. In words more eloquent than I could express, he stated:

> What was done to British citizens of Asian descent in 1968 is not a remote chapter of history. In times of populist hysteria, racism and xenophobia, it could happen again if a future Government decided to deprive some other vulnerable minority of their common humanity and their basic rights and freedoms. We would do well always to remember the terrible lesson given to future generations by the German anti-Nazi activist, Pastor Marin Niemoller:

> When Hitler attacked the Jews I was not a Jew, therefore I was not concerned. And when Hitler attacked the Catholics, I was not a Catholic, and therefore, I was not concerned. And when Hitler attacked the unions and the industrialists, I was not a member of the unions and I was not concerned. Then Hitler attacked me and the Protestant Church—and there was nobody left to be concerned.

The legal and political wrangling concerning the Act and the European Commission's decision continued for some years.

Coupled with the Commonwealth Immigrants Act was a severe quota the British had maintained since 1968 which limited the entry of Asians from East Africa into the United Kingdom to a few thousand heads of household per year plus their dependents.

Despite the legal mishmash, after Idi Amin issued his expulsion proclamation, British Prime Minister Edward Heath stepped up to the plate, and pluckily announced that Great Britain would accept up to 30,000 Indian emigrants from Uganda. He did so in the face of considerable political and public turmoil. Ultra-conservative Members of Parliament brayed about the inevitability of escalating racial hostility, thereby serving to increase racial tension. The National Front, a political party on the far right restricted to "whites-only," augmented its public support by inciting anti-immigration protests and marches. Many local councils, including

Leicester, placed advertisements in the *Uganda Argus* and other newspapers warning Asians not to come to their cities and towns.

The Prime Minister, although he was urging other countries to accept Asians, stuck to his guns. Toward the end of the three month deadline, up to thirty aeroplanes each day were embarking from Kampala bound for England. In the end, the United Kingdom received about 27,000 Asians who held British passports.

Once in Great Britain, the government placed the emigrants in old Royal Air Force barracks converted to temporary housing. About eleven of these "resettlement centres" existed in counties such as Suffolk, Lincolnshire, and Warwickshire. Sometimes, the toilets and other facilities were less than adequate but the British did provide our tragically displaced people with shelter, food, and medical care. The Asians refugees had to endure the frigid cold of an English winter in these barracks but, as soon as they were able, they left to join relatives or friends or to acquire their own homes.

Canada proved to be another welcome sanctuary. As soon as Amin issued his order, the Aga Khan worked tirelessly to convince foreign governments to accept refugees. He and the Canadian Prime Minister, Pierre Elliott Trudeau, had attended Harvard together, and were good friends. The Aga Khan called Trudeau personally to ask for the assistance of the Canadian government.

Trudeau dispatched the Canadian High Commissioner in Kenya to Kampala to look into the issue, and, on receipt of his report, Canada announced that it would accept 3,000 Asians. Many younger Asians, especially professionals and business people, queued quickly to seize the opportunity of starting over at a new frontier, and wasted no time in filling the Canadian allocation. The Aga Khan commented that Canada had extended a level of cooperation, understanding, and help that was absolutely remarkable; it is reported that Canada ended up taking some 6,000 expellees.

Some countries such as India did little or nothing to help, and other countries such as the United States did so grudgingly. It was not until October, for instance, that the United States agreed to absorb 1,000 Asians who were stateless.

Many panic-stricken Asians fled in trains, known as "Kampala Specials," bound for Indian Ocean port cities in Kenya and Tanzania, in order to travel by ship to India and Pakistan. The hardships and horrors inflicted on some of the Asians on these trains was unimaginable.

By the time the ninety day deadline expired only about 500 Asians, who had irrefutable proof of Ugandan citizenship, remained in Uganda voluntarily. But, Amin declared, in a public speech, that those 500 souls would have to leave the cities, relocate in the countryside, and earn a living by subsidence farming. This declaration scared most of the remaining Asians into a hasty exodus.

In all, the diaspora saw about 80,000 Ugandan Asians scatter, like detritus in a hurricane, to the United Kingdom, Canada, the United States, India, Pakistan, Belgium, Holland, Switzerland, West Germany, Austria, Sweden, Norway, Mauritius, Malawi, Kenya, Malaysia, Australia, New Zealand and other European and African nations, and even some South American enclaves.

The physical, emotional, and economic toll the expulsion took on the Asians was cataclysmic. At the beginning of August 1972, they were living quietly and peacefully, anxious about the Amin regime but with no notion that their lives were about to change irrevocably.

By the end of November 1972, they had lost their possessions, homes, businesses, schools, Jamatkhanas, temples, churches, and country; they had been transported, with little or no choice, and often with scarcely a change of clothes, to strange and foreign lands with different cultures and customs and often different languages; and they had suffered separation from relatives, friends, and neighbours, sometimes never to be found again.

The treatment the Asians received varied from country to country but it was often harsh, shoddy, or discriminatory. However, what is of equal importance is that Asians who fled to Great Britain and other nations were the recipients of countless acts of kindness and generosity. Many people gave Asians shelter and employment, and helped them learn the language of their new country. And, once the Asians had their feet under them, they were able to take advantage of boundless opportunities, and become thriving and productive citizens of their new homelands.

CHAPTER SEVENTEEN

My Family's Diaspora

Veil of Terror

In August 1972, I was seventeen years old, and the world was my oyster. I grooved on my cosmopolitan London life, I was ecstatic to be home for Zebby and Rustam's marriage, I revelled in the wedding celebrations, and, like teenagers everywhere, the best part of all was visiting my old haunts, hanging out at the Amber Court Club, and catching up with my friends.

Then Idi Amin unleashed the verbal equivalent of an atomic bomb on us. But, like the rest of the Indian community, at first we didn't realize that the proclamation signalled the end of our way of life in Uganda. You see, in Africa, political dramas exploded every day, and we had learned to pay scant attention to them.

Even when we grasped that Amin really was going to kick us out of the country, I think most of my family still believed, probably as a defence mechanism, that the order was temporary, and that Amin would allow us to return.

Once the reality of expulsion settled in, a veil of terror shrouded our daily lives. We dreaded the spectres of arrests, beatings, and home invasions. We had no idea what might befall us in the future—a future that was to drop on our heads, within ninety days, like a hammer hitting an anvil. The weather, at that time of year, was unremittingly hot, and only exacerbated our misery.

Back in 1962, when the country achieved independent statehood, Bapa chose Ugandan citizenship for all of us. I doubt if he gave more than a moment's thought to any other alternative. Bapa was a righteous man. In his eyes, he owed all his loyalty to the country that had given him the opportunity to build an immensely successful business; that was the birthplace of all his children; and that he expected to be our home for the rest of our lives. On a more practical note, he thought that Ugandan citizenship would protect us better in the constantly unstable political climate.

I'm sure the proclamation shattered Bapa to his core but, unlike the rest of us who railed at the injustice of it all, he was stoic in the face of the epic tragedy. He said little but, in his quiet and determined way, picked himself up, and started planning for the safe evacuation of his family and his wealth.

Bapa, Bahadur, and Nizar continued to go to work but the rest of us hunkered down in the house almost all the time. We never risked a trip to town or to the market. We feared harassment or worse from the soldiers who patrolled the streets with their jeeps and guns, and the local Africans were militant and antagonistic. I managed to go to the Club now and again but was always home by dusk. The only other outings for us women were to the Jamatkhana. Early each evening, we participated in a special ceremony at the mosque, praying for peace and safety.

As an example of the ludicrous climate of fear that prevailed, Amin had banned mini-skirts, and the military was arresting girls who walked down the street wearing them. The army was even patrolling the Parvatiban Muljibhai Madhvani Girls School to check hem lengths.

The girls at the school wore skirts with the hems let out as much as possible to ensure that skirts reached the mandated two inches below the knee. Even before the ban, Bapa used to tell Ma to buy an extra half yard of material so that my skirts were not so short. This directive did not please me at all. Needless to say, I was all about miniskirts and hot pants.

One morning, I was waiting in our front yard for Bapa to pick me up and drive me to the photography studio on Main Street. I needed to have a photo taken for my passport. When he arrived, I hopped in the car, and we were about to leave, when he noticed that I was wearing hot pants. He was aghast, and his fear rendered him angrier than I had ever seen him. We returned to the house, and he furtively hustled me inside to change.

Rashida Takes Flight

Rashida was the first member of our family to leave Uganda forever. She possessed only a Ugandan passport but her British work permit was still in effect. Bahadur drove Rashida to the airport at Entebbe where, she met up with Mobina Jaffer. Mobina's grandfather was Bandali Jaffer, the plantation owner for whom our Nanabapa had worked in Bujuta so many years before. Mobina's husband was Rustam's brother, Nuralla, and they had all had flown in from London for Zebby's wedding.

Their leavetaking was arduous. They booked a flight on BOAC to London four or five times on consecutive days but, each time, circumstances caused cancellation of the flight. Fortunately, Mobina's dad, Sherali, owned a hotel in Kampala where they were able to stay.

Each morning, they braved the civil turmoil and threatening soldiers to drive thirty-two interminable kilometres to the Entebbe airport. Each morning, they joined the thronging line-up of people waiting anxiously to board the aeroplane. Each morning, the airport security personnel subjected them to a degrading strip search. But, the searchers weren't the brightest bulbs in the chandelier, and, each time, they neglected to search Rashida's handbag where she had secreted jewellery belonging to Ma, Zubeda, and her.

Each afternoon, termination of their flight forced them to return to Kampala. At long last, they cleared Ugandan air space, and flew to London and safety. Even then, Rashida's misery continued as the British customs officials seized her cache of jewellery. She later retained a lawyer, and sued successfully for its return. One down, eleven of us to go.

Rustam, Zebby, and Almas Escape

Rustam, on behalf of himself and Zebby, applied to many different nations, and endured days of exhausting line-ups. The United Kingdom officials were not interested in even talking to him. Rustam sought entry to Canada as an engineer, and Zebby as a fashion designer. They had never set foot in that country, but they were hopeful because they could claim ties to it. Rustam's sister, Firoz, and her husband, Alykhan, had immigrated to Vancouver, British Columbia in 1969, and had settled in White Rock.

Canada granted permission based on a points system. The magic number was fifty. English language skills were worth ten precious points, and French another ten. Each year of education yielded one point, and youth was good for several more. Rustam was optimistic because he had no trouble scoring fifty points, and could claim Zebby as a dependent.

The Canadian consular office in Kampala issued numbers to applicants, and, each morning, the local newspaper printed the numbers that entitled their holders to an interview the following day. Rustam's number came up quite quickly, and he and Zebby showed up apprehensively for their critical interview.

The consular official approved their applications but Rustam, in a heart-warming show of loyalty, told the official that they could not accept unless Almas and her friend, Nasim Charania, could come, too. Both of them had applied for entry to Canada, Almas as hairdresser, and Nasim as Montessori teacher. Miraculously, the incredibly kind official agreed to fast track their applications, interviewed them the same day, and gave all of them his stamp of approval. Then they endured yet another series of endless line-ups to obtain their medical clearances.

They were slated to leave the next day, but Almas protested that they needed to return to Jinja to say farewell to their family. She must have been wearing her charm on her forehead because they received permission for the slight delay. Their quick visit to Jinja was immeasurably precious to us because we didn't know if we would ever see them again.

After our wrenching and tearful goodbyes, Rustam, Zebby, Almas, and Nasim departed for their gruelling drive to the airport, and lifted off in a Canadian military transport plane.

They flew to Montreal where the Canadian government housed them in army barracks. They slept in bunk beds. Another military flight to Vancouver followed. The price they had to pay was that, once they found work, they had to reimburse the Canadian government for the cost of their flight. They did so gladly, and with gratitude. Four down, eight to go.

Bapa convinced Bahadur to apply for immigration to Canada as well but, at the time Rustam and the others left, the Canadian consular office had not yet notified him to come in for an interview. Once his number did come up, Bahadur decided not to leave without first helping Bapa to secure their finances, and without taking Bapa, Ma, and Nizar with them. Given that Bahadur had a wife and two small children, his decision was remarkably brave. Then the issue became moot as Bapa and Bahadur were among the select group of businessmen Idi Amin "invited" to stay to train the Africans to take over their industries.

My Agonizing Departure

I was a Ugandan citizen by virtue of my birth but, according to Amin's rules, I was stateless. Bapa solved that problem by procuring a British passport for me on the black market. He knew of an expert forger in Jinja who, for a wad of cash, created the counterfeit document. When I started off to town, in my hot pants, with Bapa to have my photograph taken, it was for that passport picture. By the time Bapa was able to complete all the arrangements necessary for me to leave Uganda, it was October of 1972, and the ninety day deadline was looming.

On the morning of my departure, I walked slowly around my bedroom. I trailed my trembling fingers across the spines of my books and records. I left David Cassidy and Michael Jackson hanging forlornly on my wall. I said "goodbye" to all my possessions. They represented familiarity, comfort, and security, and were so much a part of my sense of self. I could not fathom that I would never see most of them again.

When the time came to leave, I clung ferociously to Ma and Zubeda and my tiny nieces. The air was redolent with our terror. We sobbed. The certainty that I would never again talk, laugh, or cry with them was suffocating me. I had convinced myself that they would never make it out of Uganda alive. Bapa had to wrench me away, and force me into the car.

Bapa and Bahadur drove me to the Entebbe airport. They didn't allow the women to come because it was far too perilous. During the journey, which took almost two hours, fear petrified all three of us.

The once peaceful highway was a cacophonous bedlam. Vehicles full of terror-stricken Asians, laden with suitcases roped precariously on their roofs, jammed the lanes. Local Africans along the roadside harangued us. An endless succession of military roadblocks slewed across the highway. We saw soldiers dragging people from their cars, rooting through their luggage, and strewing it around.

At each checkpoint, I managed to display an outward calm but my palms were sweaty, my blood was racing, and terror suffused every muscle and sinew of my body. Soldiers loomed right in our faces, gesticulating rudely as they pointed their weapons at us. They demanded to know where we were heading, and who was leaving. In anticipation of this harassment, Bapa had stuffed his pockets with clumps of cash, and was able to bribe his way through all the barriers.

The commotion at the airport was just as chaotic. Indian families huddled in the departure lounge, desperately trying to shrink within themselves to escape notice. But, they couldn't stop their children from screaming and crying. People hugged one another in tearful farewells. Armed soldiers roamed everywhere. The customs officers were belligerent, bullying, and nasty. They jacked open suitcases, dumped their contents on the floor, and strip searched people without compunction.

I was slightly more fortunate. A search of my luggage yielded some large, colourful "GoGo" watches I had bought at Draper's Department Store in Kampala before the insanity overtook our lives. The customs officer eyed them greedily but, before he could confiscate them, Bapa caught his eye, and raised a finger, signifying that he would pay him cash to leave me alone.

The flight from Entebbe to London took almost nine hours, and by the time I reached the sanctuary of Rashida and Mansur's home in Stoke Newington, I was exhausted and shattered. Guilt about being safe, while my family remained in peril, and guilt about being glad to be safe, coursed through my veins. Five down, seven to go.

The Remaining Rahemtullas Plot their Exodus

Back in Jinja, Bapa, Bahadur, and Nizar continued to work at the factory, training their staff to take over the business Bapa had built. They had no choice but to leave Ma, Zubeda, and the girls at home each day even though they dreaded a home invasion.

Bapa was artful in his use of bribery, and he paid cash to secure protection for his home and family. Cash payments could work wonders because even the soldiers and their families didn't have enough to eat, and cash was a far more valuable commodity than stolen property.

Shortly before the expulsion proclamation disrupted our lives, Bapa had ordered and paid in advance for equipment from the manufacturing company in Germany with which he had dealt for several years. His intent was to outfit a new plant, and establish a new process for producing carbon dioxide.

Bapa had long-standing business relationships with the manufacturer's German representatives which had morphed, over the years, into close personal relationships. They were the gentlemen who had stayed at the Crested Crane Hotel, and dined at our home so often. Those special bonds, enhanced no doubt by Ma's home cooked meals, reaped life-saving dividends for our family. Bapa was able to secretly arrange with his German friends to refund his substantial investment less a commission.

In January of 1973, Bapa and Bahadur convinced Ugandan officials to allow Bahadur to travel to London and Stuttgart, ostensibly to finalize arrangements for the equipment. His clandestine mission, though, was to facilitate the transfer of the money from Stuttgart to Bapa's bank account in London.

When Bahadur returned to Uganda, Bapa and he informed the government that production of the equipment was coming along splendidly, and would greatly enhance the profitability of the business. However, its arrival in Jinja would consume another few months.

Meanwhile, on the home front, Ma made it her quiet but implacable mission to salvage as many of our personal belongings as possible. Our circle of family friends included the owners of a packaging and moving company. As a huge favour to Ma, they sent a lorry to the house; parked it in the gravelled lane behind our garden; crated a lot of our effects under Ma's censorious eye; and transported them to a freight depot for shipment to Rashida and Mansur's home in London.

By virtue of this adroit manoeuvring, Ma managed to save her china, pots and pans, and other household items; her saree collection; her heavy Pfaff sewing machine; some paintings; Shalina's bedroom baby furniture; a Grundig stereo player in a magnificent mahogany cabinet; my record collection; a smattering of my books; and one of my poofy party dresses, complete with crinolines, which Shalina wore a few years later at one of her birthday parties. Our prized painting, "Elephants at Amboseli" by David Shepherd, survived, and now hangs in Zebby and Rustam's home in North Vancouver.

Ma's jewellery was another matter. Bapa was friendly with a few of the foreign ambassadors, and when they travelled to Kenya, they were kind enough to smuggle Ma's valuables across the border. The border guards did not search their vehicles as the ambassadors claimed diplomatic immunity. They then dropped the jewellery off with Zubeda's parents in Kisumu.

One of our many blessings during that harrowing time was that we were able to stay in contact with Ma by telephone once or twice each week. She would call Zebby and Almas in Vancouver, followed by calls to Rashida and me in London. Then Rashida and I would call Zebby and Almas so we could compare notes.

The government tapped the phone lines so Ma could not say much but the mere tone of her voice was enough to tell us that they were still okay. We carried on guarded conversations in Kutchi but even then we were wary, and talked in simple code language.

For instance, we would ask Ma if she had received any visitors, and if she said no, we knew that no soldiers had barged into the house that day. During every conversation, our hearts were beating out of our chests in case we heard something bad. Knowing that survival in Uganda was growing ever more perilous, I could scarcely imagine the horrors they must be facing. It meant the world to me to hear Ma's voice, and know that they were still alive.

Those six months of agonized waiting were surreal. I spent a lot of time at my bedroom desk studying for my "O" levels. Rashida and Mansur worked so I was often home alone, and dread overwhelmed me. I felt like a hollow husk. I splashed tears constantly on the pages I was studying. My food was tasteless. Fear sometimes strangled my vocal cords so acutely that I could scarcely speak. Sinuous terror crept and snaked through every crevice in my body. I prayed incessantly. I bargained with Allah. "If You will steer my family to a safe harbour, I will never ask you for anything again, and I will be a good person."

And yet, as is always the way, life continued. In the Spring of 1973, my friend, Gita Gosai, and I wrote our "O" levels. They are the equivalent of Grade 12 exams in Canada. Each exam was two or three hours long. I wrote chemistry, biology, English, physics, and math. I failed math but passed the other four subjects, and that was sufficient, in Great Britain, to apply for post-secondary education.

Being a teenager, I still enjoyed fleeting moments of fun, such as Gita and I singing *Harambe, Harambe* to the mummies at the British Museum. But, I paid a price for each brief moment of forgetfulness as worry and guilt battered me immediately afterward.

At the London Jamatkhana, each Friday, a particularly nasty woman from Jinja tracked down Rashida and me like a heat-seeking missile. She then offered a vitriolic commentary about how horrible things were in Uganda, and how many people the soldiers were killing. Her vicious gossip upset Rashida and me terribly. It reached the point where Rashida, Mansur, and I would play a game in the Jamatkhana to scope out the woman, and devise strategies to dodge her.

The one bright star in our personal galaxy was that our darling Mariam Masi and her seven offspring were safe in England out of harm's way. In a sense, the perversion that was Idi Amin proved to be a blessing for Asians like my aunt and cousins who had few prospects in Uganda. Like many

Asians, they had no passports but the British government rescued them, and flew them to the United Kingdom. When they first arrived, the government housed them in a resettlement centre. It was pretty decrepit and uncomfortable but at least they had shelter, and were well-treated and well-fed. The children ranged, at the time, from about twelve to thirty years old.

Before long, the state relocated them to Exeter, and helped them out with education, medical care, and housing. They lived in a cute little home in a lovely neighbourhood. In due course, they moved to Birmingham. The older four or five children soon found jobs. Some of them worked at the Cadbury chocolate factory, and the younger ones were able to attend school.

Rashida and I visited our aunt and cousins at the resettlement centre, and then in Exeter, several times. The remainder of our family was still trapped in Uganda, and our friends and other relatives had scattered to the four winds. For us, those visits were an oasis of laughter and joy. Our aunt and cousins had great senses of humour, and we craved our aunt's mothering, to say nothing of the knack for cooking Nanima had bequeathed to her. Going to see them gave us a much needed sense of connection. It was the new "normal."

By March of 1974, only a few Indian families remained in Jinja. Bapa and Bahadur had tied up all the loose ends of their surreptitious deal with the Germans. Soldiers began coming to the house to try to trick them into confessing that they were about to run away. A government official informed them that no more training of the staff was necessary, and demanded that they turn over the keys to the factory.

During the troubles, Victoria, the mid-wife, remained a loyal friend. She helped to conceal Ma's illegal shenanigans and Bapa's escape strategy from the incessant suspicious prying of the military. For their part, the family never revealed her illicit affair with Milton Obote to a soul. Had they done so, Idi Amin, without question, would have arrested her, and ordered a gruesome death.

Bapa sensed that the family had run out of time. He generously gave the servants money to return to their villages and buy cows. Many of the Africans that we knew, including our friends and servants, were all too aware of the devastating consequences they would suffer as a result of the expulsion. They knew that the country would face ruin, and that they would have no means to provide for their families. So, anguish shadowed their days as well.

By way of pre-arranged code words, Rashida, Mansur, and I knew that the family was about to flee to Kenya. About 5 a.m. one morning, Bapa and Bahadur woke Ma, Zubeda, Nizar, Shalina, and Narmin, and told them to dress hurriedly. Ma did so, and rushed outside with the others. Their hearts pounding with fear. Then, they simply disappeared from Uganda. Ma never even had the chance to say good-bye to her cherished home. She just grabbed her purse, and left forever. In some ways, I don't think she ever recovered.

Our family will always be grateful to Mansur Shariff, the brother of Zebby's friend, Rozina, who played a key role in assisting my family with their escape. Mansur's father, Jeraj Shariff, was Bapa's friend from the early days, and his children and my siblings grew up together in Jinja. Mansur used to live in Kampala but frequently travelled to Jinja to visit with Bahadur and our family. Mansur's family had left Uganda for Great Britain and Canada but Mansur had remained in Kampala to continue to manage the family business.

Even today, after the passage of forty years, my family chooses not to reveal the precise means by which they fled Uganda because some of the people who assisted them still live there.

The seven of them travelled to Kisumu where they found refuge with Zubeda's parents. They were able to let us know that they had escaped. After a short time, they travelled to Nairobi

Bahadur and his family had Canadian papers but Bapa, Ma, and Nizar had nothing. A friend of Bahadur's, Shekhar Mehta, the East African Safari Rally champion, had a friend who worked for the British embassy in Nairobi. With their help and some judicious bribery, Bapa was able to obtain the papers necessary to transport all of them to the United Kingdom.

Rashida, Mansur, and I, along with a couple of our friends, awaited the arrival of the family at Heathrow. Shedding the oppressive cloak of despair and anxiety that had weighed me down for six months was a colossal relief. I was literally jumping for joy. I remember thinking to myself that I would never worry about anything ever again. I know that will remain always as the happiest moment in my entire life. What a reunion! Twelve down, none to go.

I would like to say that the ecstasy of our reunion lasted forever. But, teenagers and human nature being what they are, I was not enamoured with being under Ma's thumb again after my years of independence in London, and we engaged in many a tussle.

CHAPTER EIGHTEEN

The Continuing Ugandan Tragedy

The Decimation of Uganda

As the years passed, the economy crumbled. The currency devalued to virtually nothing. The people were penurious. Fear of saying or doing the wrong thing paralyzed the civil service. Garbage clogged the cities and towns. Incompetent management by Africans wiped out most industries. Factories ground to a halt because repair and maintenance of the machinery was non-existent. Inept upkeep of the Owen Falls Dam resulted in a critical decline in the supply of electricity. Businesses degenerated. Buildings decayed. Potholes riddled the roads. The educational structure disappeared. Schools, universities, hospitals, clinics, and churches declined into wrack and ruin. Even the wildlife suffered devastation as the soldiers killed and butchered animals for food and ivory. The climate of terror annihilated tourism, and the dollars it generated. And, so, the squalid and sordid saga continued for eight interminable years.

After Amin ordered the killing of two of his key ministers, Oboth Ofumbi, and General Mustafa Adrisi, his vice-president, some of Amin's loyal troops finally mutinied, and fled to Tanzania. Amin accused Julius Nyerere, who was then the Tanzanian President, of waging war against Uganda.

Late in 1978, Amin mobilized troops to hunt down the mutineers by invading Tanzania, and annexing a portion of it. Observers believe that Muammar al-Gaddafi provided Amin with military assistance, but to no avail. In January 1979, Tanzanian military forces, aided by Ugandan exiles who had formed the Uganda National Liberation Army, fought their way into Uganda, and, by April, captured Kampala. Ironically, the people welcomed the demise of the Butcher of Uganda's regime the same way they had welcomed its creation, with dancing and singing in the streets.

Idi Amin fled ignominiously into exile in Libya. Finally, the Saudi royal family gave Amin sanctuary in Saudi Arabia where he lived for many years in quiet retirement. As a last kick at the cat, in 1989, Amin attempted to return to Uganda by way of the Democratic Republic of the Congo but its President forced him to retreat to Saudi Arabia.

In early 2003, Amin's family requested Ugandan President Yoweri Museveni to permit Amin to return to Uganda as his health was failing. Museveni responded by saying that if Amin appeared in Uganda he would be arrested and would have to face the music for the sins he had committed.

Idi Amin died in Saudi Arabia on August 16, 2003 without a hint of regret, repentance, or shame. While I'm certain that many people, including ousted Ugandan Asians, welcomed the news of his death, for our family, it was merely the closing of a chapter. We had all moved on, and were secure and happy in our new Canadian homeland.

History will never know the exact number of people murdered during Idi Amin's dictatorship but some observers placed the ballpark estimate between 300,000 and 500,000 souls.

While I hesitate to give Amin any more notoriety, even in death, I should mention that, through the years, several movies and documentaries have depicted the abominations of this despot.

Raid on Entebbe (1977) is a film that portrayed the 1976 hijacking, by pro-Palestinians, of an Air France aeroplane. Idi Amin gave the hijackers refuge at the Entebbe Airport where they held the crew and a number of Jewish and other passengers hostage until Israeli commandos seized control of the airport and freed most of the passengers, although some were killed or wounded. The international community criticized Amin's role in the atrocity, and Great Britain responded to the criticism by closing its High Commission in Uganda.

Another film, *The Last King of Scotland* (2006), focused on Amin's fixation on all things Scottish, leading to his actually anointing himself "The Last King of Scotland." While some of portions of the movie were purely fictional it also integrated actual events that occurred during Amin's dictatorship.

The Aftermath

After Idi Amin's ouster in 1978, Uganda was in ruins, and its people war-weary and tattered. But, the devastation, atrocities, corruption, political instability, tribal dissension, civil war, economic decimation, and flagrant violations of civil rights continued for another several catastrophic years.

Believe it or not, the ubiquitous Milton Obote re-ascended to the presidency, and took up where he left off in his unquenchable quest for absolute power. In 1985, Tito Okello, commander of the army, ousted Obote, appointed himself president, and carried on the perverse Ugandan traditions of venality and carnage.

In the early 1980s, in opposition to Obote, Yoweri Museveni had established a band of guerrillas called the "National Resistance Movement." By January of 1986, the NRM had fought its way to Kampala, and stormed the capital. Okello and his troops fled. On January 26, 1986, Museveni assumed the mantle of the presidency, and promised the Ugandan people a return to democracy.

Obote fled to Tanzania, and then to Zambia. He died in South Africa on October 10, 2005 at the age of seventy-nine. His wife, Miria, whom many Ugandans respected, and his five children, survived him. Although Obote and Museveni were bitter rivals, Museveni, perhaps in a gesture, of reconciliation, allowed the former president a state funeral in Kampala.

CHAPTER NINETEEN
Our New Canadian Homeland

Destination Vancouver

Unbeknown to us, Aga Khan III, in 1951, had uttered these pro-
phetic words:

> Your grandfathers crossed India to come to Africa. You
> have to cross right up to the Atlantic and, who knows,
> later I may send you to America....

None of my family had ever been to Canada but we decided to look
into immigrating. Ma was less than impressed with the damp English
climate, and Zebby, who was rapturous about Vancouver, held a lot of
sway over Bapa and Ma.

About a month after the remainder of my family arrived in London, I
headed for Canada on a school break to visit Almas and Zebby. I stayed
with Almas and Nasim at their apartment in the Buchan Hotel in the
heart of the West End of Vancouver. The West End was the area where
Zebby and Rustam had found accommodation after staying, when they
first arrived, with Rustam's sister and brother-in-law in White Rock.

I had mixed feelings about my first impressions of Vancouver. I liked
the city much more than I did London, and the water, mountains, and
greenery reminded me viscerally of Uganda. Having been born and
raised in Jinja, I didn't appreciate the ancient ambience of Africa when I
lived there but, when I came to Canada, the newness of everything, especially the buildings, struck me immediately.

While I was visiting my sisters, Bahadur and Zubeda, and their children, arrived in Vancouver for a "look-see." The fact that the landed immigration visas they had managed to snare in Kampala were about to expire

had motivated them. They liked Vancouver, and decided they wanted to settle here. Bahadur contacted a Canadian immigration officer to enquire whether Ma, Bapa, and Nizar would be welcome, too. The answer was "yes" so the three of them promptly flew over from London.

As soon as Ma, Bapa, and Nizar arrived, they went to the immigration centre on West Hastings Street. I went with them but waited in the reception area. The interviewer asked Bapa if anyone else needed to apply, and he replied that his daughter was in the waiting room. The official called me in, and generously awarded me landed immigrant status too. I was eighteen years old at the time. I returned to London to pack my belongings, and then came to Canada for good.

The migration of Ismailis from Uganda to Europe, Great Britain, and especially Canada and the United States marked the first time our community had to re-create itself in western nations. Years later, Brian Mulroney, a former Prime Minister, commented that the Ismailis were one of the most successful communities that had ever immigrated to Canada.

Acclimatizing to our New Homeland

My family and I felt an instant sense of belonging in our adopted city but we did suffer some challenges. During the first several years, we experienced racism in subtle and petty ways, perhaps, in part, because the local population feared the large influx of brown people they saw descending upon them.

A common illustration of racism was the difficulty we endured finding accommodation. On one occasion, Almas and I saw a "For Rent" sign for an apartment near Beach Avenue. We rang the manager's buzzer, and, in my impeccable British accent, I asked if the apartment was still available. The manager replied in the affirmative but, when he came downstairs to meet us, reversed his stance, saying he had just rented it.

Almas told this story to Wayne, a gentleman with whom she worked. He was furious, and zoomed over to the building to ask whether the apartment was available. The manager said that it was, and that Wayne could rent it. Having caught the manager redhanded, Wayne confronted the man, and threatened him with a lawsuit on our behalf. However, we didn't wish to pursue the matter, not wanting to live where we clearly were not wanted. Shortly after our unpleasant encounter with the bigoted landlord, Bapa managed to rent two apartments on Broughton Street.

The West End was a good place to put down our roots. It was a "happening" neighbourhood, and, everything being in close proximity was helpful because we didn't know our way around. We especially enjoyed strolling along English Bay and through Stanley Park in the evenings.

Compared to parks in Uganda and Kenya, it was intriguingly cultivated and civilized.

During my initial weeks in the West End, I spent quite a bit of time wrestling with the decision of what I was going to do with myself.

School Days All Over Again

I found everything in Vancouver new and confusing. I had no idea how to cope. I was thrilled to find that my childhood friend, Nasreen Adatia, and her parents had immigrated here. Nasreen was attending Kitsilano Secondary School at the time, and she encouraged me to enroll. Even though I had finished my "O" levels in London, I did so, in September of 1973. I chose to repeat Grade 12 because I needed time to get my feet under me. My decision was a wise one because attending school taught me a lot about Canadian ways and how best to integrate.

My first class at Kitsilano was social studies. Following my *modus operandi* at Hackney & Stoke Newington Polytechnic, I quickly shrank into a desk in the middle of the room but my luck could not have been worse. My teacher was the indomitable George Puil.

Mr. Puil was a legendary Vancouver figure who was cocksure and combative. He did not suffer fools gladly. He was a high school teacher for thirty-five years, a member of the Vancouver City Park Board, and a high profile Vancouver Councillor. He chaired many regional and national committees including the Greater Vancouver Regional District and the Greater Vancouver Transportation Authority. His many awards include Transit Advocate of the Year, the UBC Alumni Award of Distinction, and The Queen's Golden Jubilee Medal.

When Mr. Puil entered the room, his bushy eyebrows, piercing blue eyes, and thin-lipped smile almost scared me back to Jinja. His first act was to pin a map of Canada on the blackboard.

Unbelievably, he fixed me with his gaze, and, in his squeaky voice, asked me to name all the provinces. I was petrified but, in accordance with British tradition, promptly rose from my seat. Everyone laughed at me so I sank back down. Mr. Puil pointed to British Columbia and then Ontario, and I managed to name them. Then he gestured to Alberta, and my response was "Atlanta." Everyone giggled, which mortified me. However, I bravely stood again, and said that I would like to explain that I had been in Vancouver only a month; that I did know several of the provinces; that, in retrospect, I should have responded with "Alberta"; and that I would like someone else to continue. Mr. Puil then called on a home-grown scholar who failed miserably.

After class, Mr. Puil pulled me aside, apologized to me, and asked about my background. Ever after, I could do no wrong in his eyes.

When I graduated from Kitsilano Secondary School in June of 1974, I didn't feel ready to enter university so, beginning in September of 1974, I enrolled in a business programme at Langara College. The programme included a two-month work practicum. The Royal Bank of Canada, Hastings and Granville Branch, in a foreshadowing of my banking career, accepted me as an apprentice from March to April of 1976. The Bank did not pay a salary, but I had the opportunity to work in various areas of the branch. At the end of the two-month practicum, the personnel manager offered me permanent employment upon completion of my programme. I graduated in June of 1976, and celebrated by travelling to Disneyland with Almas and Nizar, and our nieces, Shalina and Narmin.

The Royal Bank of Canada Calls my Name

I called the Royal Bank on my return from vacation. The person to whom I spoke asked me to come in for an interview at the Visa Centre. I interviewed on a Friday, and received a job offer then and there to start on the following Monday. Thus began my career, or at least my first career, with The Royal Bank of Canada.

I worked at the Visa Centre in Vancouver handling credit and collections. Regrettably, I loathed this job. I stuck with it for one year but then became dispirited, and quit. I consoled myself by travelling for a few months in Great Britain and Europe.

When I returned to Vancouver, I knew that I wanted to pursue a financial career. But, I was concerned that I lacked the self-confidence and polish to advance up the corporate ladder. Accordingly, I decided that, before embarking on my career, I needed to apply some finishing touches to myself.

So, I enrolled in a programme at "Patricia Stevens," a private finishing academy. Despite being in the basement of a building on Granville Street, the school was gorgeous and upscale. Shirley Hickey, a classy lady, owned and operated it. My lessons included how to walk, talk, and dress, and I received some valuable tips. However, even though the tuition was prepaid and non-refundable, I left the programme after about three months because I felt the instructors were trying to mould me into a model. I recognized I was clearly not model material.

One thing I now regret was that, about this time, I shed, to the extent I could, my British accent, leaving me with diction that I consider "neither fish nor fowl nor good red herring."

Bapa was becoming anxious about my future, and convinced me to contact the Royal Bank again. I spoke to a personnel manager at the Visa Centre, and told her, rather presumptuously in hindsight, that I wanted employment at a bank branch rather than at Visa. Even though the market was at a low ebb, the personnel manager found me a job at one of their smaller branches. After that, I worked at various bank branches, at one of which I met Allison McLeod (now Allison Tucker), the first of many great friends I was fortunate to make during my banking career.

I've been blessed throughout my life with an abundance of good friends, one of whom, Sherrill Sambrooke (now Sherrill Hemsley), I hooked up with at the Pender and Bute branch. Her parents owned a home in Kelowna, with a huge swimming pool. Sherrill and I travelled there to visit them every August long weekend. I adored them, and called them "Mom" and "Dad." On one occasion, we all attended an orchard party in Kelowna. An elderly gentleman overheard me call Sherrill's parents by my pet nicknames for them. To our enduring amusement, he waxed eloquent about how kind they were to have adopted a poor little Indian girl from Africa.

While I was at Pender and Bute, the Bank encouraged me to enroll in an intense programme consisting of several university level courses. I attended all courses in the evening at Simon Fraser University. Another requirement of the programme was attendance at a two week module at the University of Calgary along with employees from all the various Canadian banks. We worked in groups consisting of people from each of the different banks. The purpose of the work group was to simulate the activities of an actual bank.

School was never my cup of tea, however, the programme remains one of the most interesting endeavours I have ever undertaken, and the reward was certainly worth the candle. After passing the final major exam, I received a diploma from the Institute of Canadian Bankers, and became a fellow of the Institute.

On January 2, 1980, I transferred to the Royal Centre Branch as a credit analyst in the corporate area. My mandate was to assist a senior corporate and multi-national account manager in administering his loan portfolio which was sizeable in terms of dollar value and complex in nature. My duties included analysing the financial position of borrowers. I also participated in real estate lending transactions, several of which were for the development of landmark projects in the Vancouver area. At the time, I did not foresee how this education in real estate lending would play a role in shaping my future career.

Shortly after my arrival, Bill Thompson who was responsible for setting up RBC's Private Banking operation in Vancouver occupied an office next to mine. I got to know Bill well, and he mentioned to me that when I was a bit older, he would love to recruit me. A career in Private Banking became my "go to" dream.

A few weeks after joining the Royal Centre team, I met Anne Lippert, a senior corporate account manager. Anne commented that she loved the way I dressed so I promptly introduced her to Zebby. It was a good match, and from 1980 until Anne retired, Zebby designed and sewed all her clothes. Anne and I have maintained a close camaraderie too for all these years. Philippa Mckenna, who was the Royal Bank's MBA trainee at that time, became another friend.

After five years, the Bank transferred me to the No. 3 and Cook Branch in Richmond as an account manager. In that position, I was able to use the corporate lending skills I had acquired to assist independent business owners with their financial requirements. As usual, I made great friends including Cathy Smith, Erika Penner, and Marilyn Homer (now Marilyn Tevington). The four of us were studying together for our Personal Financial Planning Certification. In a silly, euphoric moment, we decided that, after completing our exams, we would embark on an African safari. However, our number expanded to include Joan Norrington. One day in the lunch room, I was telling someone about the safari, and Joan overheard. I scarcely knew Joan but she came to me that afternoon, and asked if she could join us as it was her dream to go on a safari adventure. I liked Joan tremendously, and we became instant friends. The safari was not far off.

CHAPTER TWENTY

The Ups and Downs of Life in Canada

Work Searches and Experiences

I considered myself blessed to have found employment with the Royal Bank but I'm satisfied that I earned every promotion I received. Some of my siblings were not so fortunate in their early job searches.

The common refrain when they applied for jobs was that "Canadian experience" was a prerequisite. That barrier is still prevalent today. In my work, I routinely receive job applications from people in other countries saying they will work for nothing in order to obtain that elusive "know-how."

Discrimination was not the only bar, though, and we still laugh about Bapa's abortive attempts to put Bahadur and Nizar to work. He was really keen for Bahadur to buy an egg farm in the Fraser Valley, and the three of them drove out to Abbotsford to look over a likely prospect. At the time, automation wasn't yet available, and the stench was so bad that Bahadur threw up. That was the end of that.

In the early 1970s, you could buy a McDonald's restaurant franchise for about $200,000, but Bapa and the boys doubted the long-term value of an investment as speculative as a fast food chain. So, they passed.

Bahadur held a couple of jobs, and dabbled in real estate. His main interest in life, though, was to be the best father he could be to Shalina and Narmin and, later, to Farha. Bahadur and Zubeda were (and still are) ideal parents.

Despite Zebby's degree in dress design from the Paris Academy in London and having owned her own dress-making and design shop in Jinja, she could find no work commensurate with her education and experience. She finally obtained employment as a seamstress at Koret of

California, a female garment manufacturing factory, on Cordova Street, in an unsavoury part of town.

To reach Koret, Zebby had to take a bus from the West End to East Vancouver, a distance of several kilometres. She wasn't sure how to get there, and worried about travelling alone. As a result, Rustam escorted her to work each day on the bus. But the fare of twenty-five cents per person was hefty so he walked back home. He then spent several hours job hunting until it was time to walk back to Cordova Street to take Zebby home on the bus. On the upside, Rustam became extremely fit.

Koret was a decent employer, and Zebby enjoyed a good career there. Because of her ability, she rose through the ranks to become co-manager of a large sewing department. An added bonus for us girls was that we were able to buy clothes directly from Koret at an employee discount. We spent a lot of time there! Nizar joined Zebby at Koret of California in their design and cutting section, and worked there for several years.

Although Rustam was a chemical engineer, he had the utmost difficulty finding a job that matched his education and skill set. After a few months, he scored an interview with Westroc Industries near the foot of McGill Street. The interviewer, Ceneke Kotterau, asked Rustam a lot of seemingly irrelevant questions about his expulsion and re-location experiences but nothing at all about his qualifications. Rustam had nursed high hopes about the interview but left feeling quite dejected.

Imagine his surprise when the interviewer called him the next day and offered him a job. Serendipity had certainly come into play because Mr. Kotterau was a Czechoslovakian who had escaped from his country, and had relocated to Vancouver. When he interviewed Rustam, he was simply interested in comparing their experiences.

The job Rustam took was at entry level but he was still ecstatic to be earning a living. He worked there for about three years as a technician, and gradually won the respect of his employer who promoted him. Eventually, though, the plant closed, and Rustam was jobless again. He applied to the City of Vancouver's Engineering Department, and found employment as a lab technician. His job was to test for quality control of all materials such as asphalt mixes and precast concrete purchased by the city.

The most difficult issue for Rustam at the City had nothing to do with his job but rather with swearing. Rustam is a gentle soul, and was not accustomed to the salty language used by many of the employees. After awhile, though, he realized that the swearing had no meaning but was just expression by rote, and then it no longer bothered him.

Although the City did not pay him to do so, Rustam took it upon himself to organize the lab, and create a system for handling the work. He impressed his boss's boss with his capabilities, and, when a top level engineering assistant position became available, he was awarded it. In this capacity, Rustam was responsible for writing the material specifications for all tenders put out by the City. Rustam remained with the City for several years until his retirement.

Almas' friend, Nasim, who had run her own Montessori School in Jinja, became a Montessori teacher.

Almas, meanwhile, worked as a hairdresser at the Raymond Salon in Park Royal in West Vancouver from about 1972 to 1974. One day, shortly after she started there, a client named Mrs. Pattison, who was the wife of Jimmy Pattison, the legendary British Columbian entrepreneur, learned that Almas was from Uganda. She offered, on the spot, to buy her a winter coat. Almas politely said "no, thank you," but always remembered this kind gesture during her first days in Canada.

After leaving Park Royal, Almas, having seen a newspaper ad, went to work for a Japanese couple, Kay and Mas, at Fashion Tress, located at 15th Avenue and Trafalgar Street in Vancouver. She adored Kay and Mas, and they her. Almas spent about fifteen years there as an employee, and then as an owner. One of the many things that endeared Kay and Mas to me personally was that they bred Shih Tzu puppies. In my book that made them the finest kind of people.

Acquiring Permanent Residences

Rustam and Zebby were hard workers. Zebby, in particular, put in a tremendous amount of overtime. As a result, they were the first of the family to buy property. It was a modest townhome on Lillooet Road in North Vancouver. In 1985, they built their dream home on the bank of the Seymour River where they still reside.

Zebby's co-manager at Koret was a lovely lady named Marrietta. In March 1975, Marrietta told Zebby about a newly constructed house in Burnaby near her own home. It was on Montecito Drive part way up Burnaby Mountain. Bapa drove over to take a look at the house, and fell in love with it. It was big enough to house all of us and the icing on the cake was that the area was largely undeveloped, and woodland abounded. Bapa made the deal straightaway, and the house on Montecito Drive became our first permanent home in Canada.

More Blessings

On June 15, 1976, we all received a gift beyond compare when Zubeda gave birth to Farha. She was third and last daughter for Zubeda and Bahadur, and our first baby born on Canadian soil.

In 1977, after living in Canada for more than three years, and after studying and passing the citizenship test, Ma, Bapa, Bahadur, Zubeda,

Almas, Nizar, Zebby, Rustam, Shalina, Narmin, and I all received the blessing of becoming proud and loyal Canadian citizens. That was a fine day for our family.

Virgin Voyage to Asia and India

In early 1979, while I was still at the Pender and Bute Branch, Almas, Nizar, and I undertook our first whirlwind expedition to Asia and the Indian subcontinent.

Our arrival in Hong Kong corresponded with the Chinese New Year. At a shop in Hong Kong, I bartered so hard with the shopkeeper that she told me she would remember me even if I came back twenty years later. We enjoyed further New Year festivities at our next stop in Singapore which, as I can attest, truly is the cleanest city in the world.

Pressing on to Bangkok, the floating markets were the highlight for us. Small boats are laden with tropical fruits and vegetables, coconut juice, and local foods cooked right on board.

Our stay in Karachi to visit Mansur's family began inauspiciously, and ended splendidly. We ran into trouble before we even exited the airport. Our experience has been that, even though we carry Canadian passports, customs officers in certain countries tend to give us a hard time because we are brown rather than white, and they don't want us to forget it—or perhaps they are just envious. The Karachi customs officers lived up to this tradition.

First, we had to convince them that we were Canadians which was difficult because we did not speak their language. Then they insisted on opening our luggage. We had brought suitcases full of gifts, including one filled with chocolate, because gifts sent by mail most often did not arrive at their destination. The customs officers wanted us to share the gifts. I refused, and stood my ground. As a result, we spent two hours just clearing customs. We were not impressed.

At long last we emerged from the airport, Mansur's sister and brother-in-law, and their three daughters, whom we had never met before, were waiting patiently for us, and they welcomed us with open arms.

We had booked rooms at the renowned Karachi Sheraton Hotel but the family took us to their home for lunch, and the brother-in-law started to unload our luggage. He cheerfully told us that he had cancelled our hotel reservations. At first, we were apprehensive but the family had a roomy condominium style apartment, and the daughters were all good fun. One was close to Almas in age, and another close to my age. At bedtime, we dragged all the mattresses into one bedroom, and talked half the night. Another bonus was that their mother was a "blue ribbon" cook, and all our meals were sumptuous.

Some friends of the family who lived in the apartment complex married while we were visiting, and we had the chance to attend our first Pakistani wedding.

Our hosts took us sightseeing around Karachi. We were privileged to visit Honeymoon Lodge, situate on the eastern outskirts of the city. It perched precariously atop a hill, with one hundred steps leading up to it. The lodge was the birthplace of Sir Sultan Muhammad Shah, Aga Khan III.

We also rode camels, an adventure that was both funny and scary. Once seated on the camels, we discovered that their hind legs rose up before their heads. Keeping our balance was challenging, and Almas screeched during her entire ride. (That was the fun part.)

From Karachi, we flew to Mumbai. On the plane, a swarthy, good-looking Saudi gentleman sat next to me, and we engaged in a friendly discussion. He asked where we were staying. When I told him we were staying at the Taj Mahal Palace and Tower Hotel, he said that he had a room booked at the same hotel. We had arranged for a van and tour guide to meet us at the airport, and the man asked if he could beg a ride with us. We said, "Sure," but when we arrived at the hotel, it turned out he had no reservation. He claimed a mix-up, and the desk clerk found him a room. The next morning, he was waiting in the lobby. He asked if he could join our tour. He came with us but later I found out he had told the hotel staff he was part of our group. At that point, I had a quiet word with the staff, and we never saw our mystery man again.

The uniforms worn by the female personnel at the Taj were elegant yellow silk sarees. I was so taken by these sarees that we caught a cab to the store that stocked them, and I bought one which, all these years later, I still own.

Our stop in Delhi was noteworthy as well. The window of our hotel room at the Sheraton Oberoi overlooked a courtyard. We were peering down at a Hindu wedding when a gentleman knocked on our door, and invited us to come down for the ceremony. We dressed in no time flat, and joined the wedding in progress. We managed to snag a delicious meal as well. Many of our Ismaili customs derive from Hindu religious traditions so the wedding rituals were fairly familiar to me.

Srinagar is the capital of Kashmir in northern India. Kashmir is situate between India and Pakistan, and most of its inhabitants are Muslim. We visited there during an extremely cold February. While driving from the airport, we noticed both men and women who wore large ponchos and looked rather pregnant. It turned out that, under their ponchos, they were carrying clay pots containing hot coals to keep themselves warm.

In Srinagar, we booked a houseboat on a lake. It was quite a treat because the price included a cook, servant, and major domo. The houseboat contained stand-alone wood burning fireplaces and an enormous Aga stove for heat. In the bedrooms at night, our beds were outfitted with luxurious eiderdown quilts and three hot water bottles.

The lake was rife with houseboats. Vendors, in small craft, came by to sell us their wares. The highlight of this region was our visit to a carpet factory. There we observed workers weaving expensive and exquisitely designed silk carpets for Eaton's Department Store in Canada.

Our first Far East trip ended in Japan where we went to Tokyo and Kyoto by the Bullet Train.

Fatima's Birth and Tragic Death

Zebby and Rustam desperately wanted children but Zebby had trouble conceiving. She underwent several *in vitro* fertilization treatments. At last, the grand occasion arrived. They were jiggling with joy when they announced that Zebby was expecting. Zebby was the apple of Bapa's eye, and he was over the moon with happiness for her. Ironically, after all the anguish of trying to become pregnant, the early months of her pregnancy were relatively easy.

Zebby was extremely popular and well-liked at Koret, and the employees she managed were thrilled for her, too. Many of the seamstresses were Taiwanese or Chinese, and they made it their mission to fatten her up by constantly bringing her their home-cooked specialty dishes.

One day, when Zebby was about six months along, she and I were shopping together on South Granville Street. Suddenly, she was beset by labour pains. I whisked her to the Vancouver General Hospital. Just as we arrived, her water broke. I called Rustam, and he raced to the hospital in a flash.

Rustam joined Zebby while I remained in the waiting area. I was beside myself with worry. After a few hours, I dashed to the hospital bookstore, and bought something mindless to read. It didn't help.

Finally, Rustam appeared. His face told me everything I didn't want to know. He was so upset. Zebby had given birth to a baby girl, but she was so tiny she fit in the palm of his hand. Her prospects were not good. I went into Zebby's room to console her, but didn't see the baby. They had taken her away.

Rustam's sister, Noorjahan, chose the name "Fatima" for our niece, after the daughter of Prophet Muhammad. Our Fatima lived for only a day or two. When she died on July 22, 1980, Zebby was still in the hospital.

A few days later, Rustam brought Zebby to our home on Montecito Drive. She came into the house wailing, and buried herself in the willing arms of her family. We were all terribly distraught, but Zebby was drowning in inconsolable grief. And I'm sure that, for Ma and Bapa, Fatima's death brought back tragic memories of my sister, Khatun, who had died from leukemia.

Fatima's death posed another problem. Our religion dictates that only people who are baptized as Muslims are entitled to a proper Muslim funeral and burial. Our solution was to bring Fatima's small body to the Jamatkhana on Drake Street in Vancouver for a simple and heartbreaking baptism. Rustam's sister, Firoz, and her husband, Alykhan, bravely volunteered to transport Fatima's corpse, and Mobina Jaffer bought her a precious pink baby outfit for her sole appearance on this earth.

The funeral service followed on the heels of the baptism. Then, contrary to Muslim dictates, Zebby and Almas, along with a small cadre of both male and female family members, accompanied Fatima to Forest Lawn Cemetery on Royal Oak Avenue in Burnaby for burial. Fatima was the first member of our immediate family to be interred in our adopted country.

In the ensuing months, Rustam and the rest of our family worried mightily about Zebby's emotional and physical health. Losing Fatima after trying so hard and so long to conceive, coupled with a long physical recuperation from her ordeal, almost sent Zebby over the edge. Neither did it help that this tragedy was the first personal one she had endured. But, we all offered our support, and Ma and Zubeda spent a great deal of time with Zebby. She was, at her core, a strong woman. She survived, and recovered.

The people at Koret, who were like family to Zebby, were most caring and kind. She was able to take off as much time as she needed. After recuperating for several months, she returned to Koret.

None of us will ever forget little Fatima, and I think of her every time I pass by the Vancouver General Hospital.

Rashida, Mansur, Nashina, and Natasha Join the Clan

Meanwhile, Rashida and Mansur also despaired of ever having children. Rashida, had no trouble on the conception front but suffered six miscarriages. She was understandably depressed so she and Mansur decided to move to Vancouver to benefit from our family support network. They sold their business and their home at 34 Manse Road, Stoke Newington, and joined us in Burnaby in 1980.

With the proceeds from the sale of their London home, Mansur was able to buy a dry-cleaning business at Broadway and Commercial in Vancouver where the SkyTrain station is now situate. Rashida procured a job as a clerk in international trade and finance at the Canadian Imperial Bank of Commerce in Downtown Vancouver. Rashida and I had great fun commuting together. Rashida and Mansur settled into a new townhouse complex on Montecito Drive just across the street from our family home.

Rashida had always been faithful about exercise, and, on her arrival in Canada, took up swimming. One day, at the pool, she was trapped under water for a moment. Afterward, in the change room, she mentioned her scare to another woman who said that the same thing had happened to her. They got to talking, and hit it off. Rashida, for some reason, told the woman that she and Mansur were thinking about adoption. As fate would have it, the woman was a case worker at the Department of Human Resources whose mandate included adoptions.

The case worker suggested that Rashida make an appointment with her, and she did so the following day. The case worker came to inspect their home, and said that she could tell right away that Rashida and Mansur would be wonderful parents.

Within a couple of months, Rashida received a telephone call that a baby would be available just a few days later. When the great day came, Rashida and Mansur rushed off to Grace Hospital through a ferocious snow storm. A nurse brought the baby into the room where they were waiting. Rashida, who had been a bit uncertain, fell hopelessly in love at first glimpse.

Rashida couldn't stop crying as she dressed the baby in some clothes she had brought with her, and asked the nurse who could give up such a beautiful child. The no-nonsense nurse told her to just stop crying and be happy.

Allah had finally blessed Rashida and Mansur with the adoption of a precious baby girl born on January 11, 1982. I was thrilled that she was born on my birthday. I had the honour of naming her, and I called her "Nashina," after a friend of mine. Nashina was a simply beautiful baby. When she was born, she looked as white as anything but then, in the blink of an eye, turned darker.

The excitement in our home was out of this world. As soon as the proud parents brought Nashina home, Rashida and I rushed out to buy baby clothes. Rashida, who normally had no interest in buying clothes, shopped till she dropped.

Nashina was a colicky baby, who cried incessantly, and that's where our family support system kicked in. Zubeda, who is the prototype for the universal mother, could often be seen running across the street in the middle of the night, answering distress calls from Rashida.

When Nashina was about three years old, Mansur and Rashida sold their townhouse, and built a new home nearby in Burnaby.

When Zebby and Rustam saw first-hand the joy Rashida and Mansur were experiencing with Nashina, they too realized that there was more than one way to skin a cat, and they applied to the adoption agency. Natasha was born on March 6, 1983, and they were thrilled beyond belief to be able to call her their own.

After Natasha's birth, Zebby decided to leave Koret, and become a stay-at-home mom. Never one to suffer idle hands, especially her own, she dusted off her design skills, and set up a clothing design business from their house. Thanks, in part, to my word-of-mouth advertising efforts, Zebby soon had a substantial client base for whom she designed and sewed, for several years, with flair and creativity.

Nashina and Natasha were much-loved additions to our family but for Anais, not so much. Shortly after we moved to Montecito Drive, a darling ginger-coloured Shih Tzu puppy joined our family circle. She was a gift from Almas' friend, Elaine Lu, who had moved to an apartment that didn't allow dogs. Her name was "Anais" after the Persian goddess of love. She was my first dog since the accidental death of my Pekingese, Mickey, in Jinja. I was utterly infatuated with her.

Anais, unfortunately, developed a decided antipathy toward children, particularly as she got older, and the five girls were too much for her delicate nervous system. We agonized over our decision but finally agreed to give our darling doggy to a client of Almas', Mrs. Brown, who was an ardent dog lover. Anais lived for about a year with Mrs Brown before dying, and I was welcome to visit her at any time which, naturally, I did.

Bapa and Gene Kiniski—Who Knew?

When Idi Amin ousted us from Uganda, Bapa was already more than sixty years old. He felt out of his element in the Canadian business world, and decided to retire. He kept up with current and business affairs by scouring newspapers like *The Economist*, and other news and international affairs publications voraciously. He also cut out endless articles which he insisted I read.

Strangely out of character as it was for my austere Bapa, he developed a love affair with wrestling. We bought tickets at Fred Asher, the clothier and wrestling sponsor, every week, and Bapa dragged Bahadur, Almas, and me with him to watch wrestling live at the Pacific National Exhibition. Bapa had his favourites and Gene Kiniski was at the top of the list.

My niece, Shalina, has some fun recollections of her beloved grandfather. She remembers that even in Canada, in his retirement, he always wore dress pants and a dress shirt around the house, and added a suit jacket when he went out. He was always clean shaven, and wore cologne. He carried a walking cane for balance but used it more as a pointer. For breakfast, he unfailingly ate two pieces of white bread with butter and marmalade, and, for dinner, rice, *rotli* (an unleavened bread made from stone ground whole meal flour), and curry. One of his favourite sayings was that people born in India always ate "rice and curry, curry and rice."

Shalina also recalls that Bapa invariably watched the 6 p.m. and 10 p.m. television news as well as Indian movies on the VCR. He took the bus each weekday at 10:30 a.m. to the Army and Navy Department Store and the seniors' centre on Dunsmuir Street. When asked why he chose not to drive in Canada, he replied, "Why should I, I have a $100,000 chauffeur-driven vehicle," being, of course, the bus.

Ma, the Homebody

Living in Canada did not change Ma. She continued to be a homebody. Shalina also retains sweet memories of her grandmother. She likes to reminisce that Ma always wore dresses in the house which she had patterned and stitched herself, and that she wore sarees to the mosque. She carried a clutch purse, and always wore a strong perfume called "Amarige." She was particular about the creams she used on her face, and painted her finger and toe nails in bright red polish. Ma intensely disliked grey roots, and was particular about colouring her hair. Cod curry was one of her favourite foods along with Marks and Spencer rich tea biscuits. Ma also loved to take pictures, and was good at drawing pictures of flowers and people.

Almas the Entrepreneur

While I was busy building my banking career, Almas was following in Bapa's entrepreneurial footsteps. Almas, as well as Kay and Mas, had benefited from the good will the three of them had built up at Fashion Tress over the years. They had many elderly clients, with whom Almas enjoyed an excellent rapport. She lent them a sympathetic ear, and her clients could sense that Almas' interest in them was genuine. As a result, when Kay and Mas decided, in about 1980, to retire, it was a "no brainer" for Almas to buy them out.

In 1989, construction of a retirement community on Yew Street in Vancouver called "Tapestry at The O'Keefe—Arbutus Walk" was completed. The facility housed a hair salon for its residents, and Almas applied to manage it. The management company interviewed Almas, and offered her the opportunity. Almas has managed the O'Keefe Hair Salon ever since, and loves her work and her clients. Almas' friend, Elaine, who gave us our doggy, Anais, and had also worked with Almas at Fashion Tress, joined Almas at The O'Keefe.

CHAPTER TWENTY-ONE
The Wonders of Kenya Safaris

The Dress Rehearsal

Noor Panjoo, the sister of Rustam's brother-in-law, Alykhan, hailed from Mombasa in Kenya. She moved to Vancouver about five years before the influx of Asians from Uganda in 1972. She and her roommate, Bhagwant, were immensely kind to the Ugandan refugees including Zebby and Almas. For instance, Noor and her friend owned a car, and often drove folks to the Jamatkhana.

Noor worked for the Royal Bank at the Royal Centre in the audit department. I first met her when I went to work at the Royal Centre, too, and we hit it off instantly.

Toward the end of 1988, she and I travelled to Kenya for a safari. We stopped over in London, and saw theatre productions of *Phantom of the Opera* and *Les Misérables*.

Our first stop in Africa was Nairobi where we stayed with Noorbanu's son, Sadru, and his lovely wife, Mina. Both Sadru's and Mina's families and ours are friends from generations back.

One particular highlight was a New Year's Eve bash which we all attended at the Intercontinental Hotel. While I was in the bathroom, I ran into Mama Ngina, wife of Jomo Kenyatta and the First Lady of Kenya. I stuttered, "Are you...?" She laughed, and replied, "That is what everyone says!"

A pathway led from the hotel to a nearby world-class casino. I thought nothing of walking over to the casino by myself. When I arrived, I bumped into one of Mina's brothers who was playing blackjack. He interrupted his game to scold me, saying it was dangerous to go anywhere alone. He told me that when I was ready to leave the casino, he would arrange for someone to escort me back.

Noor and I finally left the party about 4 a.m., and snuck in a few hours of sleep. Mina woke us up in a frightfully cheery way, and invited us to her brother's home for breakfast. We arrived at 9 a.m. to an opulent mansion, and enjoyed a relaxing swim.

At breakfast, Noor and I chatted with a couple who owned a beach-front hotel in Mombasa. Booking a room in Mombasa at peak season was an impossibility but these kind people offered us the use of their own suite in the hotel. Needing no encouragement, that same evening we hopped on the *Lunatic Express*, a diesel-hauled train, for an overnight journey to Mombasa.

Because the train porters sometimes doubled as looters, the train stopped quite a long way from the station to discourage them. That forced us to walk quite a distance along the platform hauling our own luggage. I managed to put my back out quite severely. That evening, I asked the hotel manager for a hot water bottle. He couldn't find one so, instead, gave me two empty wine bottles in a pail with a note. It suggested that we fill the pail with hot water to heat the bottles. I didn't bother.

The next morning, I couldn't even get out of bed so Noor called for a doctor. An extremely tall Sikh physician showed up at our door. He proceeded to pull a needle large enough to poke a horse out of his bag. Noor was suspicious, and cross-examined him about the needle's sterility and the muscle relaxant it purportedly contained. Finally, she allowed him to poke me in the butt, and, within about five minutes, I was fine.

Mombasa is an African port with a harbour on the Indian Ocean. Arab traders began trading from Mombasa in the eleventh century, dealing in spices, gold, slaves, and ivory. The majority of its inhabitants are Muslim. It is a charming island city, and boasts superb sweeps of white sand beaches and coral reefs.

Giant prehistoric-looking baobab trees, called "upside-down trees" or "monkey bread trees," mango trees, and showy red acacias adorn the gardens and streets of Mombasa and its surrounding countryside.

We explored all of Noor's choice old haunts. We stopped in at the Castle Hotel for a drink where we met two gorgeous young Arab guys who were tooling around town in a Mercedes. They drove us to a famous local restaurant, which specialized in African dishes, and treated us to the restaurant's famous *nyama choma, also known as mishkaki,* (Swahili for "barbequed meats"). We hung out with our new friends for the rest of the week, and had a wonderfully carefree time.

Another thrill was the opportunity to visit Noorbanu, the lovely distant cousin-in-law who had visited us in Jinja with her paralyzed son, Zul.

Along the way, Noor and I managed to squeeze in a safari to the famous Masai Mara game reserve and the Treetops Hotel which turned out to be a dress rehearsal for the safari I organized several months later.

Nazlin and Noor with Masai (1989)

Noor and Nazlin at Treetops Hotel (1989)

The Main Event

The Kenya safari with my good friends, Anne Lippert, Erika Penner, Cathy Smith, Marilyn Homer, and Joan Norrington remains one of the absolute highlights of my life. It was raucous, dissolute, and delightful. We began our journey in October 1989.

About two months before we left, I cleverly managed to break my left wrist while playing tennis. The surgeon encased my wrist in a Plaster of Paris cast covered by a second fibreglass cast. I convinced him to remove these impediments a week early so I could travel but I did have to wear a wrist splint. I imperiously deputized Cathy to act as my porter, and haul my luggage throughout the trip.

We flew first to Amsterdam. Marilyn had never been there so, late in the evening, we took her for a walkabout in the red light district where we saw store window displays with women sitting in them. The sight was disturbing and sad.

We then continued on to Africa, and arrived at the Jomo Kenyatta International Airport in Nairobi, Kenya. Francis, who we had retained as our driver and guide, greeted us at the airport. He was a tall Kenyan in his mid-thirties who impressed us with his perfect English. I was able to impress him in return when I responded in Swahili. We were all sporting matching Vancouver T-shirts, and we won Francis over when we produced one for him as well.

During our brief stay in Nairobi, we explored the town, and visited the Nairobi Railway Museum. It contained relics from the construction of the East African Railway between Mombasa and Lake Victoria. Some fascinating and tragic stories about the railway involved the predatory lion. In 1898, while workers were building a bridge across the Tsavo River in Kenya, two man-eating lions attacked the construction camp, and killed a great many workers, both Indian and African. In 1899, a lion dragged a British engineer from his tent, mauling and killing him. In 1900, a lion actually entered a railway observation salon, in which three men were sleeping, and dragged a British police officer through a window and into the bush.

After leaving Nairobi, we drove first to the Outspan Hotel in Nyeri, Kenya near the entrance to the legendary Aberdare Forest. This hotel has two claims to fame. First, it is the drop-off point for the magnificent Treetops Hotel in the Aberdare Forest. Secondly, Robert Baden-Powell, founder of the Boy Scouts movement, lived in a cottage on the grounds. Baden-Powell's burial plot is nearby.

We were fortunate to arrive at the hotel on "Jomo Kenyatta Day," a celebration of the president and founding father of the Kenya nation. We were able to partake of a lunch buffet featuring African, Indian, and Western foods that was somewhere well beyond extravagant.

Kenyatta Day Celebration (1989)

After lunch, we embarked on our first great adventure. Packing only overnight bags, we travelled by bus into the Aberdare Forest. The bus stopped about a mile from the Treetops Hotel so as not to disturb the wildlife. We walked to the hotel, escorted on each side by guards with rifles to protect us from lions and leopards.

The original hotel sat at the top of a fig tree with eye-catching views of Mount Kenya on clear days. It lay in the path of a migratory route that elephants had used since time immemorial. The hotel's purpose was to provide a platform from which its guests could safely view the exotic African wildlife that ate, bathed, and frolicked at the watering hole and salt lick in front of the hotel.

In 1952, the hotel became world renowned when Princess Elizabeth, who was staying there, learned that her father had died, and that she would ascend to the British throne. The common expression was that she climbed the tree as a princess and came down as the Queen.

In 1954, during the infamous Mau Mau uprising, African guerrillas burned the hotel to the ground but it rose again, on stilts, in a nearby chestnut tree.

Treetops Hotel

The tiny rooms in the hotel are reminiscent of ship cabins. Our travel agent managed to reserve for us the only two with ensuite bathrooms. Usually the hotel set these rooms aside for the rich and famous, and the likes of Princess Elizabeth and Brooke Shields likely slept in them. So, even though we had to sleep three to a room, we were thrilled. Each room featured a tree trunk with hangers on it for clothes. The rooms were crowded but we didn't mind because we were too excited to sleep.

We arrived in time for an elegant high tea on the outside deck. It was very British, and we ate our fill of tea, scones, cookies, and crumpets.

Dusk fell quickly, and the night began to cool. We sat outside on a roofed veranda, quietly sipping drinks, without a whisper. Except for Anne, who always drinks Courvoisier, our liquor of choice was Kenya gold coffee liqueur. The staff brought us blankets. Magically, the animals began to stagger in to the pond and salt lick. They continued to arrive late into the night.

About 8 p.m., the staff escorted us into the belly of the hotel for dinner. We ate at a long trestle table covered by a white linen table cloth. A track for passing food careened down the middle of the table like a railway. All the posts and beams in the dining room were tree trunks.

Later that evening, when we returned to the viewing deck, a herd of elephants frolicked at the salt lick, licked the salt, sauntered into the water, returned to play some more, and generally made quite a ruckus with their trumpeting. The elephants dominated the salt lick, digging out the salt with their trunks. Observing the elephants was an extraordinary privilege. They are the largest land animals in the world, and the way they use their trunks to pick food up from the earth or yank it from trees is mesmerizing. Daily mud baths are crucial to elephant hygiene, offering them protection from the sun and removal of ticks and other debris from their skin.

The elephants allowed water buffalo to mingle with them, and drink the water. In addition, we saw loads of wart hogs with knobby faces and short tusks, antelope, and a family of hyenas, on the periphery of the salt lick. One incident we have laughed about for years was that Anne, while showering, looked out the window, and saw an elephant peering at her from across the salt lick. Her first thought was, "Oh! I don't have any clothes on!"

The next day, we returned to the Outspan Hotel, where Francis waited with our van. Off we drove, crossing the equator on our way to the luxurious Mount Kenya Safari Club resort. One of the founders of this celebrated Club was the movie star, William Holden. Other famous founders and members have included Sir Winston Churchill, Lord Louis Mountbatten, Robert Ruark, Lyndon Johnson, Conrad Hilton, Bob Hope, and Bing Crosby.

Mount Kenya Safari Club
(L-R) Joan Norrington, Marilyn Homer, Anne Lippert,
Nazlin Rahemtulla and Erika Penner

Our first view of the Mount Kenya Safari Club took our breath away. It sits on expansive grounds at the equator. Immaculately manicured lawns, landscaped gardens, and decorated ponds surround the glistening white main building. It rises against a panorama of evergreen forests at the foot-hills of Mount Kenya.

A proud pageant of massive maribou storks, multi-coloured peacocks, and cranes stalking regally around the lawn of the Club rendered us virtu-ally speechless (completely speechless would have been impossible for our little band of chatterboxes).

One of our most hilarious stories involved our check-in. The hotel clerk serving us was a drop-dead gorgeous Kikuyu tribesman, a tribe noted for its good looks. As he was describing the amenities to us, Marilyn, usually the most reserved and decorous of people, asked him if he came with the room. The lobby was rollicking with laughter.

Our rooms included fireplaces, and, as the nights tended to be quite cool, an attendant was available to stoke the fires during the night.

We found the service at the Club exquisite, and, because the price was all-inclusive, we gobbled as much food as we could eat. We golfed, rode horses, and generally relaxed. The nine-hole golf course was challenging because it consisted of criss-crossed grass.

While golfing, we met four men who were investigating a tragic air crash that had occurred nearby during the previous year. Suddenly deluged by a ferocious rain storm, we all stopped at a halfway house that, fortunately, contained a fireplace in front of which we were able to dry off, and we and our new acquaintances imbibed a drink—or two—or three.

Later, we dressed for dinner. The dinner entertainment included a charming African band, complete with pulsating bongo drums. They played some of my favourite African songs, such as *Jambo Bwana*, *Karibuni Kenya* and *Mama Salama*.

Our next stop was the Samburu Serena Lodge. This Lodge, and a few others at which we stayed, are part of the Serena Group, one of about ninety-six companies that make up the Aga Khan Fund for Economic Development, the "for profit" arm of the Aga Khan Development Network.

This particular Lodge was set on the banks of the Ewaso Nyiro River where we were treated to the sight of enormous herds of elephants crossing the river at dusk. The Lodge itself is decorated with colourful masks, beadwork, and spears from the Samburu culture, a semi-nomadic Nilotic tribe of Kenya. Here, we stayed in timber cottages, each with its own veranda. We sat on the veranda in the evening, and friendly baboons perched on the railings to visit us.

Game is abundant in this region, and we were able to view big cats, reticulated giraffes, gerenuks which are a long-necked species of antelope, wildebeests, and Grevy's zebras which are the largest species of zebra in all of Africa. Giraffes are fascinating to watch as they are so tall they can graze on acacia trees. Zebras too are compelling. The stripes on the back of each animal are unique. They are like human fingerprints. Lions find zebras and wildebeests among their tastiest prey.

Our trip was flying by at break-neck speed. We'd scarcely settled at Samburu Serena before we were on our way to the Sarova Lion Hill Lodge at Lake Nakuru. This Lodge, at the entrance to the Rift Valley, overlooks Lake Nakuru and Lake Nakuru National Park. Its grounds abound with tall acacia trees.

Wildlife in the Masai Mara Game Reserve

While we were there, because of the proximity of the lake, we had to sleep, for the first time, under mosquito netting. The high point of our morning game ride was the spectacle of countless pink flamingos rimming Lake Nakuru. And, we returned at dusk to the spectacular sight of the flamingos reflected in the Lake.

Flamingos at Lake Naivasha

During the day, we toured the dense woodlands of the Park, inhabited by mammoth black pythons that dangled from trees and even wound their way across the roads. On this tour, mud mired our van, and it took Francis plus all the girls to push the vehicle clear. Because of my broken wrist, I had the comfy job of steering.

Our next destination was the Masai Mara in the Great Rift Valley, whose magnificent scenery was featured in portions of the movie *Out of Africa*. We stayed at the Mara Serena Lodge. It stands high on a hill with magnificent views of both the savannah and Mara River. From the Lodge, guests can view the world-famous annual migration of wildebeest across the river. The Lodge, which resembles Flintstone City, lies within a gated compound to protect its guests from the hordes of wildlife that roam in close proximity to it.

We embarked on several drives to see as many different areas of the park as possible. One such drive suspended us in terror. We had just passed a herd of elephants and a nearby pride of lions when the van suffered a flat tire smack in the middle of lion territory. Everyone, except for myself, because of my broken wrist, had to exit the vehicle to help Francis change the tire. Exiting the vehicle in the Masai Mara is absolutely forbidden but we simply had no choice.

Before the trip, I'd had a nightmare about leaving the van, and being chased by wild animals, so I was shaking with terror and my heart was pounding. That made my task of manning the binoculars rather daunting. I was living my nightmare. I was certain that if a lion or cheetah charged,

Francis and the girls would not all be able to retreat to the van in sufficient time. To add to our terror, we knew that just a month before, a middle-aged American woman had taken a vehicle out alone, and, when she got stuck, feral predators actually devoured her.

If we were unable to mobilize the van, no one would be able to find us at night because the park was so vast. (This was the pre-cell phone and pre-GPS era.) Yet another daunting concern was that we would not make it back to the safety of the Lodge before the staff closed and locked the gates. In that case, we would have been obliged to hunker down in the van because wildlife hovered, during the night, just outside the gates. Hyenas could strip us to pieces in no time flat. Their muscular jaws can bite through bone and marrow. They are essential to the natural order because without them, the putrefying flesh of carrion could poison the savannah.

Luck, though, rode on our shoulders. Once Francis had changed the tire without anyone being eaten, he drove like a maniac, and we reached the gates just as they were about to close. As we entered the gates, we passed a pack of hyenas with tongues lolling at the sight of us.

When we reached the Lodge, my legs turned to jelly, and I had to lie down. However, the girls were able to resuscitate me with a Grand Marnier, and I bravely dressed, and joined the others for dinner. After dinner, we were treated to an intoxicating Masai welcoming dance, although the earthy odour of the dancers was almost overwhelming.

Despite our scary experience, we were ready, early the next morning, for a game ride where we saw an astonishing variety of wildlife including elephants, giraffes, zebras, hyenas, cheetahs, leopards, impalas, gazelles, wildebeests, and dik diks. The latter are tiny, perfect antelopes that weigh only five or six kilos, and look like goats. We also saw a lion chasing prey, a cheetah crouched in a tree, and the grisly sight of a lion devouring a zebra.

We then boarded a boat to observe hippopotami in the Mara River. The hippos are a sight to behold. Pods of them rest in the river with only their eyes, noses, and a bit of their pink-tinged faces above water. Sometimes, birds perched on their heads. The hippos made me more than a little nostalgic for Jinja.

Another high spot was visiting the Masai in their *manyattas*, (settlements or compounds).They are a traditional semi-nomadic tribe who subsist, in part, by working cattle farms. Many of them are Christian, and a few are Muslim.

They traditionally wear *shukas* (traditional African clothing worn by the Masai), with red being their favourite colour. Their sandals are made from cow hide, the men all carry wooden clubs, and the women wear ruffs around their neck, beaded earrings, and intricate jewellery for which they are famous.

We found the time-honoured Masai huts, which the women build, especially interesting. They consist of wooden poles fixed into the ground, covered by a latticework of small branches layered with animal skin and plastered with a blend of mud, sticks, grass, cow dung, human urine, and ash. The men are responsible for erecting a circular wooden acacia fence around the village.

Masai in Manyatta

At night, the men herd the livestock into the centre of the village into a *boma* (corral) to keep them safe from the marauding wildlife. Although the Masai are a traditional tribe, and, in many respects, quite primitive, the females are apparently familiar with women's liberation. Visitors to the village are expected to pay an entrance fee but, when we arrived, one woman whispered to Anne, to her delight, that we should pay the fee to her, and not to the men. Once in the village, we treated ourselves to some jewellery and bangles, and, each time, we made sure that we gave the money to someone of the female persuasion.

Cathy Smith recently undertook another trip to Kenya and was startled to observe the Masai walking around with their cell phones in hand.

Our next port of call was Lake Naivasha where we stayed at the Lake Naivasha Resort, formerly an English colonial farm house. In the 1960s, Joy Adamson lived at Elsamere on the shores of Lake Naivasha, and we visited her celebrated home. It is now a wildlife retreat and an education centre. While there, we took tea, once again in the British tradition, and, needless to say, bought copies of *Born Free*.

Elsamere (Home of Joy Adamson)
Front Row: Nazlin, Cathy & Erika
Back Row: Joan, Marilyn & Francis

We then boarded the *Lunatic Express*, and travelled overnight from Nairobi to Mombasa. We had reserved first class compartments with sleeping berths. We ate dinner and breakfast on the train. The dining car still used the original cutlery from the East African Railway. It was all quite decadent, and even included a genuine article: an elderly, colonial woman who was very British. She lived on a family plantation, and entertained us during our journey. The train climbed the wall of the Rift Valley Escarpment, and passed through many tea and coffee plantations.

After all our adventures, we were a bit giddy. We sipped a Grand Marnier nightcap from one shared sippy cup which insisted on collapsing every time we passed it from one person to the next. At each collapse, we shrieked with laughter.

In Mombasa, we stayed at the Bamburi Beach Hotel, facing the Indian Ocean, and treated ourselves to some aimless relaxation on a white beach shaded by coconut palms—a tropical paradise.

I had a grand reunion with Amir, the eldest son of Noorbanu and brother of Zul, and Amir's wife, Shamsa. Amir ran the Mombasa office of Jubilee Insurance of Kenya, a company under the aegis of the Aga Khan Fund for Economic Development. Amir and Shamsa treated all of us to dinner at the Mombasa Club.

The Mombasa Club
(L – R) Amir, Shamsa, Anne, Cathy, Joan & Erika

The Club is in the middle of the historic Old Town of Mombasa which is chock-a-block with ancient buildings, in shades of coral, housed along narrow streets. Despite the extreme heat, we saw many Arab women in the streets, shops, and markets, wearing *hijabs* (burkas). Fort Jesus, a monumental fortress, towers over the Old Town. The Portuguese constructed the fort toward the end of the fifteenth century on the backs of Indian labourers they had imported from Goa.

For me, the Mombasa Club brought back special childhood memories. My parents used to take me there for lunch on the dining terrace overlooking the Indian Ocean. My all-time favourite dessert (along with English trifle and Knickerbocker Glory—yes, I know I have issues) was the Baked Alaska served at this Club. My dear cousin, Amir, made a perfect evening even better by remembering my craving for this heavenly concoction, and ordering it for us.

The following night, Amir and Shamsa invited all of us, along with his boss and wife, who were in town from Nairobi, to the luxurious Serena Beach Hotel for dinner. The boss's wife, Rashida, was from Vancouver so she was thrilled to catch up on the local Vancouver news.

Dinner was perfection. A cool African band was playing my favourite songs. The food was buffet style. Each time we rose to replenish our plates, a male African server, dressed in white Arabic garb, pulled out our chairs, and then held our plates while we selected our food.

I cannot leave Mombasa without mentioning yet another dinner, this one at the Tamarind Restaurant. Its location is in a gleaming white building, of Arabic design, nesting on a cliff with its terrace facing the quaint Old Harbour of Mombasa. The waiters supplied us with bibs and large finger bowls, and we dove into whole succulent fresh crabs suffused with melted butter sauce—heavenly.

Back in Nairobi, we luxuriated at the awesome Nairobi Hilton Hotel, and visited the David Sheldrick Wildlife Trust. It is a sanctuary for the treatment and rehabilitation of orphaned or injured elephants, black rhinos, and other animals. For example, older elephants might be without tusks so they have no mechanism with which to defend themselves. This sanctuary is famous for Dame Daphne Sheldrick who was featured in the film *Born To Be Wild*. While there, we suffered another wildlife scare. A prehistoric rhinoceros appeared out of nowhere right in our faces, and looked as though it was about to charge. Francis, though, evinced great bravery by jumping in front of us, and the rhino skulked away.

We couldn't leave Nairobi without paying a visit to the Karen Blixen Museum on the outskirts of the city. The museum is the rambling stone farmhouse that was the centrepiece for the movie *Out of Africa*. It was quite a kick to see the original gramophone featured in the film as well as the porch chair where Robert Redford sat.

Karen Blixen Museum

(L-R) Francis, Joan, Erika, Cathy, Anne & Marilyn

A particular Nairobi highlight was dining at the regal and legendary Norfolk Hotel, first built in 1904. This experience resurrected more fond childhood memories—most of which seem to circle around food. Bapa used to take me to dine outdoors in the hotel grounds. Like Wimpy's, they were culinary masters of the Knickerbocker Glory on which I gorged whenever we were there.

At the end of our trip, we satisfied a dream of Marilyn's by bravely riding camels. We were terrified but had great fun. Then we indulged in the unique experience of dining at the Carnivore Restaurant. Its specialty is open-air meat, including wild game, roasted on traditional Masai swords over a massive charcoal pit at the restaurant's entrance.

We spent our last day lounging around the swimming pool, gloriously sated from our astounding experiences but desperately sad to be leaving. Our farewell to Francis at the airport was tearful. He had taken excellent care of us. Joan had sat in the front seat of the van with Francis most of the time. They had struck up quite a friendship, and on her return to Canada, she received an endearing letter from him.

The Royal Bank had appointed Anne as a Vice-President and Area Manager for the BC Region shortly before we left on our trip. Anne's career with the Bank was long and distinguished, and she was a mentor to many of us. Anne retired several years ago.

Cathy, Erika, Marilyn, and Joan were also long-time employees of the Bank. Erika left the Bank about the same time I did. Marilyn transferred to the Courtenay Branch shortly before our trip. She has since retired but still lives in Courtenay with her husband. Joan also retired several years ago. Cathy is the only remaining Bank employee. All of us remain good friends.

CHAPTER TWENTY-TWO
Career Triumphs and Personal Tragedy

My Dream Gig

Upon my return from Africa, the Royal Bank transferred me to the Broadway and Granville Branch for a short stint which began in December of 1989. I provided maternity leave relief for Phillipa McKenna, who had became a friend when I worked at the Royal Centre Main Branch. The head of human resources in Toronto tantalized me with the hint that, at the end of my stretch at Broadway and Granville, a nice surprise was in store for me.

"Nice" was a supreme understatement. The surprise was the realization of my dream. In March 1990, the Bank appointed me Account Manager for domestic Private Banking, and my fancy new office was on the fourth floor of the Royal Centre Tower.

Under the Private Banking model, the Bank assigned advisors, such as myself, to provide exclusive assistance to high net worth clients. Our mandate was to get to know our clients personally, to understand their individual needs and objectives, and then to guide them with innovative financial strategies and solutions.

My client portfolio consisted primarily of lawyers and accountants. Two of the lawyers were Larry Page, who, with his wife, Robyn, became a dear friend, and David McLean, one of Vancouver's premier movers and shakers, all of whom would later play integral roles in my life. My new position also enabled me to expand my career horizons by meeting many of Vancouver's most influential citizens.

One of the most satisfying aspects of my new job was being able to devote my attention to financially challenged folks, of whom Margaret Fairweather, then a partner with the law firm of Bull, Housser & Tupper, was a prime specimen. Using boundless patience and food rewards, I slowly convinced her to slide her money from under her mattress, and bring it to me for investment.

Within a week or two of meeting Margaret, she invited me to lunch with her husband, another new client. We walked down Hornby Street to an old building in a rather seedy section of town, and up a narrow poorly lit staircase. I was a bit anxious but then I met Franz.

Dr. Franz Josef Wilfling was a psychologist who practised in a homey antique strewn office. He was a burly man with a curly beard, a head of wild curly hair, and thick spectacles who filled any room he entered with the warmth of his presence. Franz was an exceptional story teller who loved to laugh at everyone and everything including himself. By all accounts, he was a superb therapist, and many of his patients became his friends.

I once confided to Franz about my annoying habit of falling asleep when I was a passenger in a moving vehicle. Predictably, he soon had me giggling about it. His diagnosis was that my Nanima had caused my problem by tying a string to her toe, and constantly rocking my cradle. He said he could fix me in just a few seconds but, regrettably, we never got around to it, and it still ticks Almas off whenever she's driving.

Franz died several years ago but I'm sure none of his friends will ever forget him or his kindness, caring, and laughter. Neither will we forget the silliness of this big, bearded man begging kisses from their two Yorkshire Terriers, Miss Critter and Buster Cornelius Von Poof the Fourth.

I made some incredibly good friends in Private Banking, and none more so than Jan McLeod, a small, pale, blond girl I met on my first day. We recognized immediately that we were soul sisters. The Hyatt Hotel was adjacent to the Royal Centre office tower, and Jan and I developed the habit of taking coffee in its Regency Grill every morning at 10 a.m. We were fixtures at the grill, and all the staff came to know us. There was method in our madness because we invariably ran into clients there, and chewed the fat with them. Jan and I worked with T.W. (Tung Wai) Wong who was later to accompany me to Uganda as part of a business delegation, and then on to Kenya for a safari.

Another favourite client, who became a close friend, was Ben Singh. Ben came to Canada from Fiji. He was a senior executive with the Inchcape Group of Companies, whose primary source of business revolved around international trade commodities. Ben endeared himself to Jan and me forever, not by way of his investment portfolio, but because, whenever he travelled to London, he returned with a pound of Thornton's Original Special Toffee for us. Jan and I always hid the toffee as soon as Ben presented it to us, and we never shared it with another soul.

Along with my legal, business, and accounting clients, I provided services to a variety of celebrities, most of whom were pleasant, down-to-earth people. One client, a well-known mining entrepreneur, invited me to fly in a private jet, on a day trip to an open-pit gold mine in the northern reaches of Canada. I had one day's notice of the trip, and had to rush out to buy a heavy coat and gloves. The temperature was -45 degrees with a wind chill, and the fluid in my nose froze. I had never been so cold in my life. It made London seem like a tropical paradise.

Dear Bapa's Death

A few months after I joined Private Banking, an inestimable tragedy struck my family and me. Bapa had always controlled his diabetes with medication but, in the last few years of his life, he was obliged to take insulin shots. That was when he started to go downhill.

One evening, Bapa felt ill, and was wheezing. He had always avoided hospitals but, by morning, his wheezing was quite bad so Bahadur and Zubeda insisted on driving him to the Burnaby General Hospital.

The emergency room staff determined that he was suffering from pneumonia. Against his protests, they admitted him to the hospital. On the third day, my friend, Noor, and I went to visit Bapa after our tennis game, in the late evening. Ma and Zubeda had just left for home.

We had a good visit with Bapa, and, although I was sick with worry, we made him laugh. I asked if he had eaten. He replied that Ma had brought him some food but he didn't feel hungry. I scolded him, and told him that he shouldn't go to sleep on an empty stomach. I called Ma, and asked her to cook up some *khechri* (a hodgepodge of lentils and rice boiled together). We eat it with all sorts of things including curry but, most often, with a small dollop of butter and yogurt or butter and warm milk. It was one of Bapa's favourite dishes, and was easy for him to digest.

I told Bapa's nurse that I was going to run home to get some food, and would have to come back after visiting hours. She was okay with that. When Noor and I returned to the hospital, I was able to feed Bapa but then he said he wanted to sleep, so we left.

Early the next morning, June 24, 1990, I was just about to leave for my Sunday golf game when we received a phone call from the hospital. We were told that Bapa had suffered a heart attack during the night, and the prognosis was not good.

Our whole family whisked off to the hospital, and gathered in the waiting room. After a few hours, the doctor joined us, and imparted the terrible news that our cherished Bapa had passed away.

Through our Jamatkhana, we are fortunate to have a burial committee. When a death occurs, the family needs to notify them, and they take care of all the arrangements. We telephoned one of the committee members to tell them about Bapa. The committee arranged to bring Bapa's body to a funeral home. Our faith requires washing of the body before burial, and funeral homes have the necessary facilities. They cleansed Bapa, and draped his body in white cloth. Then the committee coordinated transport of his body to the Burnaby Lake Jamatkhana, and finalized arrangements for the funeral.

My family and I arrived at the Jamatkhana about two hours before the ceremony. In accordance with Muslim custom, Bapa's cloth-covered body lay flat on the floor in the loggia. We covered him with a cashmere taupe shawl. Then we said our heart-wrenching goodbyes to our dear husband, father, father-in-law, and grandfather. In doing so, we took care not to touch Bapa's body. Our beliefs dictate that once the soul has departed, we must let the body be.

The ceremony began about noon. No matter how rich or poor, important or unimportant, famous or infamous the deceased, all Ismaili funerals are identical. The Mukhi, and his assistant, the Kamadia, conducted the service which included the reading of a verse from the Qur'an. A great many people attended the ceremony, and, because Bapa's body was in the loggia, our friends of other faiths were able to join in the service and pay their respects. Bapa would have liked that.

Afterward, the men accompanied Bapa's body to Forest Lawn Cemetery for burial. Nothing had changed in that regard since our days in Jinja when we buried our Nanabapa and then our Nanima. Although we had broken the rule during Fatima's burial, traditionally only men make the trip to the cemetery.

After several years of lobbying, the Provincial Government allowed us, in accordance with Muslim ritual, to inter our loved ones without caskets. Bahadur, Nizar, Rustam, and Mansur lowered themselves into the six foot deep hole to receive Bapa's body. Then they hoisted themselves from the grave, and watched as the shovelled dirt slowly covered him. I must confess that I was glad not to be at the cemetery. I could not have borne the sight of his body disappearing from us forever.

We women remained at the Jamatkhana consoling one another and our friends. Normally, the family of the deceased hosts a luncheon at a nearby hall. However, because the June weather was warm, and because Bapa had always loved to entertain at our home, we decided to break with tradition, and hold the luncheon in our backyard. We rented tables, chairs, china, glassware, and silver, and hired a caterer who prepared mounds of Indian food.

Many old people who didn't know Bapa, but attend funerals to pay their respects, came to the Jamatkhana. We invited them, along with all our family and friends, to our backyard luncheon. We even arranged for cars to transport them. We knew that we risked disapproval by bucking convention in this manner but our fears were unfounded, and it proved to be a cathartic experience for our family.

Even though Bapa was aging and his health declining, his death was still sudden and devastating. At the same time, though, I was thankful because he was such a strong and stoic man that I don't think he could have coped with a slow and undignified deterioration.

In the months that followed, I assuaged my grief by crying in private on my drive home from work. Once there, though, I put on my cheerful face as my family and I all worked together to support and bolster Ma.

I find it hard to fathom how Bapa developed such a wellspring of courage and resolution. He departed from his primitive and isolated village of Madhapur, India with only the clothes on his back, and migrated to the dark and dangerous continent of Africa. He trekked hundreds of leagues on foot through alien and perilous territory. Despite his lack of education, he built up an incredibly successful business, and became a highly respected member of the community.

At the same time, he was all about family. In the aftermath of the expulsion proclamation, he managed the safe departure of all of us from Africa. At the age of sixty-one, he re-invented himself in the strange and distant land of Canada, and established a firm foundation and home for his family here. We are all so fortunate to still enjoy the fruits of his labour. I honour Bapa's memory every day.

Beyond my Dream Gig

My tenure in domestic Private Banking was extremely successful, and I thought my career had reached its apex. However, it was about to get even better. Early in 1991, RBC rewarded me with a posting as an Account Manager for International Services in Global Private Banking. I was beyond ecstatic.

Our Global Private Banking team provided customized service and personal attention to high net worth individuals whose financial affairs extended beyond Canada's borders. We had offices worldwide in strategic financial centres, and I travelled, in the course of my work, to many exotic locales including London, Geneva, the Bahamas, Bermuda, Jersey, and Guernsey.

The Channel Islands

One of my favourite business destinations was unquestionably Guernsey which, like its sister island, Jersey, has historically offered a stable and favourable economic and tax climate. As a result, many offshore banks, fund managers, and insurers have settled there, complementing the long-established primary industries of flower growing, dairy farming, and fishing.

RBC's local office in Guernsey included several specialists in international wealth management which they supplemented with an intimate knowledge of local fiscal conditions. One of those specialists was Steve Fell.

During my several visits to Guernsey, Steve and his wife, Kerry, befriended me, and we enjoyed many dinners together. We have maintained our friendship ever since, and just last year, Steve and Kerry, along with their young daughter, Laura, stayed with my family and me at our home on Montecito Drive.

The history of the Channel Islands, located in the English Channel off the coast of Normandy, fascinated me. Archaeologists have found evidence of human habitation there dating back 25,000 years. About 8,000 BC, mounting sea levels separated the Islands from the European continent. Hunting and fishing dates back to 6,500 BC, and a burial mound built by Neolithic man, in about 4,500 BC, may be the oldest or one of the oldest manmade structures in Europe.

From the early tenth century, the Channel Islands were part of Normandy, France, and this link to Normandy survives even today in local Norman law, names, and language. Since the thirteenth century, the islands have been governed as British Crown Dependencies, independent from the United Kingdom.

In the mid-nineteenth century, Victor Hugo spent fifteen years in exile on Guernsey where he wrote many of his well-known works including *Les Misérables*.

World War II had a devastating impact on the Channel Islands, and about half of Guernsey's population fled to England. The Germans invaded and occupied the Islands in 1940, and built a maze of fortifications, known as the Atlantic Wall, which still exists today.

As will be evident from these memoirs, I love both the history and ambience of grand hotels. In Guernsey, I always stayed at the Old Government House Hotel which certainly met my criteria. First built in 1796, as the governor's official residence, it opened its doors as a hotel in 1858. Except for the war years, from 1940 to 1945, when it served as the General Staff Headquarters for the German occupying forces, it has operated as a hotel ever since, and retains its heritage of comfort and elegance.

I found Guernsey enchanting, and explored everywhere—from the quaint capital of Saint Peter Port to meandering cliff-top trails, wetland habitats, beaches, sandy dunes, wooded valleys, jagged harbours, and country lanes. I even trekked to the miniscule islands of Sark and Herm which ban public transport, and oblige everyone to walk, bike, or hop on a passing tractor.

Next Stop Sardinia

I loved every aspect of my work in both domestic and Global Private Banking. And, as added bonuses, my job allowed me to meet a tremendous number of interesting people, many of whom became friends, and to indulge my passion for glamorous travel.

A perfect example arose from a brief meeting with William Switzer, a noted designer and maker of both high end and period furniture. Bill met with me shortly before embarking on a business trip to Great Britain. His firm had recently furnished the Canadian Embassy in London, and was about to have a furniture showing in Kensington.

I mentioned, in passing, that I was leaving on a business trip to London and Guernsey. Bill's response was, to say the least, unexpected. He told me that his wife, Frances, intended to travel from London to Sardinia for a week's stay, and nothing would do but that I should accompany her. I protested that I couldn't take the time off but Bill overrode me, saying that he would fix it with my bosses, and that I shouldn't look a gift horse in the mouth. Who was I to argue?

So, Frances, whom I had met only a couple of times, and I flew to Sardinia. We arrived at our luxurious resort, where she had reserved a nicely appointed chalet, late in the evening. When the porter brought in our luggage, I was amazed to see a large hamper, which Frances had ordered from Fortnum & Mason, filled with pasta, fruit cake, Scottish wild smoked salmon, sundried stuffed olives, rose petal jelly, biscuits, and a plethora of other delicacies. Again, who was I to argue?

Frances was a colourful and gregarious soul. Among her many interests, she designed jewellery, and had a heyday in Sardinia searching for beads and trinkets. The next morning, I slept late, and arose to find Frances gone. A short time later, she returned, and announced that she had met an interesting American couple who owned a car dealership in Mount Vernon, Washington.

That reminded me of my concern about driving the narrow and winding roads of Sardinia but Frances said not to worry. Her new friends had rented a car, and would take us with them. As it turned out, we travelled everywhere together, even popping over to Corsica. Each afternoon, we stopped, at Frances' insistence, at a fancy coffee house for cappuccino and brioche.

I considered myself a clothes horse but I paled beside Frances. We made endless excursions to exclusive clothing stores, and, at Frances' urging, I fell from grace, and indulged in the purchase of a gorgeous crimson Ferragamo suit.

My Geneva Reunion with Shenaz

Far and away my most gratifying personal experience during my tenure in Global Private Banking occurred during a business trip to Guernsey and then Geneva in 1995.

After expulsion, I had lost track of my close friend and distant cousin, Shenaz Khimji. Shenaz's aunt, Banu Walji, had relocated to Belgium, and her daughter, Shabnam, had moved to Vancouver. Shabnam had become a family friend, and when Shenaz's brother, Shaukat, who lived in Toronto, visited her, she brought him to our home for a visit.

Shaukat told us that Shenaz lived in Geneva with her husband and two daughters. Coincidentally, I was planning a trip to Switzerland the following week. As soon as I arrived, I called Shenaz's home. Her husband answered. He advised me that Shenaz was not at home but that he would pass along a message.

Shenaz returned my call immediately. She was greatly excited to hear from me but told me that she had suffered a miscarriage, and was in the hospital. However, she invited me to go to her home in Nyon to meet her husband and teenage daughters, and gave me directions to get there by train. Her husband picked me up at the station.

My arrival floored the two young girls, Sabrina and Shahzia. They expected to greet an elderly woman hidden behind a burka, and couldn't contain their glee when I pranced excitedly into the house, still looking relatively young, wearing designer jeans. The girls had to run upstairs to compose themselves lest their giggling offend me. We all still laugh about this episode.

The girls put together a tasty breakfast for us, and then the family took me to the hospital to visit Shenaz. Our reunion was ecstatic. After visiting for awhile, Shenaz was tiring so the girls showed me around Nyon. It is an immaculately clean little town on the shores of Lake Geneva surrounded by vineyards. A thirteenth century castle with five round towers overlooks the historic Old Town through which we traipsed. Afterward, they and their father treated me to dinner at the Cafe de Paris, which is famous for its butter based sauce served with a beef rib or sirloin steak known as *"entrecote"*, deliciously crisp *pommes frites* (French fries), and green salad.

The year after my visit to Geneva, Shenaz, her husband, Sabrina, and Shahzia all came to visit us in Burnaby. However, because it was raining incessantly, we took off for Hawaii on the spur of the moment, and enjoyed a super time in Honolulu.

Since our reunion, Shenaz and I have rebuilt our relationship, and today are as close as when we were children. As an added bonus, my bond with Sabrina and Shahzia is special to me as well. Shenaz and I have seen one another almost every year, and have taken several trips together including a memorable one to Tunisia.

On one of my trips to Geneva, I bought us both matching sleeveless red dresses in remembrance of the smoking dresses that her mom had made for us in Jinja, that we had both so loved. We donned them immediately, and wore them out to dinner.

Unhappily, Shenaz's marriage did not work out, and she and her husband divorced.

Tropical Storm Luis

After my first meeting in Geneva with Shenaz and her family, I flew to Toronto, where I overnighted. The next morning, I rushed to catch a plane to Bermuda. Consequently, I did not hear about the predicted Category 4 tropical storm *Luis* until I was in the air. The man in the seat next to me commented that he was not sure we would be able to land. We did manage to reach our destination but were the last plane to make it. The cab drive to the Hamilton Princess Hotel was unnerving because I could see shopkeepers and homeowners boarding up their doors and windows.

At the hotel restaurant, I ran into a fellow passenger, Sharon Lewis. Because we were in the same boat, we introduced ourselves, and it turned out that she worked for RBC in Toronto. I was staying in an executive suite, and, because Sharon was quite frightened (as was I), she forsook her own room for the pull-out couch in mine.

Luis turned out to be a Category 2 tropical storm, and that was sufficiently scary for me. The sound of the howling wind and the waves crashing on the beach in front of the hotel were terrifying. I was supposed to meet with some bank executives flying in from Miami but they didn't arrive until a few days later at which time we were able finally to transact our business.

CHAPTER TWENTY-THREE

Uganda Beckons

Welcome Back?

When President Museveni assumed power, he set out to secure peace and unity for the country, and to establish policies to restore the economy. In 1987, Museveni agreed to participate in a wide-ranging economic recovery programme supported by the International Monetary Fund (IMF) and the World Bank.

The Ugandan government began to move and shake on the global economic trade and investment front under the aegis of the Uganda Investment Authority. For example, a 1993 issue of the Authority's quarterly bulletin, *The Uganda Investor*, advertised calls for the construction of lodges in national parks; reported on possible joint venture linkages with Nordic countries; described the prospects for increased trade with, and investment from, Thailand; and summarized arrangements by The Uganda Manufacturer's Association to host an International Trade Fair to coincide with the Preferential Trade Area Summit the government was hosting in Kampala.

One of the initiatives the IMF recommended to President Museveni was that he invite the exiled Asians back to Uganda either to reclaim their property or to receive compensation for its loss. The Ugandan government's agreement to do so was, to say the least, extraordinary. We first caught wind of the proposal when a buddy of Bahadur's sent him an advertisement from a British newspaper.

Entitled "Uganda's Privatisation Programme," the ad stated that "the following enterprises are included in this programme for reform, restructuring, divestiture, trade sale, joint venture partnership, management contract and/or leasing." One of the listed enterprises was Bapa's company, Jubilee Ice & Soda Works. The ad ended by saying that interested overseas investors were invited to contact the Public Enterprises Reform & Divestiture Secretariat for details. We interpreted this notice as a request by the government for exiled Asians to return to Uganda, and reclaim, or receive compensation for, their assets.

Could We, Should We...?

At first blush, we all treated the news of the possible repatriation as a joke which, ironically, had been our first reaction to Idi Amin's expulsion order. But, as we mulled it over, the idea intrigued us more and more until Bahadur and several of his friends decided to return to Uganda to check things out.

For years in Jinja, Bapa's most prized possession had been a battered brown briefcase. He kept all his important documents in it, and he kept the briefcase itself in the safe in our home. We always made fun of him because the briefcase was so tattered and scruffy, and he was so anal about it. But, he would never let us buy him a new one. When he, Ma, Bahadur, Zubeda, Shalina, Narmin, and Nizar frantically escaped Uganda, Bapa had his briefcase tucked securely under one arm. He transported it to England, and then to Canada where it resided for years on the top shelf of his bedroom closet.

We had never checked the contents, but, shortly before Bahadur was to leave for Kampala, I woke up in the middle of the night, and remembered the briefcase. We hauled it out of the closet, and found that our clever Bapa had kept a record of the leasehold titles to all his properties. Were he still alive, he would have had the last laugh because those papers from his disreputable briefcase made the reclamation process a thousand times easier for us. I suspect he had kept them for just that eventuality.

Bahadur's Reclamation of our Assets

Bahadur landed in Kampala in the early Spring of 1992, intending to stay just long enough to take a quick look-see, but ended up remaining for close to three months. He engaged Mr. Suresh Gandesha, a lawyer in Jinja, to help submit asset claims for our properties.

Mr. Gandesha, a Hindu who hailed originally from India, lived for many years in Jinja. He immigrated to England as a result of the expulsion but later returned to re-establish his law practice. In the past, Bapa had retained him for legal work, and, because Bapa trusted him, Bahadur trusted him as well.

Bahadur started the ball rolling on the asset claims. In Uganda, the government owned all property, and granted long-term leases to tenants.

When Idi Amin expelled us from the country, Bapa owned leasehold titles to the carbon dioxide factory and Portello production plant at 1 Home Road, to our first home at 39 Ripon Garden Road, to our second home at 7 Nalufenya Road, and to a commercial building on Iganga Road. In addition, he was the trustee for the leasehold title to the property owned by Nanabapa which had passed, after the death of Nanima, to Ma and Mariam Masi.

Some of the titles were in the names of various family members, and Bahadur asked us to send him affidavits of verification along with powers of attorney authorizing him to deal with the properties on our behalf. These documents, the papers from Bapa's briefcase, and a copy of Bapa's will were sufficient for Bahadur to obtain Certificates of Repossession for the leasehold titles to all the properties. In the course of doing so, he managed to negotiate with the government for the addition of twenty years to each leasehold term to compensate for the twenty years we had lost.

But, re-establishing title to the carbon dioxide and Portello production plants, both situated in the same compound, led to a Mexican stand-off with the East African Development Bank (EADB).

The IMF had given funding to Uganda to rehabilitate industries. The EADB was the recipient of some or all of that funding, and had lent about (Can) $150,000.00, by way of a working capital loan, to the then owner of Jubilee Ice & Soda Works. The EADB had secured the loan by way of a floating debenture over the company's assets. However, the owner managed the company poorly and incurred several other debts. The result was that customer and supplier confidence had eroded, the facilities had deteriorated, and the owner had defaulted on repayment of the EADB loan.

When Bahadur learned of this bleak situation, he immediately notified the EABD that our family, as the original owners, wished to take physical possession of the assets, and run the company. On this basis, he did everything in his power to convince the EADB to forgive the loan or, at least, to forestall receivership to give Bahadur time to work out a deal.

Bahadur quickly found, though, that trying to formulate a solution satisfactory to everyone was well-nigh impossible. Bribery and corruption were still rampant, and much of the negotiations were verbal as the Ugandans seemed allergic to committing anything to writing. In the end, his efforts proved futile. The EADB called its debenture, and appointed a receiver-manager. Thus, they took effective ownership of the equipment and other assets while we retained leasehold title to the land and buildings.

The whole experience was hard on Bahadur physically and emotionally. Because Jinja had few amenities or facilities for a long-term stay, he frequently had to travel back and forth between Kampala and Jinja. He returned to Burnaby victorious in re-possessing our properties but frustrated about the intransigence of the EADB at a time when the Ugandan government was pressing so hard to re-vitalize industries. When he arrived home, he was tired, gaunt, and fed up with Uganda.

At that time, limited opportunities to sell the properties existed so Bahadur delegated to Mr. Gandesha the task of managing the properties on behalf of the family. Mr. Gandesha negotiated for the payment of rent from the squatters occupying the homes and carrying on businesses in the commercial buildings.

As Bahadur had no interest in returning to Jinja to operate the carbon dioxide and Portello businesses, we decided to sell them, and we retained Mr. Gandesha's services to seek out a buyer. Although he received some offers, none came to fruition.

Returning to my Roots

In August of 1993, Mr. Gandesha telephoned to say that the EADB had requested that a family member come to Uganda to continue nego-tiations. Because I was a banker and an experienced negotiator, Bahadur and I decided that I should go.

The rest of the family expressed total disinterest except for Ma who was angry, upset, and terrified. She was convinced I would come back to Canada in a body bag. I hated to cause her such emotional pain but I knew, in my heart, that Bapa would want me to complete the reclama-tion process. I chose not to add to Ma's angst by revealing that I was undertaking the trip with gut-wrenching trepidation. I was concerned for my safety, and reluctant to re-open doors to a past that I had no desire to re-live.

Nonetheless, I left for Uganda in August, 1993. I detoured, on the way, to Birmingham to visit my Mariam Masi. Her son, Mehboob, who was one of my favourite cousins, said that he would like to come with me so we set off for Uganda together.

My arrival at the Entebbe Airport marked my return to my African roots. I suffered instant pangs of nostalgia along with sad memories of the day I left, in 1972, amid the fear and commotion of all the other depart-ing Asians. I had a brief lapse where I thought, "What am I doing here?" But, I recovered rapidly, and we proceeded to Kampala where we stayed at the Fairway Hotel. Sherali Bandali Jaffer owned the hotel, and his son, Aneez, managed it. Aneez and I had attended school together, and remained friends. He was most kind to us during our stay.

On my first weekend, Meenaben Madhvani, widow of Jayant Madhvani, invited me to the Madhvani estate in Kakira. Meenaben caught me up on her daughter Nimisha's distinguished diplomatic career.

At the time of my arrival in Kampala, the Ugandan government had just appointed Nimisha First Secretary of Trade and Investment with the Ugandan Embassy in Washington, D.C. Her primary duties in that office were to concentrate on the promotion, in the United States, of investment opportunities in Uganda. She is currently Uganda's High Commissioner to India, the first Indian woman to undertake the role of emissary from an African country.

My trip to Kampala revived fond memories, in a most unexpected way, of another childhood friend with whom I had lost contact after the expulsion. Each balmy evening, we sat outside on the hotel patio for dinner. The hotel offered pungent nyama choma but I usually settled for a vegetarian pizza. On my last evening, I was chatting with a gentleman named Salim, and he turned out to be the husband of Fatima Velji, my left-handed intellectual pal from Jinja days. I learned that Fatima had become a lawyer, which didn't surprise me at all.

Before leaving Vancouver, some relatives of an Ithnasheri woman named Mumtaz Kassam urged me to contact her when I reached Kampala. I did so, and found her to be charismatic and amiable.

According to Mumtaz's own resume, she had fled from Uganda in 1972; studied at the College of Law at Lancaster Gate; worked as a commercial solicitor in London for six years; and then returned to Uganda. She set up shop to assist former Ugandans to reclaim their properties and businesses, and she established a management company to manage their real estate assets, including the reclaimed properties.

Mumtaz had infiltrated her way into Museveni's inner circle, and seemed to know everyone In Kampala. We went to several parties together, where the liquor flowed like the Murchison Falls, and she introduced me to a great many people from the various embassies.

She also introduced me to Mayanja Nkangi, with whom we both got along famously. A well-educated man, he held a Bachelor of Arts degree from the University of London, and a Master of Arts degree from Oxford University, and was a barrister at Lincoln's Inn. He had, at one time, been a lecturer in Monetary Economics at Lancaster University. He was the Prime Minister of the Kingdom of Buganda, and had held a variety of posts in the Ugandan government. When we met him, he was the Minister of Finance and Economic Planning, and a power player in Museveni's command structure.

Mr. Nkangi was about sixty years old, and quite a handsome man. His grey hair brushed straight back from a high forehead and segued down into bushy sideburns that joined up with a dashing moustache. His complexion was an attractive mahogany, and his eyes always looked charmingly startled. He was a nifty dresser, and favoured impeccably tailored navy blue suits complemented by white shirts with wide blue pinstripes and blue and red patterned ties. He was a cool guy so I nicknamed him "Cool Dude" which, fortunately, he found amusing.

Mumtaz wanted to take over management of our reclaimed properties but Bahadur and I were content to leave it with Mr. Gandesha because we trusted him, and he was our eyes on the ground in Jinja. To Mumtaz's credit, she didn't push us about the issue.

Mehboob and I along with Rohit Kotecha, a friend of Bahadur's, drove down to Jinja to confer with Mr. Gandesha, and to inspect the family holdings. For me, the visit, after an absence of twenty years, evoked a wistful melancholia, a tinge of homesickness for my stolen life in Uganda, and an engulfing gratitude for my reincarnation in Canada.

The first difference we noticed was that a reddish-brown mud had replaced most of the well-maintained tarmac on the roads, and potholes riddled the road surfaces. After we traversed the highway over the Owen Falls Dam, we stopped at my cherished home at 7 Nalufenya Road, Bapa's pride and joy.

When Idi Amin drove us out of Jinja, Dr. Kafuku, an African physician whom we knew vaguely, had taken possession of the house. His widow and children still lived there. Mrs. Kafuku was a courteous lady, and allowed us to do a walk-through, a privilege she had earlier accorded to Bahadur.

I was astounded and saddened to find that everything was virtually as my parents had left it when they took flight. Our furniture still occupied the same floor space, Ma's drapes still hung from the windows, and the original paint still covered the walls. But, everything was run-down and dirty, and the windows were cracked. Ma's "spit and polish" kitchen was dull and vacant of life. When I went into my bedroom, a huge lump worked its way into my throat when I saw my very own childhood furniture and tattered posters of David Cassidy and Michael Jackson still hanging where I had abandoned them.

Our next stop was the Muslim graveyard just down the way, the resting place for Nanabapa, Nanima, my great grandmother, and my older sister, Khatun. Once well-tended and a place of serene beauty, the cemetery was now a shambles, overgrown with grass and weeds and marred by shattered tombstones. At the present time, as I've mentioned, the government is pressing to develop the cemetery land over the bones of our departed loved ones.

Jinja itself looked like a ghost town. The streets were almost empty of vehicles and people. The buildings were in shabby disrepair, and the detailed Indian storefronts dilapidated. The once vibrant Main Street looked merely squalid, and the roads were reduced to dirt. Little remained of the Jinja pier where our families and friends once picnicked. Our Jamatkhana was a poorly kept and decrepit hospice. At that moment, I thought that if I had ever nursed any subconscious desire to return to Jinja, the seedy, neglected, and depressive state of the roads, structures, and even the inhabitants would have dissuaded me.

One last surprise awaited me when I ran into my friend Maira Butt's dad, Anwar, the mechanic and East African Safari Rally driver, on Main Street. He told me that he owned Bapa's formerly ritzy 1953 green four-door Pontiac Chieftain. Its rusted hulk was sitting in his backyard.

I so regret that I didn't think to tell my friend, Franz Wilfling, psychologist and car restoration buff extraordinaire, about the vehicle. I have no doubt that Franz would have flown with me to Uganda to gauge the Pontiac's restorability, convinced me to buy it and ship it to Canada, and then returned it to its former lustrous elegance.

I stopped in at the Victoria Nile School to say hello, and look around. I received an overwhelming reception from the students. During afternoon recess, three young ladies, wearing the same style of uniform I had worn as a child, treated me to an escorted tour. I was pleased to discover that the school had fared well despite the years of upheaval and destruction.

My friends and I took afternoon tea at the Crested Crane Hotel. We sat in the same room where Zebby and Rustam had held their wedding reception, and where we had first heard rumours of, and laughed about, Idi Amin's threatened expulsion.

None of the partying or side trips, though, eclipsed my primary purpose in returning to Uganda. I was hell-bent on convincing the EADB to release its hold, one way or another, over the business assets.

A banker for the EADB arranged for us to tour the carbon dioxide plant and Portello factory. Walking onto that property was one of the most difficult moments of my life. I was so glad that Mehboob and Rohit were with me to lend their moral support.

I could feel Bapa's presence all around me, and that brought back heart-rending memories of myself, as a child, constantly underfoot in the factory. In the throes of those emotions, I suddenly decided that I wanted to return to Uganda to carry on Bapa's legacy.

The fly in the ointment was the EADB. Under its supervision, the company had used all or some of the borrowed funds to rehabilitate and refit both the carbon dioxide and bottling plants. Equipment was purchased from the United States whereas Bapa had always acquired equipment from a manufacturer in Stuttgart.

Meenaben Madhvani had invited us to visit Kakira again after we finished up in Jinja. But, she got word through to us, at the last minute, that we should stay away for our own safety. Employees at the sugar cane plantation had attempted to effect strike action. In their fervour, they had set on fire and virtually destroyed huge fields of sugar cane. Disappointed at this turn of events, we talked about returning to Kampala that evening but our tour of Jinja had been so draining that we decided to spend the night at the Sunset Hotel. Even that stay brought to mind nostalgic recollections. The hotel was in a residential complex which Anwar Jaffer, the son of H.K. Jaffer, a director along with Bapa, of the Eastern Province Bus Company, owned when I lived in Jinja. I used to play in the main house with Anwar Jaffer's two sons.

The next morning, after one final drive through Jinja, we trekked back to Kampala. I attended immediately at the offices of the EADB, and advised them that I had experienced a change of heart. I no longer wanted to sell the land and buildings that housed Jubilee Ice & Soda Works. Rather, I wished to return to Jinja, with some of my family members, to revive Portello as the most popular soft drink in Uganda.

I began serious negotiations, at the outdoor patio of the Hilton Hotel, with two pleasant, middle-aged gentlemen, one African and one British, who represented the EADB. They found me to be an equally pleasant little Indian girl. I neglected to mention to them my career in banking with The Royal Bank of Canada.

My pitch to the EADB representatives covered several bases. I reminded them that the EADB's mandate was to assist businesses that would aid in the commercial and industrial development of the country; that recent history indicated African ownership of the plants would likely fail; and that, by not permitting the family that pioneered Jubilee Ice & Soda Works to rejuvenate it, they would destroy two industries that, in the past, had proven most successful.

With regard to the carbon dioxide operation, I pointed out that Kenya, at that time, was the sole supplier of the gas; that it could export its product only if a surplus was available; that lack of availability and delays in the import of the carbon dioxide, along with transportation costs, meant that the price to users increased; that costs to start up the factory in Jinja again would be nominal; and that, as no other carbon dioxide plants existed in Uganda, Jubilee would be supplying the manufactured gas to a captive market.

By now, I was winging along in full flight. I argued passionately that, with respect to Portello, my family's original product was more to the taste of local consumers than other drinks; that when Bapa ran the business, he enjoyed a greater market share than all other soft drinks; that manufacturing our own carbon dioxide, and utilizing our own formula, mixed to our specifications, meant we would not have to pay any franchise or royalty fees; and, that, as a result, we could produce and put a cheaper and better product on the market. These arguments were identical to the ones Bapa had made unsuccessfully prior to Jayant Madhvani intervening on his behalf with the President so many years before.

The bankers were sympathetic to my intentions, and said that, because my Bapa was the original founder of the business, they would give my family first consideration. Nonetheless, our negotiations were intense. They wanted me to pay compensation to the EADB for the new equipment. I wanted them to remove it, and re-install Bapa's equipment. They refused because the EADB had no other use for the new fixtures, and, in any case, they didn't know what had become of Bapa's old equipment.

After conferring with Bahadur, I made them an initial offer of US $25,000 which they found laughable. I told them that I would have to think seriously about an increased offer, and would meet with them after the weekend.

I spent the next couple of days doing a lot of soul searching. On Sunday afternoon, I kicked back at a party hosted by Mumtaz at her home. At that function, I met several more people in the diplomatic service who were fascinated by my adventures and opinions since my arrival in Uganda.

I must say that, while I was at the party, I received gratifying encouragement to continue my quest to carry on Bapa's legacy. The other guests were unanimous in their opinion that Uganda desperately needed people like me who possessed a "can-do" attitude, along with western education, knowledge, and skills. Many of them felt certain that President Museveni himself would wish to hear what I had to say, and they strongly encouraged me to seek an audience with him.

One of the guests at the party was Michael Frost, First Secretary with the British High Commission in Kampala. We had a long chat, and he reiterated what the other folks were telling me. He suggested as well that I should make a bid to meet the President.

That evening, I went to the Jamatkhana in Kampala, which Ismailis had managed to restore to its original grandeur, and then to the Mukhi's home for dinner. Many of the other guests were Asians from Canada and Great Britain. They were visiting Kampala for the same reasons as I. We regaled one another with our often tragic but sometimes hilarious tales of our expulsion from Uganda, and compared notes on our experiences since arriving back.

I was the only woman who was there to either claim or dispose of assets. The reception I received from the men was far less positive than what I had received from the diplomats earlier in the day. Their consensus was that while I was undoubtedly a successful businesswoman in the western world, Africa was not a conducive environment for a woman to operate a business independently. At the same time, though, the men were supportive, and wished me every success.

I agonized over these disparate points of view through the night. After a telephone discussion with Bahadur, the next morning, I elected to take two further courses of action. First, I increased my offer to the EADB to US $75,000. Second, I set about to see the President. Some people may have seen that as an overly bold gesture. However, my Canadian experience had taught me to follow my gut instincts, and make my own destiny.

At the presidential offices, I found that, in order to engage the President, I had to obtain permission from the First Protocol Officer. Undaunted, I pressed on to his quarters, and he was good enough to give me a hearing.

He advised me, however, that the President was up-country, and would not be available until the following week. As I had to return to Vancouver to make sure I still had a job, I was unable to await the President's return. The First Protocol Officer kindly suggested that I should write to the President's office, and schedule a meeting during my next visit to Uganda. On that note, I returned to Canada.

CHAPTER TWENTY-FOUR

Canada or Uganda?

Still Dreaming of a Triumphant Return

Back home, I was still captive to the notion of personally reviving Jubilee Ice & Soda Works, and helping to rebuild Uganda as it was meant to be. Bahadur said he would support me in my decision but much would depend on the outcome of negotiations with the EADB, which had rejected my second offer.

EADB made the next move in the game. They advised me that they had received an offer of US $150,000 from a source that I suspected was Century Bottling Company, the bottler for Coca-Cola. When I was still in Kampala, I had the opportunity to meet with Century's chairman and managing director, who had offered me a token US $50,000 to acquire our land and buildings in Jinja. At that time, I had countered with an offer of a joint venture between Jubilee and Century.

After I left, Century apparently approached the EADB directly. Part of their proposed scheme involved closing the Jinja premises and moving the factory to Kampala. In any event, I don't believe the EADB ever received a written offer from Century, and the negotiations died on the vine.

After the latest advance by the EADB, Bahadur and I decided to embark on one more foray of our own. In October of 1993, we applied to The Development Finance Company of Uganda for a loan of US $250,000. Our proposal was that we would pay US $150,000 to the EADB, and employ the remaining US $100,000 as working capital.

We reckoned that we would need the working capital for initial start-up costs to bring in experienced engineers from the United States or Germany to re-condition and upgrade the equipment, and to buy raw materials. We figured that we could generate an immediate cash flow from the sale of carbon dioxide. Fortunately or unfortunately, we would never be sure as the Development Finance Company rejected our proposal.

Still undeterred and ever the optimist, I penned a lengthy letter to President Museveni, and sent it to Michael Frost, with the British High Commission. I asked that he attempt to pass it along to the President.

In my letter, which ran to several pages, I fired all my ammunition. I advised the President of Bapa's history, how he found his way to Jinja in 1920 with nothing but dreams, and built one of the most successful businesses in Uganda. I went on to describe my family's ordeal during the expulsion. I told him that I wished to return to Jinja to re-build Jubilee Ice & Soda Works; that I intended to advocate in Canada for foreign investment in Uganda; that my position with the premier bank in Canada afforded me contact with professionals and entrepreneurs looking for opportunities in foreign lands; and that, to that end, I would like to invite a delegation from Uganda to discuss trade and development possibilities with my Canadian contacts. Whether or not President Museveni received or read my letter, I found writing it to be a positive and cathartic experience.

Cool Dude Visits Vancouver

A short time later, Mumtaz passed along a message to me from Cool Dude. With President Museveni's blessing, he wished to bring an entourage to Vancouver on a junket to promote investment in their nation and trade ties between Canada and Uganda. She asked if I would pass the message along to the Ismaili community at the Jamatkhana, and if I would host the delegation.

The Ugandan delegation arrived in Vancouver from a similar mission in Washington D.C. While there, they had met with Nimisha Madhvani. I marvelled at the confluence of circumstances that led to two little girls who had played together in Kakira to meeting, in Washington and Vancouver, with a trio of African government officials to discuss international investment and trade. What a fascinating world!

Accompanying Cool Dude to Vancouver were Mumtaz, Emmanuel Tumusiime-Mutebile, and Keith Muhakanizi. Mr. Tumusiime-Mutebile had received his education at Durham University and Oxford University. He had taught economic tutorials for undergraduates at Oxford, and had lectured in Industrial Economics at the University of Dar-es-Salaam in Tanzania. At the time of his visit, he held a position with the Ministry of Finance and Economic Planning. Mr. Muhakanizi held a Master of Science degree in Development Economics from the University of Manchester, and a Diploma in National Economic Planning and Statistics from Warsaw, Poland. He was Economic Advisor to the

Ministry of Finance and Economic Planning. Their academic credentials were certainly impressive.

I decided to organize a private breakfast meeting for the Ugandan delegation. It was too big an undertaking for me alone so I enlisted the help of Shiraz Lalji and David McLean. Shiraz was a member of our Ismaili community, transplanted from Uganda, and a prominent Vancouver real estate developer. David, as I have mentioned, was a client of mine and Chairman of the Vancouver Board of Trade.

Shiraz accommodated the delegation at his family-owned Delta Hotel on Howe Street. David hosted a lavish breakfast at the hotel where the delegation was able to meet with, and make a pitch for investment and trade to, a number of prominent movers and shakers in the British Columbia business world.

The thirty-five or so guests included Bahadur, representatives of the Hongkong Bank of Canada and Royal Bank of Canada; the Mayor of Vancouver; the Director, International Management Consulting Services for B.D.O. Dunwoody Ward Mallette; the President and Chief Executive Officer of B.C. Central Credit Union; the Managing Director of the Vancouver Board of Trade; the Brazilian Consul General; a senior partner with Deloitte & Touche; several prominent entrepreneurs in the Vancouver business community; and my good friend, Larry Page, who, among other things, was a well-known mining entrepreneur.

For my part, I arranged for the Ugandan delegation to give an evening address to the Vancouver Ismaili community at our Jamatkhana; to meet privately with interested parties; and to tour a Vancouver based packaging facility owned and operated by a former Ugandan family.

Cool Dude very much wanted to meet Ma so I invited him and his companions to our home for dinner. Cool Dude was a cordial and decent gentleman, and he and Ma hit it off. She liked him. For his part, he was quite taken by our family, and offered us a lovely compliment, saying, "Now this is what I call a nice warm family home."

The Bloom Fades From the Rose

Meanwhile, the stew of negotiations with the EADB continued to simmer on the back burner but, as the weeks passed, my passion for returning to Jinja began to evaporate. Ma and the family were dead set against my plan. For my part, I was torn between the strong pull of the land of my birth, and the rewarding life and career I had constructed in my adoptive homeland.

Compounding the complexity of my decision was the continuing instability of the region. It became evident to Bahadur and me, during the course of our negotiations, that Uganda was still a morass of bribery, corruption, and political disruption. It had even been alleged that the notorious assassin, Carlos the Jackal, had contracted to murder President Museveni.

The bloom was off the rose, and the question of how much we were prepared to sacrifice became paramount. After more soul-searching, and with Bahadur's concurrence, I advised the EADB that, because of the lack of progress in negotiations despite my personal attendance in Uganda, we were rescinding all previous offers, and would consider only a total forgiveness of the EADB loan. And, that if the board of directors of the bank did not find this avenue viable, then we could only say that we had used our best efforts to return to Uganda and make a contribution similar to that made by our Bapa.

My Canadian Delegation to Uganda

In early 1994, with the situation still unresolved, I received an official invitation from Cool Dude to bring a delegation of business people to Kampala to see firsthand the advantages of Ugandan investment. I agreed, in part, because I wanted an audience with President Museveni, and that wasn't going to happen without a delegation to back me.

My associates on the trip included Larry and Robyn Page, my Private Banking clients, T. W. Wong, and Naren Majithia. Larry was a founding partner of the Vancouver law firm of Worrall Scott and Page, and a Queen's Counsel. He was a director of Prime Equities International Corporation, a substantial exploration and development public mining company whose shares were listed on the Vancouver Stock Exchange and on the NASDAQ Stock Exchange in the United States.

I made my sales pitch to Larry at the Caffé dé Medici Ristorante Italiano on Vancouver's iconic Robson Street. My pitch wasn't really necessary as the first words were scarcely out of my mouth before Larry said he and his wife, Robyn, were on board.

Larry had been involved in the mining business for some time, and was interested in taking a gander at the Kilembe copper mine in southwestern Uganda which was up for sale. He was also interested in gold mining prospects.

I invited T.W. Wong to join us because, at the time, Chinese investment in Ugandan enterprises was popular, and, as a result, Cool Dude wanted me to produce a genuine Chinese person. T.W. and I, along with our cohort Jan McLeod, were co-workers in Private Banking.

T.W. had worked in Hong Kong for ten years for major commercial banks as a senior private banker. He frequently visited Asia to advise clients on investments in real estate, financial markets, and business opportunities. He was well-known in the Vancouver business community, and was a good friend of mine.

Naren Majithia rounded out our little brigade. Naren was a Hindu who had emigrated from Jinja although he was older than I, and I had never run across him in Jinja. He was a heck of a nice guy, and had worked in the mining industry for many years for Murray Pezim, the flamboyant stock promoter. Naren had attended school in India with Larry's brother, and Larry recommended him. He was a director and chief financial officer of Prime Equities International Corporation.

Our entry into Uganda at Entebbe Airport again brought back shades of the old days. Mumtaz had asked us to buy two computers and a fax machine for her. When we arrived, the African customs officials began to cross-examine us on why we had this equipment with us. They never noticed that one of us was carrying a laptop computer. In fairness, laptops were relatively new, and they had perhaps not seen one before.

I managed to push Larry, Robyn, and Naren through customs but I asked T.W. to stay with me because he was a computer whiz. The officials took us into a separate room to interrogate us. That was a bit nerve-wracking. However, Mumtaz, who had come to the airport to meet us, took the officials aside, and waved a letter from President Museveni, authorizing our visit. That either scared or impressed them enough that they let us through.

We set up our headquarters at the Kampala Hilton Hotel where we stayed for about a week. Mumtaz hung out with us the whole time, and arranged for us to wine and dine several significant players in Ugandan government and industry.

The Uganda Investment Authority, with the help of Mumtaz, arranged the official itinerary for our delegation, and they filled our slate. We met, amongst others, with the Executive Director of the Uganda Investment Authority; the Deputy Minister of Trade and Industry; the Minister of Finance and Economic Planning (aka Cool Dude); the Commissioner of Geology; the Governor of the Bank of Uganda; Prince John Barigye of Bisya Mines; a representative of the National Resistance Movement Secretariat; and various private sector representatives.

We had a fun-filled time at one particular dinner with George, a prominent African state lawyer whose last name escapes me. He stands out in my mind not because of his role or connections but because he was extraordinarily charming, well-spoken, and handsome.

Meenaben Madhvani kindly hosted a luncheon and gathering for us at her Kakira estate, to which she invited members from a number of embassies. No business motives were in play. She was simply being her usual cordial self.

Toward the end of our visit, we had the opportunity to meet with President Museveni and several of his key people including the head of the Bank of Uganda. We presented the President with two Haida Gwaii paintings arranged for by Larry. The President was a commanding presence. He was most engaging, and spoke English extremely well.

Delegation: (L-R) T.W. Wong, Mumtaz Kassam, President Museveni,
Nazlin Rahemtulla, Naren Majithia, Robyn Page, and Larry Page

President Museveni had several motives in meeting with us. He
wanted to thank me for organizing Cool Dude's delegation to Vancouver;
he was interested in talking to Larry about mining ventures in general,
and the Kilembe Mine in particular; and, most importantly, he wanted to
promote opportunities for investment in Uganda.

The President was at his most gracious but what we didn't realize was
that his intent was to televise and broadcast our interview later that same
evening. He used it as propaganda to show his people how hard he was
working to lure foreign investors to Uganda. He even began the interview
by saying that he was inviting all his "tribes to come home."

One result of the broadcast was that, for the next few days, many individuals inundated Larry with phone calls begging him to invest in their
mining ventures. One such caller was a local prince who had been educated in the United States. Larry also received a call from two gentlemen
who lived in Nairobi. Larry arranged to meet with them in Nairobi and
they lunched at the Muthaiga Country Club. Earlier in the century, the
elite society of British East Africa had frequented the Club, and it was
also famous for being one of the stage sets in the movie *Out of Africa*.

I was surprised to find out that President Museveni was well-versed in
my family's history. He was most complimentary about how hard Bapa
had worked, and how much he had accomplished.

That was the President's lead-in to his pitch that I should return to
Uganda, and encourage other young people like myself to do so as well.
I had to be honest with him. I told him that lack of safety was still a

significant factor; that young Asians would not be prepared to pour their money, and their blood, sweat and tears, into building up new businesses in Uganda under the apprehension of the government kicking them out again; that we had integrated into the western world which offered much more in the way of opportunities; and, on a personal note, that Ma would not approve, and would be so terrified for me that it might kill her. What I had to say did not appear to startle the President, and, on that note, our audience with him ended.

Larry expressed sufficient interest in the Kilembe Mine that the President offered the use of his executive jet for us to fly to Kilembe to inspect it as it was in a remote area accessible only by aeroplane. When we arrived at the President's private airfield outside Entebbe, it appeared deserted.

Larry eventually found an employee who said that a gentleman named Mr. Page from the World Health Organization had just taken the plane. We were a bit suspicious about the coincidence of a man also named "Page" having just commandeered our erstwhile transportation. We surmised that President Museveni recognized that Larry was an experienced and knowledgeable mining man, and didn't want him to see the mine which was in shambles. I doubt that my "plain speaking" had anything to do with the plane's absence.

The employee did half-heartedly offer us the use of a small Cessna 250. Larry looked out at the cerulean sky with its darkening nimbus clouds, and, not knowing whether the plane was safe or the pilot skilled enough, decided to cancel. Instead, we headed back to Entebbe for early cocktails by the pool.

Before we left Kampala, Mumtaz invited us to dinner at her home in the once prestigious Kalolo neighbourhood. Larry was wearing sandals, and when Mumtaz saw his socks, she insisted that he take them off, and give them to her. The writing on the socks said, "The presumption of innocence begins with payment of my retainer." We all had a good laugh, Larry gave her the socks, and she later framed them.

Larry loses his socks

Mumtaz also regaled us with some hilarious stories. We were talking about safety, and she told us that she came home one evening to find the askari sound asleep with his nose on the butt of his rifle. She nudged him awake, whereupon he sprang to attention, and said, "Madam, while my eyes were closed I was still observing."

Our whole gang travelled to Jinja as Naren and I wanted the others to see our hometown. We dropped by Jubilee Ice & Soda Works so I could show them the business Bapa had built. When we arrived, I suddenly remembered that my ever cautious Bapa had installed a small underground storage dungeon in the factory where he stashed Dimple Scotch, Kit Kat chocolates, sugar, and flour because demand for those items sometimes exceeded supply.

I knew the location of the secret entrance under some floor boards so, while Larry, Robyn, and Naren diverted the guards, T.W. and I snuck down into the dungeon. We found the remains of the chocolates, chewed on by rats, and some wooden crates of scotch. I scoffed one bottle of Dimple, and, that evening, we drank it back at the hotel amid numerous toasts to our friendship and our journey.

After our stay in Uganda, we rewarded ourselves with a trip to Kenya. We stayed at the Mount Kenya Safari Club; Treetops Hotel; the Arc located deep within Aberdare National Park; and Little Governors' Camp in the Masai Mara National Reserve.

For our trip to the Masai Mara, we booked a charter flight on a small Cessna, and flew there from the Wilson Airport in Nairobi. The National Reserve is one of the most popular game parks in Africa. It features open savannah, hills, an escarpment, lush grasslands, acacia forests, and central plains, and lies about 300 kilometers by road from Nairobi. During the forty-five minute flight, we flew over the Great Rift Valley where we were privileged to witness the migration of the wildebeest. The 'Great Migration', as it is known, is an annual journey by more than a million wildebeests, zebras, and gazelles, to search out new feeding grounds and watering holes. The pilgrimage wends its way from the Serengeti in Tanzania to the Masai Mara in Kenya, and is fraught with danger. The route these animals follow requires them, for example, to cross the Mara River where the largest crocodiles in Africa stalk them for dinner. From the air, the migration looked like a black streak across the Rift Valley.

When we landed, a van was waiting to escort us to Little Governor's camp which consists of a small number of luxurious en-suite tents situate around a watering hole that is a haven for birds and animals. Warthogs wandered unrestrained through the camp, and elephants often dropped by around lunchtime. At night, the eerie laughter of hyenas, and the roar of the lions, punctuated our sleep.

Little Governors
(L-R) Robyn, Larry, Guide, TW & Naren

Walking anywhere in the camp was forbidden unless a guard escorted us. Early in the morning after our arrival, we left our tents only to find our askari sprawled on his back against a tree, with his rifle across his chest, snoring sonorously. As we were leaving immediately on a hot air balloon safari, we had no choice but to leave him, and bolt across the encampment to the balloon.

We survived our run, and the balloon fired up, and floated us over the Masai Mara game reserve on an epic adventure. We were able to observe the circle of life—the hunters and the hunted. We viewed wildlife waking up to the day; a newborn zebra trying to find its legs; predators stalking their prey; and half-eaten carcasses.

The balloon landed in the middle of lion country where, incongruously, we were treated to a lavish breakfast complete with red table linen, champagne, and orange juice. After this idyllic interlude, we came back to earth, and returned to Vancouver.

Breakfast in the middle of lion country at Masai Mara

Ever since then, Larry and I have kept the memory of our trip alive by saluting one another with the Swahili greetings of *"jambo, mama"* for "hello, lady," and *"jambo, bwana"* for "hello, mister."

O Canada!

On my return home, Bahadur and I reached the irrevocable decision that neither returning to Uganda nor attempting to operate Bapa's businesses from Canada made sense from either a commercial or an emotional perspective.

Our foremost concern was about the future stability of Uganda. We were simply not prepared to invest the working capital necessary to make the assets profitable. The economics just didn't work, particularly when we took into account that we might get everything up and running only to find the Ugandan government expelling us again. The destructive action of the striking Madhvani employees in burning the sugar cane fields had also reminded me that, in Uganda, danger and violence are only a heartbeat away. Once bitten, as they say. As well, we had moved on. We were happy and productive citizens of Canada, and, in the cold light of day, saw returning to Jinja as a huge step backward.

Accordingly, we decided to divest ourselves of all our Ugandan properties. Ironically, at about this time, the EADB caved, and turned the keys to the compound over to us. We never knew why they did so but their surrender may have had something to do with the fact that Zul Jaffer, a cousin of Mobina Jaffer, had approached both the EADB and us about buying Jubilee Ice & Soda Works.

I don't know what strategy Zul employed with the EADB but we struck a bargain with him to purchase the entire Jubilee enterprise. He was to pay us by instalments. I don't know whether he was successful in his endeavour but he did pay us the entire purchase price.

We sold the Iganga Road property to a gentleman from Botswana by the name of Dr. V. B. Wankiiri, and the remaining properties to African Ugandans. We offered Mariam Masi all the money from the sale of Nanabapa's building but she insisted on splitting it evenly with Ma.

Dear Mr. Gandesha helped us throughout all the negotiations but, only a few days after completing the last transaction, his assistant emailed me with the sad news that he had died. On the "small world" front, his son, Dr. Samir Gandesha, is an assistant professor in the Department of Humanities at Simon Fraser University, just a few kilometres from our Burnaby home.

Initially, only a few hundred Asians took up the Ugandan government's invitation to return. Since then, many more have gone back to reclaim and operate their businesses, and I applaud their commitment and loyalty to Uganda.

For my part, I don't regret for a moment either the time or the physical and emotional energy Bahadur and I expended to fight for our assets on the African continent. Bapa would be so proud of us. But he would, I think, be equally proud that we decided to divest those assets, and opt irrevocably for a future in Canada. I'm certain he would have done the same.

As a postscript to this chapter, I must mention that my good friends, Larry and Robyn, know a bit about bottling processes as they own the fine Saturna Island Family Estate Winery. Saturna Island, in the Southern Gulf Islands of British Columbia, has a climate like that of the northern Mediterranean, and is an ideal setting for their twenty-five hectares of vineyards. They produce superb Pinot Gris, Chardonnay, Gewürztraminer, Pinot Noir, and Merlot under vine.

CHAPTER TWENTY-FIVE
Good Fortune Rains Down on Uganda

The Return of the Aga Khan to Uganda

The Aga Khan Fund for Economic Development (AKFED) is an international development agency under the aegis of the Aga Khan Foundation. AKFED encourages local entrepreneurship and private sector initiatives. It builds or participates in building businesses and projects in developing third world nations that are in need of foreign investment. AKFED often participates in joint ventures with both local and international partners to establish corporations that will be key players in the economic development of a country. AKFED is a for-profit agency but it re-invests all of its profits in development initiatives.

When President Museveni, at the urging of the IMF and World Bank, invited Ismailis back to Uganda, he extended a personal request to Aga Khan IV to encourage their return.

But, Aga Khan IV did much more than that. President Museveni was desperate for the infusion of foreign investment into Uganda. So, under the auspices of AKFED, the Aga Khan lent an exceptional helping hand to Uganda by developing, financing, and investing in businesses and projects that would stimulate the long-term economic growth of the country. According to the Aga Khan, building businesses, and mixing business and charity, is part of the ethics of the Ismaili faith.

The Kampala Serena Hotel was a showpiece project in which AKFED held a joint ownership interest. In November 2006, President Museveni officially inaugurated the five-star hotel in the presence of His Highness, the Aga Khan. Its opening was a much anticipated bonanza for the Ugandan service and tourism sectors.

The hotel is one of a series of Serena hotels and lodges launched by or with the assistance of AKFED. The agency's aims, with regard to initiatives of this type, are to augment the local economy; to train and hire local people to service the hotels; to promote the use of local artisans; and to conserve the indigenous environment.

At the Kampala Serena Hotel, AKFED commissioned works of arts that reflected the history and culture of the people of the River Nile. During the opening of the hotel, both the Aga Khan and Museveni took time to speak to Mr. Expedito Wakibulla, a celebrated Ugandan wood carver, whose exquisite artistry graces the common areas of the hotel.

AKFED is the lead partner in the development of a hydro power project that was estimated to cost US $860,000,000. It is the largest project upon which the agency has ever embarked. The project, slated for completion in the near future, will provide a supply of energy essential to the economic revitalization of Uganda, and critically important to vast areas of the country that suffer from a lack of sufficient electricity.

In August of 2007, President Museveni and His Highness, the Aga Khan, joined together in a ground-breaking ceremony for the Bujagali PowerStation, a 250 megawatt hydroelectric power project near my old stamping grounds in Jinja. President Museveni spoke eloquently of the Aga Khan's involvement in the betterment of Uganda:

> I welcome you all to Jinja to witness the laying of the Foundation Stone for Bujagali Hydropower Project. I wish to extend special welcome to His Highness the Aga Khan and congratulate him on this auspicious occasion of celebrating the 50th anniversary of his ascension to the position of Imam of the Ismaili Muslim Community. I salute all our development partners who have graced this occasion with their presence here in Jinja.

> His Highness the Aga Khan has made significant contribution towards the social and economic development of this country. The Aga Khan Foundation for Economic Development's (AKFED) participation in Uganda ranges from manufacturing, finance and banking, the media, social services like education and now infrastructure.

In addition to this massive contribution to Uganda's infrastructure, AKFED has been involved in the construction of a string of small hydroelectric systems around small dams to provide electricity to regions of Uganda to which the national grid does not extend. The West Nile district, for example, which is one of the poorer regions of the country, now receives electricity for eighteen hours each day rather than the four hours' worth of electricity it formerly received every other day. AKFED has been able to keep the production costs and consumption prices low but still manage to generate a profit.

Two of AKFED's tenets are that its investments are long-term and require patience, and that, although it wants an expectation of profit, it takes other matters into consideration as well. A prime example is its fish net factory in Kampala. An international initiative to develop fish farming in Uganda was afoot. Fish nets were essential to getting this industry up and running but it represented a classic "chicken and egg" quandary. Without the fish nets, fish farming was not viable but without fish farming no demand existed for the nets. AKFED stepped into the breach, and established a fish net manufacturing facility with the expectation of encouraging a new local industry and, in due course, turning a profit.

Today, corporations under the AKFED umbrella, in addition to the ones I have mentioned, include Industrial Promotion Services (Uganda) Ltd., a development corporation; Kampala Pharmaceuticals Industries Ltd., a manufacturer of pharmaceutical products; Leather Industries of Uganda Ltd., which manufactures leather; Diamond Jubilee Investment Trust, an investment company; Diamond Trust Bank Uganda Ltd.; Diamond Trust Properties Uganda Ltd., a property owner and manager; The Jubilee Insurance Company of Uganda Ltd.; The Monitor Publications Ltd., involved in print media and radio; and Tourism Promotion Services (Uganda) Ltd., a company that promotes tourism, and operates in the hotel ownership and management sector.

So, despite the barbaric ouster of Ismailis from Uganda in 1972, Aga Khan IV and his people have demonstrated exceptional generosity through their massive contribution to the development of a strong and flourishing economic and social structure in that nation.

The Return to Uganda of the Marvellous Madhvanis

I cannot write about our life in Uganda or the affairs of the Ugandan nation without giving a massive shout-out to the extraordinary Madhvani clan. They exemplify the resilience and generosity of the human spirit, and their graciousness has impacted my family in many fruitful ways.

Uganda was incredibly blessed when the Madhvanis returned some years after expulsion to lift the country up on the shoulders of their economic prowess and philanthropic vision.

The Madhvani family saga in Uganda began with Muljibhai Prabhudas Madhvani, a Hindu born in India in 1894. Though he lost his mother when he was a small lad, he was able to complete his primary school education by the time he was twelve years old. Even at that age, he recognised the importance of learning English, and enrolled at a boarding school in the Gujarat to study the English language.

In 1908, when Muljibhai was only fourteen years old, he journeyed to Uganda to join his brother and two uncles, and to start a new life. Like Bapa, he came with nothing but the clothes on his back, and what must have been an all-consuming ambition to succeed. He began his business career by working for his two uncles in a retail business in the town of Iganga. He impressed his uncles sufficiently that they asked him to open a store in Kaliro. Soon after, they requested him to launch yet another store in Jinja.

Once Muljibhai settled in Jinja, he incorporated Vithaldas Haridas & Company, and thus began his ascent into the business stratosphere. In 1918, Muljibhai's company acquired a little more than three square kilometres in Kakira in order to construct a sugar manufacturing facility.

In the late 1920s, Vithaldas Haridas & Company joined the ranks of cotton ginners, and in 1930, opened the doors to Kakira Sugar Works on the Kakira property. Muljibhai continued, during the next twenty-eight years, to expand his commercial, industrial, and trading concerns. During those years, he was at the forefront of Uganda's industrial and commercial growth. As well as cotton ginning and sugar refining, his diverse business interests included textiles, beer, jaggery, oil, maize, soap, tin, tea, and coffee manufacture or production along with a host of other enterprises.

Muljibhai's eldest son, Jayant, was born in 1922. After finishing school in Uganda, his father dispatched Jayant to Bombay, India for his higher education. While there, Jayant acquired both Bachelor of Science and Bachelor of Laws degrees.

In 1946, Jayant and his brother, Manubhai, joined their father in running the family businesses. Through the next couple of decades, fuelled by the uncommon vision and work ethic of the father and sons, their commercial and industrial complex prospered enormously. At one time, it accounted for ten to twelve percent of Uganda's gross domestic product.

Muljibhai was far more than a mere businessman. He was an exceptionally generous philanthropist who was intensely loyal to Uganda, and dedicated to the country's economic and social well-being. His charity began at home. He was a concerned and caring employer who extended free education, housing, and medical benefits to his employees and their families. But, his charitable enterprises extended far beyond his own business boundaries. He held a strong and unwavering belief in the value of education. He established various schools in Ugandan towns, including an agricultural college near Jinja, and he set up a trust fund for education.

In Jinja alone, Muljibhai financed, or contributed to the financing of, the hospital where Shalina and Narmin were born, the secondary school I attended, the town hall where my family strolled in the evenings, and other structures and improvements that benefitted my family and other Jinja residents.

Muljibhai exhibited a robust commitment to public service. At various times, he was President of the Uganda Cotton Association, the Uganda Planters Association, and the Uganda Chamber of Commerce. In 1938, the British government bestowed upon him the honour of making him a Member of the British Empire.

Muljibhai died at the home he had built in Kakira in 1958. A family mausoleum adjacent to a lake on the family estate commemorates his memory.

After Muljibhai's death, Jayant assumed the role of the family and business patriarch. By all accounts, he inherited his father's brilliant business acumen and selfless dedication to philanthropy.

During the 1960s, Jayant and his brother, Manubhai, vastly enlarged the company holdings. They expanded their manufacturing and production concerns, and also expanded geographically into other regions of Africa. In 1962, in honour of their father, the siblings founded the Muljibhai Madhvani Foundation, a charitable trust, to promote scientific and technical education in Uganda. To further this aim, the Foundation granted annual scholarships to poor but deserving students who wished to study at Ugandan universities. I surmise that the Foundation disintegrated during the turbulent years during and after the reign of Idi Amin but, several years ago, it repossessed its assets, and resumed its mission to support higher education.

Tragedy struck the Madhvani family in 1971 when Jayant suffered a heart attack and died during a business trip to Dehli, India. His widow, Meenaben, his sons, Nitin and Amit, and daughter, Nimisha, survived him.

The wealth, power, and influence of the Madhvanis could not protect them from the ugly winds of discrimination. Indeed, Amin detained Manubhai Madhvani in the notorious Makindye Prison for three weeks in 1972 to set an example to the Asian community that no one was safe. The prison was Amin's personal torture playground. Few who disappeared behind its forbidding doors were ever seen again. An estimated 150,000 souls died at Makindye Prison. Manubhai's family suffered untold anxiety, believing that they would never see him again. Against all odds, though, he was released from prison, and lived a long and productive life. In fact, he died on May 16, 2011, in London. Amin's expulsion order did not except the Madhvani family. They fled from Uganda like all the rest of us, and the government seized their businesses.

Not too long a period passed after the toppling of Amin before Jayant's wife, Meenaben, and his son, Nitin, returned to Uganda at the invitation of Milton Obote. They found their assets trashed, their business empire in ruins, their sugar cane fields trampled and overgrown by bush, and their mansions in disrepair. Over the next few years, they fought laborious and complex legal and commercial battles to re-acquire their assets, and rejuvenate their businesses. Ultimately, they succeeded beyond all expectations. The World Bank held the Madhvani name in such esteem that, even though Uganda had no creditworthy credentials, it saw fit to lend the Madhvani Group 50,000,000 pounds sterling to restore Kakira.

Since then, under the stewardship of Muljibhai Madhvani's successors, the Madhvani Group has once again rocketed to the pinnacle of the business world. Kakira, the headquarters for the Madhvani Group, is now an estate of at least 9,500 hectares. The Group employs in excess of 10,000 people, and, at last estimate, their assets were worth more than US $200,000,000.

Their diversification has continued at an incredible pace, and their business interests encompass sugar manufacturing, sweets and confectionary manufacturing, electrical generation, floriculture, tourism, safari lodges, insurance, construction, software applications, packaging, production and sale of consumer goods, beverages, and other ventures too numerous to mention.

I've cited just a few examples of our family connections in this book— Jayant Madhvani lobbying the President to ban the import of carbon dioxide from Kenya in order to assist Bapa's business; our adoption of our Pekingese, Mickey, from a Madhvani litter; their hospitality in allowing the use of their Kakira estate for picnicking and swimming; my attendance at the Parvatiban Muljibhai Madhvani Girls School; Meenaben's kindness to me during my return trips to Uganda; and Bahadur's enduring friendship with Suri Madhvani.

Bahadur and I have both enjoyed the privilege of visiting Kakira since its rejuvenation, Bahadur to visit Suru, and I at the behest of Meenaben.

The contributions the Madhvani family and the Madhvani Group of Companies have made to Uganda are incalculable.

CHAPTER TWENTY-SIX

Setting Sail on New Career Seas

Wealth Management Heaven

I had assumed that I would be an employee of RBC forever but the Bank's acquisition of Dominion Securities heralded a sea change in my professional life. By acquiring Dominion Securities, RBC's intent was to offer its clients in-house expertise in wealth management.

During my tenure in Private Banking, I had joined forces with Dean Alexander at RBC Dominion Securities and had shared a few of my clients with him. He was a really good guy, and taught me a lot about money management. I was thrilled when, at Dean's recommendation, the Manager of RBC Dominion Securities invited me to lunch, and asked if I would be interested in joining their group.

I think he pursued me for three reasons. They needed more women in their fold; they wanted access to my considerable client base; and they knew that I was able to acquire clients and maintain excellent relations with them. I took a huge risk because, for the first six months while I obtained my accreditation, my salary was minimal. My hope was that, because of the clients I could bring with me, I would make up for it in commission income.

This career path was one I had always nursed an interest in pursuing. I knew in my heart that I was up for the challenge, and realized that it was a once-in-a-lifetime opportunity. So, in April of 1997, at the age of forty-one, I took the plunge. I left the safe and secure haven of the Bank for a brand new career in wealth management.

My six months of training, including six weeks in Toronto in the heat of the summer, were gruelling, and the learning curve was precipitous. The exams I wrote to obtain my licence as an investment advisor were the toughest I had ever encountered.

The prize was membership in the Canadian Securities Institute, and acquisition of the coveted licence. On my first day as a full-fledged associate, a client gave me (Can) $1,000,000 to invest. During my first six months, I was honoured that many of my RBC clients entrusted me with their funds, and, as a result of their confidence in me, I did extremely well.

Another prize I won by joining RBC Dominion was my priceless friendship with Jerri Hass. When I arrived at my new office, the ratio of male to female associates was about thirty to eight. Jerri was one of the few other females, and she was most generous in showing me the ropes.

Jerri and I soon discovered that we were both addicted to retail therapy, and were two of the best bargain hunters ever. We were joined at the hip in our shopping expeditions. On one occasion, in San Francisco, I wanted to explore Fisherman's Wharf while Jerri was keen to visit the Union Square shops. We reluctantly agreed to part, and meet later for lunch. But, sometime before the time of our rendezvous, I walked into a store, and found Jerri at the same counter for which I had headed. Our connection was obviously not severable.

Another thing we have in common is that Jerri comes from a large family. She is the fourteenth of twenty children so she has always been completely at ease with my family. Jerri's and my close relationship continues, and we often shop, travel, golf, explore art galleries, and lunch together. Because we have worked in the business world for so many years, and were once in the same industry, we are fortunate to be able to "talk shop" and shop at the same time.

I loved every aspect of my work at Dominion Securities, and, as with the Bank, I expected to remain there until death or retirement. Then, the volatile, flamboyant, quick-tempered, magnetic, and surpassingly generous David McLean gusted into my office with the force of the tornado I had experienced in the Bahamas.

Moving and Shaking with The McLean Group

Earlier that morning, in October of 1999, I was walking down Burrard Street when I bumped into a homeless man that my friend, Jan, and I had befriended. I gave him a bit of money but he looked hungry. So, I dug into my bag, and gave him an apple and a banana. He said that it had been a long time since he'd seen fresh fruit. I continued on my way, and, just as I was entering Park Place, where I worked, I experienced an overwhelming sense, as I had several times before in my life, that something momentous was about to happen. I shrugged it off, and forgot about it until 10 a.m. when my telephone rang.

David McLean was on the line, and announced that he would like to drop by about 11 a.m. to talk to me. Naturally, I said that would be delightful but, inwardly, my "fight or flight " response kicked in immediately.

David had been my client for many years, and had never before come to my office. I had always met with him at his office.

David became a client when I was with the Royal Bank, and I always enjoyed assisting him because he was such a results-oriented person. He never presented me with a financial problem but always with a financial need and a workable solution. As well, he was most generous in referring other clients to me.

For the next hour, I was on tenterhooks wondering whether he was going to pull his accounts or tell me that other investors he had referred were going to pull theirs. Never could I have imagined the real purpose of his visit.

When he arrived, we chatted for a few minutes, and he apprised me of what was happening with his proposed film studios. I was outwardly calm but sweating bullets when he came to the point of our meeting. He and his family had talked, and had agreed that they wanted me to join The McLean Group of Companies to oversee leasing for *The Landing*, their head office building, and to assist them with financing for the film studios. David was aware of my background in real estate financing.

I felt like a mosquito felled by an elephant gun. I stammered that his offer was a lot to absorb, and that I was beyond flattered but would need to think about it. David asked me to meet with him and his wife, Brenda, at the end of the day. I met with David, Brenda, and their son, Sasha, in David's office, overlooking Burrard Inlet, and they outlined the job proposal. They let me know that they needed a quick decision as they wanted me to start on November 1. David suggested that we lunch together the next day.

I spent an agonizing and sleepless night weighing all the pros and cons—my love for my new investment management career; my loyalty to RBC Dominion which had been so welcoming and good to me; my allegiance to my clients, so many of whom were dear friends; fear of the unknown; the vagaries of private enterprise; and a concern that if the new job didn't work out I would have a reputation as a bit of a professional vagabond. On the other side of the ledger, the opportunity David and Brenda were offering me was without parallel. I would be able to put to use everything I had ever learned, even my experiences as a child observing Bapa conduct business in his factory. Finally, I thought about what advice Bapa would have given me, and I knew that he would say, "go for it."

I ended my tenure with RBC Dominion by calling each and every one of my clients to tell them my plans, and to refer them to my colleagues, Jeff Lunter and Dean Williams, in both of whom I had full confidence. Those calls were wrenching, and I was so grateful that most of my clients were understanding and happy for me. Many of them have remained friends.

So began my third career with The McLean Group. David McLean is a force of nature. He was a successful Vancouver lawyer before becoming a private enterprise entrepreneur. His achievements are considerable, and include several honourary doctorates of law; the Order of British Columbia; Chairmanship of the Board of Directors of CN Railway, the Vancouver Board of Trade, the Canadian Chamber of Commerce, Concord Pacific Group, and the Board of Governors of the University of British Columbia; and dozens of other business, charitable, and community honours and endeavours.

Brenda McLean is an accomplished woman whom I admire tremendously. She holds a degree in art history, and, among her many accomplishments, has served as a director of the Vancouver Art Gallery, the Vancouver Hospital & Health Sciences Centre, and the Queen's University Council. She plays a significant role in the company business, and is active in community education and health issues.

When I joined The Mclean Group, it was a major player in the Vancouver commercial and residential real estate markets including acquiring, developing, leasing, and managing properties. Among other things, it owned a large bank of industrial land on which it wished to build, lease, and manage film studios, and I was to play a key role in achieving those goals.

One of the perks of a financial career was the opportunity to learn so much about so many things, and that was certainly the case with the film studios. Although I was not involved in all aspects, I was usually at David's side, and I was like a sponge, soaking up all the knowledge I could. For example, David and I, together with some of his other associates, flew to Los Angeles to inspect some studios, to find out what was unique about them, and to pick up tips on how to construct them. We learned, for instance, that no noise at all can be permitted to penetrate the sound barrier between the outside and inside of a studio, and the ceilings must be at least 18.29 metres high. Who knew?

I was not, of course, involved in the actual construction. My mandate was to arrange the construction financing, to supervise construction draws, and, as it was a syndicated project, to give investors timely updates on the progress of the project.

Another of my responsibilities was to lease out the approximately 16,258 square metres of retail and office space in The Landing. It was a building constructed in about 1900 as a supply depot for miners heading for the gold rush. The McLean Group had repaired, reconstructed, and renovated it to an elegant standard, and its location in Vancouver's Gastown on the edge of the harbour was enticing to prospective tenants.

David and Brenda were remarkably generous employers. When David bumped a vacation I was planning, he and Brenda, to atone, treated me and a friend of my choosing to a stay at the famous Villa Delia Hotel and Tuscany Cooking School in Italy.

Owned by the Umberto Menghi family, the hotel is a rural sanctuary on a large estate in the Tuscan countryside noted for its gentle green hills, olive groves, vineyards, wineries, medieval villages, and ancient farms. Even though I have never been noted for my cooking skills, I was delighted at the opportunity to visit this renowned vacation retreat.

I invited my friend, Frenny Bawa, to accompany me. Frenny and her family came originally from a small town in Uganda but I met her when she worked at RBC for a short time after receiving her Master of Business Administration from McGill University.

When I asked Frenny if she'd like to come with me to Tuscany, she told me not to dare ask anyone else, and that her contribution to the trip would be two business class tickets she could obtain on points. That worked for me.

Umberto's sister and her husband ran the villa and cooking school. Frenny was a good cook already, and attended all the classes, where they taught us to make pasta, sauces, broths, Tuscan bread, biscotti, and delectable desserts. I skipped several classes, and the day we were to learn how to make pasta from dough found me exploring Chianti country. Ma would have been so ashamed.

We didn't eat what we cooked. Rather, the chefs at the villa prepared elaborate five or six course meals for us. In the evenings, we sat in the Villa's charming courtyard drinking wine and enjoying the camaraderie of our fellow guests.

Three such guests were Peter D'Souza, a Goan who had been the British Airways agent in Kampala, and who lived in Vancouver, his wife, Rita, and their daughter, Amber. I had not met Peter before but in another one of those "small world" moments, he turned out to be a good friend of my brother, Bahadur.

Our hosts had organized a trip to the annual summer opera festival in Lucca, the birthplace of the Italian composer, Giacomo Puccini, and we took in two of his operas. I'm not an opera fan, by any means, but I couldn't miss the chance to be able to casually name drop my visit to the Puccini Festival in Italy. Rita, Amber, and I took another side trip to the town of San Gimignano to browse through an antique book selling fair.

One of my oddest vacation vignettes occurred on a Sunday morning when Frenny and I accompanied our cooking school mates to services in a tiny Catholic church in the local village.

My purchase of a painting in a small art gallery in the Tuscan hill town of Siena presaged another oddity. The painting was an original but the painter had created several identical originals. A few years later, I was at Jerri Hass's home, and hanging on her living room wall was the same painting which she had purchased in the same gallery a few years earlier. That was freaky.

At the villa, we met a young "dot.com" millionaire from California and his mother. He was hilarious, and we became instant friends. Frenny and I mentioned that we were booked on a train to Milan after school ended, and he said that his mother would like to go as well. He promptly hired a Mercedes SUV and a driver, and we travelled to Milan in style. He went so far as to cancel our hotel reservations, and to re-book us into a luxury suite at the Four Seasons Hotel. At that point, though, we balked, and, though we stayed in the suite, we insisted on paying for it ourselves. We hung out in Milan for a few days, and then finished our vacation in Florence before heading back to Vancouver and work.

By the summer of 2003, I decided to depart from The McLean Group. Exhaustion had overtaken me, and I was facing a hysterectomy operation. I felt that I had given my all to the company, and had little more to contribute.

I don't regret for one moment joining The McLean Group. The business know-how I acquired, the fascinating people I met, and the generosity of David and Brenda will remain with me always. Neither, though, do I regret leaving. It was time to go, and, had I remained, I would have missed all the fresh experiences that awaited me, beginning with a trip to India and Dubai.

CHAPTER TWENTY-SEVEN

More Travels, More Career Twists,

and More Personal Tragedy

India and Dubai—The Perfect Remedy

After expulsion, Dr. Thakkar, our Jinja physician, and his wife, Rama, returned to India where they owned a residence in Mumbai. After a time, they settled in Kent, England where Dr. Thakkar continued to practise medicine. Now retired, and in their eighties, they live in Stanmore in northwest London. Their daughter, Chinchu, lives with them. Their other daughter, Shefali, followed in her mother's steps by marrying a physician, and they live in California.

In August of 2003, Dr. and Mrs. Thakkar visited us at our home in Burnaby. On their return to London, Rama kindly called me several times to enquire how I was doing after my hysterectomy. In October, she announced that she was on her way to Mumbai where they spent every winter. She suggested that I come for a visit, and that she would invite her daughter, Chinchu, to come as well.

Never one to turn down a trip anywhere, I conscripted Zebby to accompany me, and, in December, off we trekked through Mumbai, Dubai, Delhi, Agra, Cochin, Goa, and Muscat. Some of these sites I'll describe later on but I'll mention a few highlights here.

Before we left home, we had decided to visit Dubai to spend some time with our cousin, Sherbanu, sister of Noorali, who lived there. Then we learned that Aga Khan IV would be in Dubai on December 13, his birthday, to lay the foundation for an Ismaili Jamatkhana.

We hit a snag, though, because Ismailis from around the world were congregating in Dubai, and, when we reached Mumbai, Air India informed us that no tickets were available to fly to Dubai. Disappointment clouded our morning but, when we told Rama of our problem, she flew into action. She made one telephone call to a friend who had Air India connections, and invited him to lunch. Within a few hours after the luncheon, we had tickets in hand.

In Dubai, Sherbanu had managed to reserve a hotel room for us and lent us a car and driver to escort us wherever we wanted to go. We spent two energy packed weeks there.

We met all kinds of interesting people from different countries. Rustam's sister, Noorjahan, and her daughter, Shenin, were in Dubai for the momentous event as were several cousins from both Kenya and Canada. We did not witness the actual foundation laying ceremony but, along with a massive crowd of other Ismailis, joined in a two day celebration in spacious tents set up with all the amenities. On the second day, the Aga Khan honoured all Ismailis with an audience.

Zebby and I had the opportunity to participate in one of Dubai's spectacular desert safaris. A Land Rover, fitted with a roll cage to protect the passengers, took us on a roller coaster ride far into the sand dunes. It was quite the joyride, similar to sailing on a stormy ocean, and we were lucky not to get seasick.

Our destination was a desert camp. Just as we arrived a wild sand storm blew up, and we spent days afterward combing sand out of our hair. Traditional Bedouin tents sprawled through the campsite. Our hosts and servers, in conventional Arab clothing, greeted us warmly, and made us feel welcome. A procession of richly decorated camels also met us. We declined the opportunity to ride on a camel as I had "been there, done that" many years before in Karachi and then in Kenya.

After drinking in the flaring sunset, we relaxed in a tent on low cushions, and partook of an authentic Arabian barbeque and buffet dinner, gagged on thick and bitter Arabic coffee, and munched on fresh dates. Inside the tent, belly dancers swayed to oriental music around a campfire, and Zebby had her hands adorned with henna.

We didn't think anything could match our desert safari but our luxurious three night cruise, a few days later, through the lush tropical backwaters of Kerala, in western India, came close. We had travelled to Cochin where we boarded the Oberoi motor vessel *MV Vrinda*.

The *MV Vrinda* is a small elegant boat with seven cabins featuring floating sinks. Its owner had just launched the service, and I believe we were among the second set of passengers. Prince Michael of Kent was among the first group. Rama had secured our tickets for a song. A few years later, when I tried to book passage for my friends and me, the cost was far beyond the reach of our pocket books.

We drifted along serenely, winding through canals and lakes. About 5 a.m. each morning we relaxed on the boat's veranda, drank masala chai, idly observed the fishing boats embarking on the water, and watched the orange sunrise behind a row of palm trees. Each evening, we watched the equally glorious pink and mauve sunset from the roof top deck.

I celebrated my birthday on the vessel. The crew was extremely gracious, and the cook asked Zebby what kind of cake I would like. Zebby responded that I wasn't too fond of cake but would love an Indian sweet. The cook arranged for delivery of both the sweet and a birthday cake from the mainland in time for my birthday dinner.

The last highlight of this journey was the opportunity to attend the lavish Hindu wedding of a famous movie star's relative. Indians dress incredibly well for weddings so Zebby and I simply had no choice but to buy new finery for the occasion. The party continued for four days, and I saw and met many Bollywood actors. I was simply agog at the rich diversity of food, clothing, and jewellery, and had great fun people watching.

Nazlin, Rama Thakkar, Chinchu and Zebby In Mumbai

Career Shake-ups

By the summer of 2004, my sabbatical had lasted almost a year. During that time, I had recovered from surgery, travelled to India and Dubai, hot-footed it off to Geneva when Shenaz called me for support after separating from her husband, golfed till I dropped, and considered taking a position under the auspices of the Aga Khan Foundation.

AKFED was a majority shareholder in Roshan, a leading telecommunications company in Afghanistan based in Kabul. I received a provisional offer to manage a sales force operation for Roshan but first had to travel to Kabul to see if the job and living conditions would suit me.

Their understandable rationale was that hiring and re-locating me would be an expensive proposition if I decided to back out as soon as I arrived. I knew that the lifestyle would be quite different. For instance, I'd be living in a hostel for ladies, and would not have the freedom to move around on my own.

Regrettably, I never had the chance to explore the opportunity because Ma put her foot down. Even she had heard of the Taliban. The days when Ma could give me orders were long gone but, as obstinate as she was, I had too much love and respect for her, especially at her age of eighty-four, to cause her any grief or anxiety.

In August, my friend, Margaret, invited Lynn Ramsay, a senior partner with the national law firm of Miller Thomson, and me over to her home for a barbeque. We were relaxing on the deck, looking out over the garden, and munching on burgers, when Margaret and Lynn jolted my conscience by telling me it was time to get back to work. We brainstormed a few ideas, and Lynn suggested that her client, Wolfgang Duntz, the President of Bowen Island Properties Ltd., might be able to use my talents.

Lynn was not one to let the grass grow. Two days later, she and I set sail on the twenty minute ferry ride across Howe Sound from Horseshoe Bay to Snug Cove on Bowen Island. We met with Wolfgang who admitted that he needed a consultant. I signed a three month contract, and started work the following week.

The three month engagement turned into six months. I found the unique perspective of participating in development on a small island fascinating. But the help I could offer began to peter out, and I found the daily commute from Burnaby to Bowen Island fairly taxing. Wolfgang and I parted on good terms, and I still lunch occasionally with him and his lovely wife, Hedda.

I didn't lack employment for long. When I left on sabbatical, I had registered with a head-hunter. In March of 2005, I received a telephone call out of the blue. Weiler Smith Bowers, a structural engineering firm in Burnaby, was looking for a chief operating officer.

I knew Gerry Weiler. When I was with The McLean Group, he had worked on the structural design of the film studios. Gerry had built his reputation in connection with the construction of big box stores. He employed a unique tilt-up construction design where the builder put up three walls, and then tilted up the fourth cement wall by crane.

When Gerry learned that I was interested in the job, he agreed to interview me, I met the other partners, and received a job offer. I was essentially a jack-of-all-trades. I managed human resources; kept track of the financial picture; handled all equipment purchases; undertook office upgrades; and generally supervised office operations.

At first, working outside the Downtown Vancouver core was a refreshing change, particularly as my commute was only about ten minutes by car. Ultimately, though, boredom set in, and I found I missed the hustle and bustle of downtown life. After five years, I called it a day, and left the firm on good terms with everyone.

Dear Ma's Death

During the last several years of Ma's life, my friend, Susan Jaffe, was a welcome addition to our family. As with so many of my friends, Susan originated as a client. I brought her home for dinner one evening, and she and Ma discovered that they were kindred spirits. We dubbed Susan Ma's official sitter, and the two of them spent many evenings together. Because they enjoyed one another's company so much, they managed to overcome the language barrier. That plus the fact that we all suspected Ma understood a lot more English than she ever let on.

Except for chronic high blood pressure and, during her later years, dreadful boils on one leg, Ma never had many real medical problems. She often complained that her legs hurt but her unsympathetic family attributed her grousing to the fact that she never exercised or walked anywhere.

Nonetheless, Ma had the habit of visiting doctors all the time, complaining about a myriad of ailments. Their uniform response was to placate her by handing out what amounted to a pharmacopoeia of prescription drugs. Finally, one specialist Ma saw cottoned on to the problem, and actually hospitalized her to clean the drugs out of her system.

In Ma's early eighties, though, she began to decline visibly. I'm sure it was simply old age. My bedroom was next to hers, and my habit was to sleep with one eye open so I'd know if she was in difficulty. One night, I heard her get up to go the bathroom, followed by a dull thud. I raced into her bedroom, and found her marooned, partially on the bed and partially on the floor. She was not coherent. I screamed for help but it took a few minutes for Bahadur and Zubeda to respond. We managed to hoist her onto the edge of the bed, and then we called for an ambulance. Bahadur and Zubeda accompanied her to the hospital.

Zubeda phoned before Almas and I left for work to report that Ma had suffered a stroke but was still in the Burnaby General emergency room as no beds were available. Later in the morning, Zubeda called again to tell us that Ma had been hospitalized but was doing poorly. As we did with Bapa, our family converged in the hospital waiting area. A young physician, who happened to be a friend of Shalina and Narmin, advised us that Ma's stroke was massive, and that her heart was slowing down. They would keep her comfortable but it was only a matter of time before she passed.

We all filed quietly into Ma's room and stood around her bed, reciting prayers and chants, another Muslim tradition, to help the soul leave the body in peace. Ma's grand-daughter, Narmin, was the apple of her eye. She called Narmin her "diamond." We told Ma that Narmin was coming on the next flight from North Bay, and I believe that she tried to hold on but she couldn't quite make it. Narmin arrived within an hour of Ma's death. She drew her last breath on November 4, 2005.

We held the traditional ceremony for Ma at the Burnaby Lake Jamatkhana. We covered Ma's white cloth draped body with the saree she wore to Shalina's wedding. In the last few years of Ma's life, she looked frail and old but, in death, the years fell away, and she looked surprisingly good. Zebby, Almas, and I broke with ritual, and touched her. One of us even kissed her dear face. We just couldn't bear to let her go.

My niece, Natasha, was the only one of us composed enough to speak, and she recited a verse from the Qur'an. As was customary, the men in the family accompanied Ma's body to the Forest Lawn Cemetery for interment near her husband Mohamed and Fatima, the grandbaby she never met. We held the post-funeral luncheon at a Jehovah Witness hall.

Our religion calls for us to observe a forty day mourning period so we went to the Jamatkhana each evening to meditate and to pray for the peace of Ma's soul. The meditation and prayer helped us to deal with our loss.

We Muslims believe that the body is temporary and the soul eternal. Accordingly, reincarnation is not part of our faith. And yet, one of us comments, each time we see Shalina and Mahmood's sweet, sweet daughter, Marissa Jena, that, in looks and temperament, she is Ma. I know it's just genetics, and Marissa is her own wonderful person, but I find it comforting, once in a long while, to imagine otherwise.

After Ma's death, by family consensus, my sister-in-law, Zubeda, received Ma's prized diamond earrings because she had taken such loving care of Ma and Bapa in their later years. My niece, Shalina, was the recipient of Ma's inexpensive but equally treasured wedding band. A few years prior to her death, with encouragement from my siblings and me, Ma bequeathed her substantial jewellery collection to our family members.

The Last Station of my Peripatetic Career

Gowlings, a well-known and well-respected national law firm, that has existed for more than a century, was searching for a human resources manager for its Downtown Vancouver office. A friend of mine who, was a head-hunter, thought this position would be perfect for me.

So, I am now well into yet another career as human resources manager to the Vancouver branch of a law firm comprised of more than 700 legal professionals Canada-wide. In our office alone, we have about seventy lawyers and a hundred staff members. My job is a huge challenge but I absolutely love it.

CHAPTER TWENTY-EIGHT

I've Been Everywhere, Man

India the Third Time Around

In 2007, some of my Kenyan safari buddies decided that I should escort them on yet another trip of a lifetime—this time to India. The travelling circus included Anne Lippert and her husband, Wolfgang; Allison Tucker and her husband, Bill; Cathy Smith; and myself. To the immense disappointment of Erica, Joan, and Marilyn, they were unable to join us.

We spent several months planning the trip and obtaining visas. We braved inoculations for yellow fever, cholera, tetanus, typhoid, dengue fever, and meningitis; and swallowed malaria tablets daily.

On October 17, 2007, we began our journey by flying to London. Our ten hour stop-over at Heathrow was a joy for me as Maira, my old friend from Jinja, worked at Heathrow Airport for Jet Airways. Since expulsion, Maira and I had seen each other only twice. When I was leaving for Canada in 1973, she came to the airport to see me off, and, on one of my trips to Guernsey, in 1995, we had dinner together at Heathrow.

The airport was in the process of opening Terminal 5, and chaos reigned including a plethora of problems involving luggage transfers. Maira, though, had arranged for her fellow employees to make sure our luggage arrived, and to transfer it safely to the British Airways plane bound for India.

I introduced my friends to Maira during dinner at Heathrow, and then they trooped off to shop so that Maira and I could visit. We spent two hours hugging and catching up. Maira, predictably, bawled her eyes out which led us to reminisce about our parting in Jinja when she had blotted her homework with copious tears.

Even though Maira's parents knew firsthand about the difficulties of an arranged marriage they had insisted that she adhere to the same tradition. Consequently, her marriage was not a happy one. Maira gave birth to three children. She named her youngest boy "Nazeesh" after me, which thrilled me no end.

Being the astute world traveller that I am, I know that liquor is frightfully expensive in India so, at the airport, we prowled the duty free store, and bought as much liquor as we could carry, and then some. Our choices included gin for Allison, Bill and me because we love our gin and tonic aperitif while travelling; Scotch for Wolfgang and Bill; Courvoisier for Anne which she had also imbibed on our Kenyan safari so many years before; and Grand Marnier as a nightcap for the rest of us. Thus fortified, "happy hour" and nightcaps became our evening ritual.

After spending nine hours travelling from Vancouver to London, enduring a ten hour lay-over at Heathrow, and flying a further eight hours to Mumbai, exhaustion was wearing us down. Upon arrival in Mumbai, our van and driver were waiting for us at the airport. Although the distance to the hotel was only about twenty-five kilometres, traffic was chaotic, the drive took forever, and the heat was searing. Passing by the filthy Azadnagar slum which we had been able to smell as soon as we exited the aircraft was heartrending. The grimy streets were a crazed patchwork of honking cars, lorries, scooters, bicycles, crazy pedestrians, weaving rickshaws, meandering cows, and stray dogs.

Our destination, the Taj Mahal Palace and Tower Hotel, was a welcome sight. The original portion of this hotel opened its doors in 1903, and is one of the iridescent pearls of Mumbai. Located on Marine Drive, lined with palm trees, it commands a dazzling vista that includes the Gateway of India and the Arabian Sea.

The hotel is a panoply of elegance, displaying Moorish, Oriental, Florentine, and Indian influences; carpets of hand woven silk; columns of onyx; chandeliers of brilliant multi-faceted crystal; vaulted ceilings of alabaster; and a priceless array of international artwork and antiques. A myriad of distinguished guests, ranging from the Beatles, Mick Jagger and Deep Purple to the Duke of Edinburgh, the Prince of Wales, Jacquie Onassis and Bill Clinton, have stayed at the hotel. About the same time as our visit, Brad Pitt and Angelina Jolie occupied the Presidential Wing. All of the staff dress in authentic Indian garb, speak excellent English, and are gracious to a fault. We stayed in the newer tower of the hotel, with a view of the Mumbai harbour. Before departing Mumbai, the front desk staff permitted us an escorted tour of the Presidential Wing located in the original part of the hotel.

Tragically, exactly one year after our visit, Mumbai suffered three days of terrorist attacks; gunmen stormed the hotel, took hostages, and barricaded themselves inside. As a result, the hotel suffered substantial damage.

On arrival at the hotel, the expressions on the faces of my friends were priceless. I was acclimated as I had stayed there on my earlier Asian trip but I don't think any of them had ever seen such opulence. Being worn out, we spent a quiet afternoon eating, swimming, and relaxing by the pool. I was itching to check out the shops, and Anne and I ventured out on a reconnoitring trek beyond the hotel grounds.

Refreshed and eager after a good night's rest, I left the lobby to look for our van. "Lippert" being the last name of Anne and Wolfgang and the first in our alphabet of names, I saw a tour guide holding up a board that read "Lispert." For some reason, I found this sign hysterically funny, and when the rest of the group emerged from the hotel, they found me doubled over with tears pouring down my face. They thought I'd gone nuts until they saw the reason, and they all laughed. Wolfgang made the mistake of telling us that some of his staff at work referred to him as "Oolang," and hence we have called him that ever since.

On our first day in Mumbai, we explored as many of the attractions as we possibly could. One highlight was the Hanging Gardens terraced on a hillside slope overlooking the Arabian Sea, which featured hedges pruned into the shapes of fantastical animals.

Our next stop was the Mahatma Gandhi House Museum where Gandhi himself lived for several years. I was interested to learn that Gandhi's birthplace was in the Gujarat, the state from which my parents and grandparents hailed, and that the house reflected Gujarati architecture.

After leaving the Museum, we trekked to several grand Victorian and Gothic edifices, infused with Indian styling, built in the late nineteenth century during the zenith of British imperialism. Crawford Market, completed in 1869, both fascinated and repelled me. It is a massive structure that includes a clock tower, replete with handsome Victorian carvings, a striking frieze over the main entrance that portrays Indian peasants toiling in wheat fields, and an indoor stone fountain designed by the father of Rudyard Kipling. The bazaar-like atmosphere boils with people and vendors who sell fruits, vegetables, meat, poultry, cheese, chocolates, textiles, cosmetics, jewellery, turtles, guinea pigs, parrots, puppies, and anything else one could possibly imagine.

We took endless photographs of ourselves in front of the Gateway of India at Mumbai Harbour. Built in the sixteenth century and decorated with elaborate turrets and carvings, the arched gate is a splendid monument, constructed of yellow basalt and reinforced concrete. Its design reflects both Hindu and Muslim architectural styles. It is a triumphal entrance to Mumbai from the water but, ironically, behind the gate is a cacophony of beggars seeking alms from tourists.

Late in the afternoon, at the prestigious Nehru Planetarium, Cathy suddenly felt nauseous, and, to her dire embarrassment, promptly puked all over the van. We hurried back to the hotel, left the driver to clean up the mess, and sent Cathy to bed. The next day, she was fine but poor Wolfgang was feeling quite sick. Picking up bugs in foreign countries is pretty routine, and I'm lucky that no one has ever become seriously ill while travelling with me.

After an invigorating early morning swim, we headed off by ferry to Elephanta Island which is home to the labyrinthine Elephanta Caves. They consist of a series of ancient caverns, dating from perhaps the seventh century, carved from basalt rock formations, and filled with sculpted statues of Hindu deities and Buddhist shrines.

The island is a sanctuary to hordes of monkeys who scurry about, and don't hesitate to harass tourists for food. Anne seems to be a magnet for animals. Back at the Treetops Hotel in Kenya an elephant had shocked her by peering at her from across the salt lick when she was starkers. This time, a pesky monkey grabbed a box of hand wipes right out of her purse, climbed a tree, found upon investigation that they were not edible, and in a pique, threw them into a rock crevice. An elderly man took a lot of trouble to retrieve the box for Anne but she didn't want to accept a mangled box that a monkey had manhandled.

The following day, saw us reluctantly leave Mumbai, and fly to Kochi, formerly called Cochin, a lively city in the State of Kerala. Kochi lies on the southwest coast of India overlooking the Arabian Sea close to the junction with the Indian Ocean. The history of Kochi is compelling. At one time, it was a significant centre for the Indian spice trade. Through the centuries, Portuguese, Dutch, British, Chinese, and Arab explorers and traders have influenced its history, and exploited its resources.

In the sixteenth and seventeenth centuries, the Portuguese occupied Kochi for about 160 years. We visited St. Francis Church, originally built in 1503, where we viewed the first burial spot of Vasco da Gama. His remains were later transported back to Portugal.

Our further exploration of Kochi took us to the Mattancherry Synagogue, first built in 1568, and the oldest Hebrew temple in India. The interior of this synagogue has a floor inlaid with hand-painted blue willow Chinese tiles that artisans added in the eighteenth century, a spectacular Belgian chandelier, and huge scrolls of the Old Testament. We learned that the Jews of Kochi suffered mightily at the hands of the Portuguese, who ruled Kochi at the time of the Inquisition.

Another "wow" moment for all of us was the sight of gigantic Chinese fishing nets suspended in the harbour. Outside of China, they are unique to Kochi, probably introduced by Oriental traders centuries ago. They are affixed on the shore, and their operation is ingenious. Every few minutes, they descend into the sea, and then a team of fishermen raise them by tugging on a system of rope pulleys. Although the nets are huge, each lowering into the sea reaps only a few fish and crustaceans. The fun part, though, is that passersby purchase them within moments, and, if they choose, hand them to nearby street vendors to cook on the spot.

Chinese fishing nets in Kerala

Speaking of street vendors, western India is famous for *bhel-puri*, a mouth-watering snack, which they sell from street stands. Freshly made every day, and served cold, bhel-puri ingredients include puffed rice, cubed potatoes, tamarind sauce, roasted peanuts, finely chopped onions and tomatoes, green chillies, coriander, and chutney. While we did not partake in the offerings of the street vendors for fear of developing "Delhi-Belly," none of us had any concerns about eating all our meals at the various hotels and resorts which offer both Indian and Western dishes on their expansive menus.

Anne was the only one of us who didn't eat Indian food. The rest of us gorged ourselves all day every day, and imbibed copious amounts of hot and sweet masala chai.

Ayurvedic therapy is a form of traditional or alternative medicine that originated in India, and Kerala is the ayurvedic capital of the world. So, back at our hotel, the Taj Malabar, we luxuriated in some ayurvedic treatments.

After a good night's rest, we commenced upon a four hour drive to Thekkady along a captivating road that passed through serene country landscapes, luxuriant green spice plantations, and impenetrable jungles. Our hotel was the Taj Garden Retreat where we stayed in well-appointed thatch-roofed cottages on an estate that cultivated coffee, spices, and fruit trees.

Although the hotel featured an ayurvedic spa, our guide suggested that he take us into town for therapy from the locals. We did so, and received the most miraculous treatment. The therapist drenched us in oils, then placed us in ovens, with only our heads sticking out, and baked us in extreme heat. It was remarkably soothing.

Never one to ignore my shopping fetish, I found a street of small shops in Thekkady where I bought pendants for my niece, Farha, and me. Inside each pendant was a tiny scroll with verses from the Qur'an.

After our stay at Thekkady, another four hour drive brought us to Munar, where I was able to fulfill a childhood dream. Back in Jinja, we used to watch Indian movies at the Odeon Cinema, and the clips of the sprawling tea plantations of Munar, the tea capital of western India, entranced me. I had always hoped one day to visit them.

Winding our way up into the mountain range known as the Western Ghats, we passed massive working tea estates dressed in green foliage. Men and women, clad in colourful Indian outfits, could be seen busily picking tea from bushes by hand. The sight of women carrying large bundles of tea on their heads, against the backdrop of lush green tea bushes, was a humbling sight. On arrival at the hill station in Munar, we settled into deluxe villas at the Windermere Estate which produced cardamom, coffee, and vanilla as well as tea. Being a tea region, rain is plentiful, and the shrouded and misty greenery is surreal.

Garden paths meander among the villas. In the centre of the gardens was a tiny hut with bar stools where, in the best British tradition, we sampled tea, cookies, and crumpets. After dinner, we gathered in the Lippert suite where we indulged in our dwindling liquor supply, having already polished off a bottle each of gin, Courvoisier, and Grand Marnier.

On our way back to Kochi, we spent a few unforgettable hours exploring the placid azure backwaters of Kerala. They consist of complex interconnections of rivers, lakes, canals, lagoons, and estuaries that empty into the Arabian Sea.

A cruise on a traditional houseboat with an arched roof, took us past swaying palm trees; lush overhanging vegetation; small villages; women washing their long hair in the water; fishermen in long, narrow canoe-like vessels; and workers loading coconut meat, cashews, and other produce onto boats.

Cruising the backwaters of Kerala in a houseboat
(L – R) Anne, Nazlin, Cathy, Bill and Allison

After this quaint excursion, we flew to Delhi, the capital of India, and stayed at the gorgeous Taj Palace Hotel. There, we ran into a slight snag. The hotel had "lost" our reservations, and wanted to accommodate us in another hotel. I refused so the staff treated us to a complimentary lunch while they sorted out the mess. In the end, they gave us three excellent rooms on the executive floor.

Downtown shopping was our first order of business. We began by exploring some of Delhi's finest jewellery stores, and then went hunting for pashmina shawls. These exquisite shawls are hand spun and woven of fibre from cashmere goats, sometimes mixed with silk. The authentic article is so fine it is possible to thread it through a ring. I have dozens of them, some of which were Ma's.

A continuous problem I faced with Wolfgang was his propensity to tip everyone. Tipping and handing out money is a slippery slope. Pimps send women and children out to beg, and, if we gave money to even one of them, a slew of beggars would have swarmed us.

While walking down the street, a man with a shoe cleaning kit cornered Wolfgang, and asked to clean his shoes. As per my instructions, Wolfgang said he didn't need his shoes cleaned to which the man replied, "But sir, you do." Wolfgang looked down, and saw that bird droppings covered his vamps. So, he succumbed to the shoe shiner's ministrations. Afterward, I disillusioned poor, innocent Wolfgang by explaining that the man had undoubtedly spread the droppings himself.

We returned to the hotel and congregated in the bar, expecting to dine with my friend, Miriam Webber. Miriam was spending two months doing charitable work in Delhi. She was excited to see some friends from home, and was terribly disappointed when she arrived to find that, because of the earlier reservation mix-up, the hotel had no record of us. While she was searching for us, we were within several metres of one another, but we never made contact. A short time after that, and unknown to us, Miriam contracted dengue hemorrhagic fever, a life-threatening illness. Luckily, she recovered, and her husband, Phil Webber, another good friend of mine, came to India to escort her home.

The high spot of Delhi for me was the *Jama Masjid* (place of worship for followers of Islam) in Old Delhi. Completed in 1656, it is probably the best-known Masjid in India, and its courtyard can accommodate up to 25,000 faithful worshippers.

Our next destination was Agra. On the way, I insisted on a pit stop for lunch at the ubiquitous McDonald's so that I could satisfy my craving for yet another of my all-time favourite foods. McDonald's paneer wrap is a fried Indian cheese wrapped in flatbread and topped with a salad, mayonnaise, salsa, and cheddar cheese. It is delectable. I was able to convert Allison and Cathy but not Anne.

In Agra, we settled in at the Oberoi Amarvillas where almost every room has a commanding view of the Taj Mahal. Agra is an ancient and charming town noted for its red sandstone and white marble buildings. While there, we meet two famous Bollywood movie stars, Ashwarya Rai and her husband, Abhishek Buchan, in the elevator.

Agra's main claim to fame is the Taj Mahal. Constructed entirely of white marble in the seventeenth century, by the Mughal emperor, Shah Jahan, in memory of his deceased wife, Mumtaz Mahal, the majesty and architectural elegance of the Taj Mahal is indescribable.

Front row (L – R): Allison, Nazlin, Anne;
Second row (L – R): Bill, Cathy, Wolfgang—at the Taj Mahal

We also visited factories to watch the hand weaving of silk rugs, on which one family may work for up to a year, and the carving by artisans of intricate designs in marble furniture. Allison and Bill bought a cream marble end table which the seller had them sign on the back for identification when they received it in Vancouver.

I fell in love with a black marble octagon shaped dining table with elephants emblazoned in the marble. Although I consider myself a seasoned barterer, I could not negotiate a price reduction so I got fed up and left. I still regret leaving my table behind.

The next morning, one of us mentioned to a server at breakfast that we were travelling by road to our next destination, Jaipur. Typical of the attentive service in Indian hotels, when we reached the lobby, the desk provided us with a care package containing our lunch.

In exotic Jaipur, known as the "Pink City," for its painted pink buildings, the Oberoi Rajvilas was our headquarters. It is a gem of an hotel surrounded by a moat where every few suites have their own private swimming pools, and many of the rooms include sunken marble baths.

In the hotel grounds, rising out of a lotus pool was a tiny, eighteenth century Hindu temple where a *maharaj* (Hindu priest) conducted ceremonies. As a child in Jinja, many of my friends were Hindu, and I often visited their temples. As well, a tenet of Ismailism is an acceptance of all religions. So, on this particular evening, the day before the second anniversary of Ma's death, I stopped in, and the maharaj prayed with me. He gave me a bright orange thread over which he had prayed. I was to wear it on my wrist until it dropped off, and so I did.

For our next adventure, we were up at the crack of dawn to catch a flight to Udaipur so the hotel arranged for us to enjoy a continental breakfast in the lobby. While we were eating, we noticed two fellows, who were obviously western tourists, doing breakfast nearby, but thought nothing more of it.

In Udaipur, we embarked on a captivating boat ride across Lake Pichola to reach the Oberoi Udaivilas Hotel nearby to the Taj Lake Palace Hotel famous for the James Bond movie *Octopussy*.

On arrival, while relaxing by the swimming pool, we ran into the same two fellows from breakfast, Dino and Terry. We struck up a conversation, and soon found out they were from Vancouver. Dino is a well-known periodontist, and Terry operated an exclusive lady's apparel and jewellery store. That evening, Anne and Wolfgang hosted a wine and cheese party in their suite, and invited Dino and Terry. Afterward, a shared evening meal sealed our new friendship. Terry and Dino remain good friends.

Early in the morning, I visited a tailor to order some custom made silk pants and tunics for my sisters, my nieces, and myself. Cathy, Allison, and I served as models. Terry came with us, and insisted on alterations which accentuated the beauty of the garments. The tailors worked like crazy, and actually delivered the completed clothes to my room in the middle of the night.

Our last stop before returning to Mumbai was Goa. We stayed for four nights at the Fort Aguada Beach Resort, built on the ramparts of a sixteenth century Portuguese fort, with its own beachfront on the Arabian Sea. Life didn't get any better than that.

Back in Mumbai, we decided to stay at the Taj Lands End, located in the Juhu Beach area of Mumbai close to the airport. I knew I was almost out of time, and needed to indulge in some serious shopping. I ditched my companions, hopped into a rickshaw to hit the shops, and spent a small fortune in four hours—my personal world record.

I stormed two exclusive saree retailers. At the second one, I hooked up with two male personal shoppers who had exquisite taste. I bought dozens of sarees and other Indian outfits for my sisters and nieces. A small glitch occurred at the second store when I found my credit card blocked because I'd spent so much that Visa thought it might have been stolen. Fortunately, I had a fall-back credit card. The two attentive personal shoppers even accompanied me down the street to buy a suitcase to cart everything home. It was a perfect shopping spree.

The Taj Palace in Mumbai features some elegant boutiques. All of us girls ordered custom made outfits, and Wolfgang commissioned a silk jacket. We arranged for their delivery to the Taj Lands End, and they arrived on time but did not fit too well so we had to taxi back to the Taj Palace for rush repairs.

On our return to England, Bill, who is a Brit, showed us around his London, and we ended our sensational expedition tippling in The George, one of London's oldest standing pubs.

I wish I could introduce all my friends to the magnificence of India. I know that my words of description are in no measure adequate so I'll turn again to Mark Twain's *Following the Equator* where, well over one hundred years ago, he wrote this passage that still resonates today:

> This is indeed India! the land of dreams and romance, of fabulous wealth and fabulous poverty, of splendour and rags, of palaces and hovels, of famine and pestilence, of genii and giants and Aladdin lamps, of tigers and elephants, the cobra and the jungle, the country of a hundred nations and a hundred tongues, of a thousand religions and two million gods .... mother of history, grandmother of legend, great-grandmother of tradition... the one land that all men desire to see, and having seen once, by even a glimpse, would not give that glimpse for the shows of all the rest of the globe combined.

Travel Odds and Sods

I could fill another book with stories of my travels, by land, sea and air, with family and friends but I shall settle for mentioning just a few more brief anecdotes about my trips. Travelling with Zebby is a hoot because she has an obsession about the cleanliness of hotel bedding. As a result, she always packs an inflatable mattress along with her own sheets and pillow cases. Frankly, I'd much rather leave the suitcase space available for the loot I acquire.

On my first trip to Boston, in 1991, with some friends, Ann Lippert and I saw our first "Au Bon Pain" on the Harvard Campus. It offered good quality fast food including soups and homemade breads. Then we started seeing them everywhere. Ann and I wrote to the owner to ask about acquiring a Canadian franchise. Ann wanted the franchise for all of western Canada, and it would have cost, at that time, a few hundred thousand dollars. We went so far as to fly back to Boston to meet with the owners but, in the end, decided not to pursue the matter. We should perhaps have seized the opportunity because "Au Bon Pain" outlets are now fixtures in many parts of the world.

On our Caribbean cruise in 1994, I travelled with Susan Jaffe, her husband, Dave Woolley, Dave's son and his son's friend, Rashida, Zebby, Almas, Shalina, Narmin, Farha, Nashina, and Natasha. The kids had a super time. They all had their hair braided, and I was enormously popular because I bought them cards entitling them to as many soft drinks as they wanted. Nashina and Natasha were especially pleased because, as young teenagers, they were just discovering flirting, and were able to practise on the bartenders.

Although many of my trips are now a blur, I shall never forget being in Neuchatel, Switzerland on June 25, 2009. Shenaz, Almas and I were eating lunch at a Lebanese restaurant when we heard the news that Michael Jackson had died the day before. We were devastated as were my nieces back home.

CHAPTER TWENTY-NINE

My Ugandan-Born Nieces,

their Husbands and Offspring

Thoughts on All My Nieces

I have left the best until almost last. I can't imagine my life without my five nieces, three great-nephews, and one grand-niece. I am so proud of them all. Before I get to my Ugandan-born nieces and their offspring, I have a few things to say about all of my nieces.

Shalina, Narmin and Farha, the children of Bahadur and Zubeda, all grew up in Burnaby. Nashina and her parents, Rashida and Mansur, lived a short distance away, and Zebby and Rustam raised Natasha just a hop, skip, and a jump across the Ironworkers Memorial Bridge in North Vancouver.

My nieces all call me Naz Aunty but, because our age difference, especially with the older girls, is not that great, they treat me more like a big sister. I was supportive of them when they were growing up, and I like to think they looked to me for guidance. Shalina says that I was able to see their perspective with a "young heart." I certainly tried to inspire them to work hard, enjoy life, and become strong women.

That is not to say that I wasn't strict. Like their parents, I impressed upon them the need to excel in school, and helped them with their homework. Shalina remembers that she often asked me to read and critique her essays. However, unlike Rashida did with me, I never tweaked Shalina's ear!

It won't surprise anyone that I take credit for instilling a sense of fashion in my nieces. When they were kiddies, they played dress-up with my clothes and stiletto heels. As they grew older, I shepherded them on many shopping trips. If I taught them nothing else, I taught them about the latest trends in fashion. They accompanied me on many of the trips I've mentioned, and our ports of call over the years have included the Caribbean, Disneyland, Mexico, Boston, and New York.

My nieces are kind enough to claim that the example of my career and travel experiences inspired them, and that they benefitted from my financial advice. They are also generous in expressing gratitude for the traditional way in which our family raised them, that being the concept that it takes a village to raise a child. Of course, I was only one small person in that village. Bapa, Ma, Rashida, Mansur, Zubeda, Bahadur, Zebby, Rustam, Almas, and Nizar collectively constituted a formidable parenting force for five little girls. And that's without even mentioning the extended families of Mansur, Zubeda, and Rustam.

Shalina, Mahmood, Noah, and Marissa

Shalina obtained her Bachelor of Science degree in Biological Sciences from Simon Fraser University, received a Diploma in Dental Hygiene from Vancouver Community College, and qualified as a dental hygienist. She finds her work as a dental hygienist hugely rewarding.

Shalina met her future husband, Mahmood Ladhani, through her friend, Ronnie Bains, with whom she attended Simon Fraser. Mahmood and Ronnie's brother, Dilbir, were close friends in high school. Ronnie and her mom brought up Mahmood's name to Shalina whenever they could for about two years. They must have had a premonition. Shalina and Mahmood finally met in January of 2000.

Mahmood was born in Mengo, Uganda. He came to Canada at the age of one as a result of Idi Amin's expulsion. Once they settled in Canada, his dad, Madatali, worked two jobs, and his mom, Roshan, worked hard too, so that Mahmood could play hockey and soccer, and enjoy all the other perks of life in Canada. His parents instilled an excellent work ethic in him, as well as passing on to him the importance of family. Mahmood has two older sisters, Karima and Ashifa. Ashifa is married to Victor Valdez and they have two daughters, Alysha and Shalina.

Mahmood obtained a diploma in Financial Management from the British Columbia Institute of Technology. He also holds an Executive Master of Business Administration degree from Athabasca University. He is a Personal Banking Area Manager for BMO Bank of Montreal, and is responsible for facilitating retail banking operations.

Shalina and Mahmood shared a lot of the same interests, and rapidly became best friends as well as boyfriend and girlfriend. Shalina loves to recount that, on their first date, he took her ice skating because the sly devil knew that she couldn't skate, and that gave him an opportunity to hold her hand.

Fun and laughter filled their courtship. They were avid fans of the Vancouver Canucks hockey team and the now defunct Vancouver Grizzlies basketball team. They golfed and played softball all summer. He regularly sent flowers to Shalina at work, and he was clever enough to send flowers to Zubeda as well.

Mahmood proposed to Shalina just eleven months after they met but, being a traditional young man, he first asked for Bahadur's consent. Knowing that "11" was Shalina's favourite number, he invited her, on November 11, to the Observatory Restaurant on Grouse Mountain where they shared an intimate, romantic dinner. After dining, and despite the late hour, he insisted on taking Shalina to Ambleside Park in West Vancouver. At 11:11 p.m., he sat her down on the park bench where they had shared their first kiss, and proposed to her. As Shalina was an avid reader and belonged to various book clubs, he even thought to attach the engagement ring to a book marker.

They married on September 2, 2001 on Zubeda's birthday. At the reception, Shalina spoke movingly about her love for her mom and for Ma. She called her mom an angel, and that is so true.

Amyn Hirji and Asif Bhalesha are treasured friends of both Shalina and Narmin. Bahadur and Zubeda treat them like sons. Amyn is a wonderful singer, and, at the reception, he sang a popular Indian song, which moved the guests to tears. Asif, a talented photographer, shot the wedding photographs.

Wedding of Shalina and Mahmood
(L - R) Narmin, Zubeda, Shalina, Mahmood, Bahadur and Farha

Rahemtulla clan and friends at Wedding of Shalina and Mahmood

Ladhani Family at Wedding of Shalina and Mahmood

Shalina cracking sapatia at her wedding

September 4, 2002 heralded the arrival of a new treasure for our family. Shalina gave birth to a son at 4:35 a.m. in Vancouver's BC Women's Hospital & Health Centre. Zebby was present with them in the delivery room as Shalina had been staying with her and Rustam on enforced bed rest. At the hospital, a flood of memories engulfed Zebby as she remembered the birth and death of her precious Fatima. But, karma may have been at play because sharing the experience with Shalina helped to complete Zebby's process of healing.

The baby surprised everyone by showing up five weeks early, and weighed in at almost two kilograms. Mahmood and Shalina named him Noah Mohamed Ladhani. "Noah" was the namesake for the Prophet Noah or "Nuh" in Arabic. It is a Hebrew name which means "to rest." They gave him the middle name of "Mohamed" to honour Mahmood's paternal grandfather, the late Mohamedali Suleman Ladhani, and Shalina's paternal grandfather, my Bapa, Mohamed Rahemtulla.

The day after Noah's birth, I rushed off to the Pacific Centre, and bought him a huge teddy bear. It was almost as big as me. I had to lug it back to my office on foot, and the other pedestrians had a good laugh.

When I got in my car to drive to the hospital, the teddy bear did not fit. I had to drive across town with my car top down, and the bear strapped into the passenger seat. It was all worthwhile, though, and Noah still keeps his gift in his bedroom.

As Noah was the first grandchild for Shalina's parents, the first male grandchild for Mahmood's parents, and the first great-nephew for me and my siblings, we were all over the moon with delight. Ma had predicted Noah's gender, and she was an ecstatic great-grandmother. She couldn't remember his name so, for the first few months of his life, she called him "Nivea." Sadly, her darling "Nivea" was the only grandchild she ever had a chance to know.

Shalina and Mahmood with Ma and Noah

Noah was a mellow baby who smiled endlessly, and was never demanding. Shalina and Mahmood called him their "Angel Baby." Noah has always been a coordinated little guy. He was even an expert crawler.

From the moment Noah could walk, he's had a hockey stick in his hands. His dad and both his grandfathers have spent endless hours playing hockey with Noah to prepare him for a star-studded career in the National Hockey League with the Vancouver Canucks. His other favourite sport is soccer; he plays baseball in the spring and summer; and, he has started lessons in golf. Mahmood is a "hands-on" dad, and coaches Noah's hockey, soccer, and baseball teams.

Noah attends Southridge, an independent school in Surrey. His parents chose this school because it instils a strong sense of academics, arts, service, sports, and community as the cores of education. Southridge emphasizes the helping of other less fortunate people through service.

As an employee of BMO, Mahmood takes a personal leadership role in fundraising for charitable institutions such as BC Children's Hospital, the World Partnership Walk, and the United Way. Because of Mahmood's involvement, Noah is learning to appreciate how a community can make a difference.

Noah's favourite subjects are math and physical education. Learning about tall structures, aeroplanes, and ships fascinates him. His favourite authors are J.K. Rowling and Chuck Temple. His favourite foods are his grandmother Zubeda's macaroni and cheese, butter chicken and rotli.

Susan and I once embarked on a shopping expedition to F.A.O. Schwarz, New York's legendary toy store. Susan bought a colourful piggy bank in the shape of a clock tower but I liked it so much she gave it to me. I keep it on my desk, and each year, I fill it with "toonies," the Canadian two dollar coin, for Noah on his birthday.

The family waited impatiently another six years for Shalina and Mahmood to produce a second child. When they finally obliged us, they came up with a winner. Shalina delivered Marissa Jena Ladhani on October 24, 2008 at 6:50 pm at Richmond Hospital. She weighed a healthy three and a half kilograms. Zubeda was overjoyed to be present in the delivery room for the birth of her first granddaughter.

Mahmood chose his daughter's name. "Marissa" has two meanings, "Of the Sea" or "Wished for Child." Her middle name, "Jena," comes, of course, from Ma. I've mentioned how like Ma Marissa is in both looks and temperament. She even has Ma's round face and chubby cheeks.

Shalina and Mahmood call Marissa their "Spirited Baby," and they also call her "Jhan" which means "Allah is gracious." She is very clear about what she likes and does not like, and doesn't hesitate to let everyone know. She is also a girly-girl. She loves dressing up, and she's motherly toward both her brother and her dollies. In fact, her parents call her "Mommy Marissa" because she's so caring and nurturing. She is forever changing her dollies, feeding them, and walking them in a stroller. Marissa enjoys art, and will hopefully collaborate with her Aunt Narmin in artistic endeavours in the future.

Marissa loves to play pretend, make play cookies, pizza and chai, and amuse herself with puzzles and mega blocks. While Noah is doing his homework, she sits beside him, and pretends to do homework as well. Her version consists of scribbling and colouring. She has inherited Zubeda's palate, and can eat Indian food until the cows come home. Her favourite is also rotli. Most evenings, Marissa and her dad share ice cream. Even though she's only three, gymnastics is her favourite sport.

Shalina and Mahmood with Noah and Marissa

Shalina is a kind and considerate person, and Mahmood, despite his high stress job, is thoughtful and patient with Noah and Marissa. Mahmood is a humble person, and we have great respect for him. We are blessed to have him in our family.

Narmin, Azaad, Khalil, and Aleem

Like Shalina, Narmin received her Bachelor of Science degree from Simon Fraser University. She majored in Biology, and minored in Environmental Toxicology with an Honours Thesis in Molecular Biology.

After Narmin finished university, she was in a quandary about her future. She did not enjoy laboratory research, and, because of a health condition, didn't think she could handle the rigours of a medical career. So, she enrolled at the British Columbia Institute of Technology, and obtained a Diploma in Environmental Health (Honours) which supported her Certification as a Public Health Inspector (Canada).

Narmin says that choosing this career path was an excellent decision, and one that would shape her future. As well, she had the good fortune of working with experienced mentors who were willing to take a chance on her, and recognized talent in her that she did not know existed.

The second event that would shape her future occurred in 1997 when she met Azaad Kassam in the back seat of a friend's car. Azaad had returned home for summer vacation to visit his family. He had obtained his Bachelor of Science degree from the University of Alberta in Edmonton, and was about to enter his third year of medical school at that institution.

Azaad was born in Nairobi but his family moved to Calgary in 1974 because the political situation in Kenya, while obviously better than that in Uganda, was still a few nickels short of a dollar in terms of stability and safety.

Azaad, Shalina, and Narmin, along with four other new friends, did everything together that summer, and had the time of their lives. The experience marked a turning point in Narmin's life. Until then she had been painfully shy but this group of convivial friends allowed her to open up, and let her dazzling personality shine through.

Azaad returned to Edmonton in September of 1997. At that time, he and Narmin were just summer friends. But, in June of 1998, Narmin moved to Edmonton too, and their friendship blossomed. They soon became best friends, confided in each other about everything going on in their lives, and supported one another unconditionally. (They were obviously a bit slow on the romantic uptake.)

The purpose of Narmin's transfer to Edmonton was to undertake a practicum with Health Canada (First Nations) to support her certification as a Public Health Inspector. It was her first time away from home, and the practicum was supposed to last only six months, after which we expected her to return. However, it's been eleven years now, and we're still waiting.

The gods of all faiths were smiling when Narmin touched down in Edmonton. Bahadur and Zubeda said they would feel comfortable only if she lived with a family so I put her in touch with some friends of Ben and Angela Singh who, in turn, were close friends of mine. Bill and Helen Chrapko welcomed Narmin under their roof for six months, and she then shared accommodation with their daughter, Wendy, for another nine months.

Bill, who was a retired public health inspector, and Helen adopted Narmin symbolically as their daughter, and, as Narmin says, they became her "Canadian" parents. Bill and Helen have remained an integral part of Narmin's support system.

While Narmin was in Edmonton, Health Canada afforded her the opportunity to travel to different parts of Canada to participate in national working groups. That gave her a terrific opportunity to see areas of the country she probably would not otherwise have visited. On her first trip to Ottawa, Ontario, she experienced a sense of déjà vu as soon as she stepped off the plane, and knew that, in the future, she would live there.

In 1999, Narmin's and Azaad's career paths separated them almost by the width of a continent. Azaad moved to Montreal, Quebec to pursue his residency in Psychiatry at McGill University, and, in 2000, Narmin left for a job in Calgary, Alberta. The federal government appointed her Environmental Health Officer to one of the largest First Nations in Canada, the "Blood First Nation and Peigan First Nation." As part of her mandate, she had to endure a three hour weekly commute to Lethbridge, Alberta to work directly in aboriginal communities. But, as she describes it, the grass roots public health experience she acquired had a life-long positive impact on her. She learned to understand the value of listening, and the power of both education and perseverance to effect change.

Although Narmin enjoyed the field work and learned a lot, she thought that she could contribute more at the strategic and programme development level. Later in 2000, opportunity knocked, and she had the chance to apply for a position in Ottawa, working under a mentor, for the *National First Nations Environmental Health Program*.

Three months later, she moved to Ottawa to manage a national programme in the aftermath of "Walkerton." That was the tragic incident where the deadly E. coli bacteria contaminated Walkerton, Ontario's town well. It then seeped through the water pipe system into the homes of the residents, killing several of them and sickening over 1,000 more.

Narmin undertook a steep learning curve but worked long hours to educate herself. Still wanting challenges outside her comfort zone, in 2001 she left the programme to accept a policy position with Environment Canada. After a two year stint in that department, she returned to Health Canada in 2003 to head up the *National Travelling Public Program*. Their mandate dealt with the public health inspection of conveyances and facilities including trains, ferries, cruise ships, aeroplanes, flight caterers, and airports.

Once Narmin was in Ottawa, she and Azaad resumed their relationship but finally realized that romance trumped friendship. They began dating, and, for the next four years, helped to burn up a lot of Greyhound Bus tires commuting each weekend between Ottawa and Montreal. In December of 2002, unbeknownst to Narmin, Azaad asked Bahadur for his daughter's hand in marriage. In an excess of either caution or diplomacy, he asked permission from her "Canadian" dad, Bill, as well.

Azaad proposed to Narmin on a Cayo Coco Island beach in Cuba under a blanket of stars that illuminated the clear, still night. He wrote a poem for her, and the last line contained the proposal. You can't get much more romantic than that. Narmin was utterly surprised, and her first response was "What do you mean?" Fortunately, her second response was "Yes!"

Life is sometimes passing strange. Azaad's father, Firoz, grew up in Kisumu, and he had retained fond memories of gazing at a shy, beautiful girl in the schoolyard. That girl was none other than our dear Zubeda.

Azaad's mom, Yashmin, grew up in South Africa and Firoz and Yashmin also have two daughters, Anar and Farah.

Narmin and Azaad were in accord about their marriage plans. They both desired a small, spiritual, and romantic wedding. They married at a Jamatkhana in Paris, and held their wedding dinner at the Chateau Chantilly, an historic manor house where Princess Zahra Aga Khan, the daughter of Aga Khan IV, was married. They honeymooned in Venice, Italy.

Wedding of Narmin and Azaad
(L – R) Shalina, Zubeda, Azaad, Narmin, Bahadur, Farha

When they returned to Canada, a terrific job opportunity awaited Azaad in North Bay, Ontario, at the general hospital, and they moved there in August of 2004. They planned to live in North Bay for only two years but have now been entrenched in the town for several years.

During that time, Azaad has been actively involved in the Northern Ontario School of Medicine as a teacher of residents, lecturer, and member of the board of selection for the medical school. He has also gained valuable administrative experience by sitting on the Board of Directors of the North Bay General Hospital, and is Chief of the Department of Psychiatry. In addition to those duties, he practices both in-patient and community based psychiatry.

Once they put down their roots in North Bay, Narmin continued to work as a senior policy advisor in the management of the National Travelling Public Program. She has contributed to Canada's *Quarantine Act*, which the government enacted after the "SARS" scare, and to revisions of the World Health Organization's *International Health Regulations.*

Allah has blessed Narmin and Azaad with two darling children. Khalil Kassam entered this world on August 30, 2007. They had multiple motives in choosing the name "Khalil." It means "Companion of God." It is an alternate name for the Prophet Abraham who is the common link among Jews, Muslims, and Christians. Khalil Gibran, who wrote "The Prophet," is Narmin and Azaad's favourite poet. And, believe it or not, "Khalil" is the Kryptonian name of Superman.

I feel that Khalil and I have always had a special connection. He shows a maturity far beyond his years, and his mom and I have often commented that he must be an old soul from Bhuj. Despite his young age, Khalil is kind-hearted, respectful, and gentle.

Khalil loves good books, even ones that are quite advanced for his age, and can't get enough of them. He feels quite at home at the library. He can devour ten books in one sitting. He routinely enlists anyone who is around to read to him—even first time visitors to their home.

Acting may be in his future as he'll pick up found objects in the house, employ them for skits, and enlist his brother and a host of imaginary friends to participate. He can't wait to start kindergarten, and even pretends to do homework.

He already appreciates good food, and is quite willing to try different cuisines. He nurses a passion for fruit, and eats a whole plateful each evening before bedtime. Housework, shovelling snow, and playing outside all engage his interest. Last but far from least, Khalil is the best big brother. He takes Aleem under his wing, and always looks out for him.

And that brings me to Aleem Kassam, born in North Bay on February 7, 2009. "Aleem" means "teacher or scholar," and is one of the ninety-nine names of Allah "servant to the most knowing."

Similar to Marissa, Aleem is their "Spirited Child." Also like Marissa, he is abundantly clear about his likes and dislikes, and does not hesitate to make sure everyone else knows as well. His physique is stocky and strapping, and Mahmood and Noah predict a career for him in hockey or rugby.

Aleem is quite the renaissance toddler. He is a charming little guy, popular with women of all ages. Again like Marissa, he's a glutton for Indian food, and is in seventh heaven when Grandma Zubeda, the cook, visits. Like Khalil, he's passionate about books. He adores his older brother, and shadows him constantly.

Narmin and Azaad are terrific parents. I would say that Narmin's best attribute is her thoughtfulness for others. For instance, she is a self-proclaimed card snob, and expends a great deal of time choosing the perfect card for each recipient.

Narmin and Azaad with Khalil and Aleem

Narmin's passion has always been art, and she is completely self-taught. She loves to experiment with different media and styles. She uses oil, acrylic, pointillism, pencil, charcoal, and watercolour, and her methods range from realism to abstract. The title of the illustration on the front cover of this book is *"Aleem's Elephant."* Narmin used acrylic on canvas, in an abstract textural style, to create this illustration. She dedicated it to Aleem as a gift to celebrate his birth. The elephant represents strength, honour, stability, patience, luck, fortune, and protection, and also pays tribute to Aleem's African roots.

The Hockey Rivalry

Mahmood is a die-hard Vancouver Canucks fan but Azaad, having lived in Edmonton for so many years, bleeds Edmonton Oiler colours. The next photograph illustrates graphically that the hockey loyalties of the kids follow those of their dads.

Noah, Khalil, Marissa, and Aleem

CHAPTER THIRTY
My Canadian-Born Nieces

Farha

Farha of the irresistible smile and soulful eyes is Bahadur and Zubeda's youngest daughter. Now in her mid-thirties, she has coped, since she was a small child, with a severe illness. She suffers from epilepsy, a disorder that results from the generation of confusing electrical signals within the brain, causing recurrent seizures.

Seizure symptoms vary. On a relativity scale, Farha is fortunate because her seizures usually occur only once or twice a month, and, for the most part, they are *petit mal* seizures. The symptoms of a petit mal or "absence" seizure consist of staring, along with subtle body movement, sometimes accompanied by a brief loss of consciousness. Occasionally, a *grand mal* or "tonic-clonic" seizure will sweep Farha up like a tsunami has her in its grasp, but, thank goodness, that happens only once in a blue moon.

A neurologist at BC Children's Hospital diagnosed Farha's illness when she was four years old. Ever since, she has been a frequent visitor to the hospital. Many different neurologists have worked with her to find the most suitable medication to control her symptoms. Surgery is a useful tool to treat some people with epilepsy but it is not an option for her because the problem area is too close to her vision centre. All her physicians have been compassionate and caring, and their common goal has been to help Farha grow up healthy and able to function normally. She says that her physicians have taught her that she has to be independent and rely on herself.

Finding the right type and dosage of medication requires a delicate and shifting balancing act. Any particular cluster of pills may work for awhile but then Farha's body may grow immune to it, or the dosage may no longer be sufficient. Another problem is that the medication can engender significant side effects. For example, it slows down functions such as speech, and it may adversely affect her kidneys, liver, vision, and immune system. It can even exacerbate carpal tunnel syndrome.

At present, Farha has her condition well under control. She has had a lot of experience recognizing the warning sign of an impending seizure. It presents as an aura. She knows that she has just a split second to pop a pill or lie down. The seizure generally passes within about ten minutes, and then she is back to normal. Although epilepsy sometimes retreats with age, she will likely have to deal with it for the rest of her life because the epicentre is so close to her optic nerve. She has learned to take one day at a time as stress can cause a seizure.

Farha has repaid the many neurologists who have cared for and about her by volunteering, on innumerable occasions, to be a test subject for different drugs. Her neurologists also ask her, once in awhile, to give speeches to the parents of children newly diagnosed with epilepsy, and she does so gladly. She encourages the parents to fight the disease, to have patience, and to never give up.

I have begun my portrait of Farha by discussing her illness, not because it defines her, but because her lifelong battle not to allow it to do so illustrates a profile in profound courage. While we all keep an eye on Farha, we are careful not to infringe upon her fiercely independent nature. Having said that, she is extremely thankful for the care, support and encouragement she receives from our extended family.

Farha acquired a passion for cooking from her mom and her two grandmothers so, after high school, she gravitated naturally toward a career in food services. She attended Vancouver Community College for three years, and received a diploma along with the honour of being chosen class valedictorian. She now works in food services at the BC Hydro building in South Burnaby.

Bahadur, Zubeda and Farha

Farha inherited a love of sports from her dad. When she was growing up, Bahadur, Narmin, and she used to watch hockey and football games together on television. She is a fervent fan of the Vancouver Canucks hockey team. She works at Rogers Arena at a concession stand. As a perk, she also gets a call-up for some of the other big ticket events. She had a blast serving people from all over the world at the 2010 Winter Olympic Games, the 2010/2011 Vancouver Canucks Western Conference Finals, and the 2010/2011 Vancouver Canucks Stanley Cup Finals.

One of her favourite possessions is a book about the Vancouver Canucks which commemorates forty years of Canuck memories. Her best-loved players, even though they have long since retired, are Kirk McLean (Captain Kirk) and Trevor Linden who led the team to Game 7 of the 1994 Stanley Cup finals against the New York Rangers. Even though they lost the final game, the series remains one of the greatest events in Vancouver sporting history. She is an ardent fan of the BC Lions football team as well, and works as a cashier at a BC Place Stadium concession.

She has inherited Almas' penchant for cross-stitch, and produces some exquisite work depicting African and Indian motifs and even some Disney characters. She also finds time to volunteer at the Jamatkhana.

Farha was married for a time but, unfortunately, it didn't work out, and I pray that she'll have a second chance which she so deserves. My darling niece possesses the biggest heart in the world.

Nashina

Nashina is a down-to-earth, all-round nice girl. Growing up, she was constantly at our house after school as it has always been command central for the family.

Nashina with Mansur and Rashida

When Nashina was sixteen years old, she began working part-time in the retail industry. After graduation, she joined the retail workforce full time but found that it did not satisfy either her career or financial aspirations. So, she opted for Vancouver Career College, and studied to become a medical office assistant. She applied herself assiduously, and, when she graduated from the College, received a Medical Office Assistant Diploma, Medical Pharmacy Assistant Diploma, Standard First Aid Certificate, and CPR "C" Certificate.

Within two weeks after graduation, she found a job in Burnaby at the office of an ear, nose, and throat specialist; however, Vancouver Coastal Health was on her radar as a possible employer. One evening, at a party, she met a manager from VCH and a month later, she landed the job of her dreams as a medical office assistant at Vancouver Coastal Health.

Vancouver Coastal Health is a regional public health authority that provides health services throughout the Greater Vancouver Region. Its mandate includes home and community care, the provision of mental health services, and preventive health and addiction services. Nashina is a full-time float which means that she covers shifts for people who are on vacation or away ill. She likes the variety of the different jobs, and is passionate about her work. She feels that she is making a difference by assisting people who really need help.

Nashina had always been infatuated with dogs but had never owned one. Adopting a puppy was at the top of her bucket list, and when she began looking for one, she chose a puppy that was chocolate brown with blue eyes. As soon as she held the puppy in her arms, she knew it was meant to be. She was a pit bull/Rottweiler/lab cross. She intended to name her "Nala", but the seller mistakenly started to call her "Hannah," and by the time Nashina went to pick her up, that was the name to which she responded. Hannah is a gentle soul.

Nashina's home is a condominium apartment at Victoria Hill in New Westminster overlooking the Fraser River. The development is just across the road from stately Queen's Park, a heritage treasure of the Royal City. Her proximity to Queen's Park is ideal for both Nashina and Hannah. They often roam through the park, and are especially fond of the off-leash area.

My niece is so dog-crazy that, every day, she adds considerable time to her commute in order to drop Hannah off at her personalized doggy day care centre known as "Chez Parents." Rashida and Mansur look after Hannah five days a week. Like me, another of her passions is reading, and her tastes are eclectic. I gave her a Kindle E-Reader, and she's glued to it. She is also a keen artist, and creates abstract art using acrylics. She has a sketch book full of drawings, and is a serial doodler.

Both Nashina and Natasha were Sikhs by birth but were baptized into our Ismaili religion. Nashina has never felt an overwhelming need to search out her birth family but, in case she changed her mind, her mom gave her a paper setting out a scant bit of information.

Nashina gathered that her birth mother was about eighteen years old when she became pregnant by a university student who was studying English and history in India. The birth mother told her social worker that they had met only a few times, and that the birth father no longer wanted anything to do with her. The paper said that "the birth mother comes from a culture where pregnancy without marriage is completely unacceptable. There was no choice given to her; the child must be given up and one pretends there was no pregnancy at all. A marriage has been arranged for her very soon after she delivers the baby."

Nashina seems to be pretty philosophical about the adoption issue. She says that, after reading the document about her birth circumstances, she is so thankful to have been adopted into such a loving and supportive home and family. In her view, it is not the person who gives birth to a child but the people who raise the child who are truly the parents.

Like all parents and children, Nashina and her mom and dad have their moments of discord but, by and large, she thinks that her parents are just about perfect, and she can't imagine where she would be without them. She comments that Rashida has taught her a valuable lesson, that is, not to depend on other people but, rather, to rely only on herself.

Natasha

Natasha is blessed with the gift of the gab. She's worked in the hotel industry and other customer service related positions but, has had trouble finding her niche.

Zebby and Rustam with Natasha

Without detracting at all from Natasha's love for her adoptive family, she had always felt an overwhelming need to look for her birth family. Here is Natasha's story, in her own words:

"I have wonderful parents and a wonderful extended family. I wouldn't trade them for all the tea in India. But, for as long as I can remember, I've wanted to learn about my origins.

In 2005, my Dad and I were returning from an Eid celebration, and started to argue about my need to search out my birth parents. When we arrived home, Dad gave me an envelope containing a letter, dated April 9, 1983, from the Ministry of Human Resources.

Back when my parents received this letter, Mom wanted to destroy it. As far as she was concerned, I was their daughter, end of story. They never opened the letter. Unknown to my Mom, though, Dad kept it for all those years.

Dad and I unsealed the letter, and read it together. It contained some biographical information on my family but did not include any names or other facts that might help me in my search. Even the scant information on the page moved me to tears, and Dad cried along with me.

I felt that a new chapter was opening in my life's journey. But, at the same time, I was fearful of what continuing my quest might uncover, and I did not want to hurt my parents. As a result, I did nothing for four more years.

Finally, in April of 2009, I began the quest for my birth family, and, after many twists and turns, I found my birth mother, two brothers, and a sister. My first contact was with my elder brother. I called him, and said that I was sorry to bother him but I wanted to know if his mother's maiden name was "X." The response was abrupt. He wanted to know why I was asking. At that point, I just blurted out, "Because I'm the daughter she gave up twenty-six years ago." Diplomacy has never been my strong suit. He hung up.

To give him credit, he called back within seconds, and apologized, saying that he knew nothing about my claim. I replied that I'd like to meet with him. I asked him to bring photographs of his family, and said that I would bring my documents.

We agreed to meet at Starbucks. When I walked in, the first thing I saw was a huge Indian guy. He rushed up, and gave me a massive hug. He said, "You look exactly like mom." That moment, that hug, and those words will remain with me always. I had found my place in the world.

The next day, I drove to meet my bio-mom and sister a couple of blocks from their home. My bio-mom fell to my feet and wept. She looked up and said, "Not a day has gone by that I haven't thought about you." That was exactly what I needed to hear to fill the biological hole in my life.

My bio-mom told me that when I was born she held me for five minutes, and then I was gone. She knew she couldn't care for me, and the government worker had assured her I was going to a good family who would love me and look after me.

The process of discovering my birth family was a clandestine operation in that I told my Mom nothing about it. At last, though, I worked up the courage to do so because I wanted to share everything about the momentous event with her. Mom was understandably upset, and wasn't too receptive when I asked if I could bring my bio-mom and sister to our home to meet Mom and Dad.

When they came to visit, Dad was happy to meet them, shared stories of when I was little, and hauled out the family photo albums. I was worried to death about my Mom's reaction but I should have known better. My Mother is innately gracious and hospitable to her core. I think she's incapable of being anything else. What touched me especially was Mom's evident pride in me when she conversed with my bio-mom.

I spent Christmas of 2009 with my birth family, and that was a fulfilling moment in my life. However, while my bio-mom gave birth to me, my Mom allowed me to live my life. She is the person who rubbed my back when I was sick, supported me through thick and thin, and helped me build my future. I will always be grateful to my parents for adopting me and giving me a wonderful home and all their love and attention."

Farha, Natasha, Shalina, Nashina and Narmin

CHAPTER THIRTY-ONE

Home Building Epic

The Big Decision

The year 2008 saw me embark on my craziest project yet. When Ma was alive, we undertook quite a few renovations to our home on Montecito Drive to make it liveable for her. After she died, the lay-out of the house didn't quite work for Bahadur, Zubeda, Almas, Nizar, and me, to say nothing of our constant stream of sleep-over guests.

We debated about whether we should sink more money into a dated house or pull up stakes, and find new living quarters. At that time, no thought of rebuilding on our present site had permeated our collective consciousness.

We retained a realtor who showed us two perfect newly constructed homes his brother-in-law had built, and the impeccable workmanship impressed us. We asked the realtor to take a look at our house. He did so, and pronounced it eminently saleable. Then, one rainy day he returned, and brought along his brother-in-law, Bob Minhas, the contractor, for a cup of tea. Bob surprised us by saying that we would never find another lot as good as the one we had, and that we should think about tearing the house down, and replacing it.

For some reason, Bob's suggestion made an insane kind of sense. Bahadur, who was usually cautious about change, startled Almas and me by saying, "Why not?" For Bahadur that constituted an enthusiastic endorsement. Almas, Nizar, and I were keen. Coincidentally, Rashida and Mansur had bought a condominium at Victoria Hill in New Westminster, and wanted to give condo living an experimental try. So, they would be able to lend us their nearby home. Bob promised to complete construction within one year. The stars seemed aligned in our favour.

I had never given a thought to constructing a house but saw it immediately as an intricate challenge, and an opportunity to carry on Bapa's, and perhaps our Mistri ancestors', passion for home building. So, by May, we moved everything into storage, and took up residence at Rashida and Mansur's house.

The New Home

Bob established an immediate rapport with our family, and we worked together to produce plans that would accommodate the needs and preferences of our various family members. Bahadur, Zubeda, and Nizar gave Almas and me *carte blanche*, and we set about the process of building our dream home.

Almas and I were pretty demanding but we knew exactly what we wanted:

- a modern home that would incorporate traditional Tudor touches such as wainscoting, crown moulding, french doors, recessed window seats, and window shutters to remind me of the Tudor house I had dreamed of owning when I lived in England
- an interior design that would reflect clean lines, spaciousness, harmony, and effortless flow from room to room
- an ambience that would instil a sense of comfort, cordiality, warmth, and welcome
- decor and furnishings that would commemorate our heritage and experiences in India, Uganda, Great Britain, and Canada.

I think that Bob, Almas, and I succeeded in achieving these goals.

7330 Montecito Drive

The front entry hall is reminiscent of our foyer at 7 Nalufenya Road in Jinja which was large enough for us to entertain guests. The walls of the entry hall are a lush butter cream. The floor covering is lead coloured Italian porcelain tile partially overlaid by a Gustav Klimt silk and wool rug, in a gold design, woven in India. The main piece of furniture is a dark cherry hall table which Almas, in keeping with our tradition in Jinja, faithfully replenishes with arrangements of fresh flowers. The showpiece of the entry hall is a large Hermes silk scarf given to me by David and Brenda McLean which I had framed. It depicts two leopards, and its title is *Jungle Love*.

The floors of the living and dining rooms are a rich Brazilian cherry, and a pale gold Indian rug graces the living room floor. The colour of the living room walls is cork—a subtle shade of golden tan, the ceiling is a rich cream, and the ceiling over the recessed fireplace a desert tan.

The fireplace itself is marble, and on the mantel resides our photograph of Aga Khan IV. In the centre of the mantel is a tall urn potted by Bill Boyd. Bill is an internationally renowned artist who lives and works on Galiano Island, one of the southern Gulf Islands of British Columbia. The shades of the urn are gold and mustard topped by a lid with a gold plated knob. Bill finishes his pottery with a silicate zinc-crystal glaze, and infuses his works with an Asian flavour which blends perfectly into our home. At the same time, though, his art is distinctly Canadian.

In the living room stands a glass-fronted dark cherry cabinet. By way of tribute to the positive British influences on our lives, select pieces of English china reside in the cabinet. Its contents include five Royal

Doulton figurines which our friend, Susan Jaffe, kindly gave to Almas; an Old English Johnson Brother dinner plate and serving platter, being the only surviving pieces of Ma's dinner set, which Bapa had bought for her in London; and three Royal Grafton tea cups which were wedding presents Margaret's mom received when she married in 1941.

Burgundy fabrics clad the dining room chairs as well as the sofas and armchairs in the living room. The plush burgundy and gold hues of these two rooms are representational of a traditional Indian look.

The main floor also has a guest bathroom, a bedroom and sitting room for Almas, a small study for Bahadur, and a large room that stretches across the whole rear of the house. It includes the family room, dining nook, kitchen, and small wok kitchen. My aim for the family room is to create an African ambience but that is still a work in progress.

On the wall of the dining nook portion of the room, we have hung a painting by Narmin of a poor and endearing Austrian boy happy to receive a new pair of shoes. A massive round glass table dominates the nook, and anyone who comes to our home is likely to find at least one or two people at the table eating a meal, reading the newspaper, or just hanging out.

The kitchen and wok kitchen feature dark maple cabinets and Giallo Santa Cecilia granite countertops. Walls and a door separate it from the remainder of the great room. Its purpose is to protect the house from the pungent odours of Indian cooking. Zubeda, bless her heart, spends much of her day closeted in this tiny space, cooking for the entire family. We usually let her out in the evening.

From the entry hall, a staircase heads up to the second floor. I'm especially fond of the balustrade which consists of wrought iron spindles and a Brazilian cherry wood railing. Halfway up the stairs lies a landing with a recessed wall. In the recess, we have hung a large Heidi Lange black and white batik rendering of a Kenyan woman, exquisite in the intricacy of its design. Heidi is a Swede who spends a good part of each year living in the Rift Valley of Kenya. The culture and traditions of African tribes fascinate her, and her work hangs in art galleries and museums internationally. I was fortunate enough to acquire this particular piece in Nairobi.

Off the large second floor landing are a guest bedroom and ensuite bathroom; a master bedroom and ensuite bathroom for Bahadur and Zubeda; and my bedroom and ensuite bathroom, and study. I took enormous pleasure in decorating my bedroom, and, naturally, I stayed true to my love of the colour purple. I had long dreamed of possessing a huge walk-in closet, and the one I now have fulfills my fantasy. Andy Warhol carpet pieces on the closet floor lend a touch of whimsy.

My study is a warm golden straw colour with cream cabinets and a wall-to-wall bookcase. I've always been quite the bibliophile, and my bookcase is home to an eclectic selection of books I've collected over the years. My goal is to fill the remaining shelves with antique and special interest books. To that end, I'm now haunting used book stores. So far,

I've acquired the complete works of Charles Dickens, Rudyard Kipling, and William Shakespeare along with a collection of Agatha Christie mysteries. I'm going to be reading until I'm at least ninety-nine.

Nizar's bedroom and his living room, which doubles as a recreation room and bar, are in the basement level of the house. This floor includes a laundry room, a powder room, and a hobby room for Almas. Some of Almas' cross-stitch embroidery pieces of African women grace the walls of the hobby room.

A Round of Thanks

Almas and I will be forever indebted to our friend, Susan Jaffe, who gave so generously of her time and artistic sensibility. She spent endless weekends trekking all over the Lower Mainland with us searching for everything from just the right shade of fabric for a couch to the perfect slab of granite for a countertop.

Like Bapa, when he built our home at 7 Nalufenya Road in Jinja, my attention to detail was painstaking. I will be ever grateful to Bob for his patience and flexibility in creating exactly the home I envisioned.

Bob, in turn, has been kind enough to say that building our house was a privilege. He appreciated that we knew what we wanted, and did not change our minds. And he has told us many times that he realized he was building a real home rather than just a place for people to live.

I would like to think that Bapa would be proud of Almas and me. Building and decorating our home was the most difficult and rewarding project I have ever undertaken, and I will never, ever, ever do it again!

CHAPTER THIRTY-TWO

Where in the World Are We Now

Ismailis in Canada

The last thirty years of the twentieth century witnessed the scattering of Ismailis, as well as Indians of other faiths, throughout Asia, Africa, Australia, Europe, and North America. The seminal event was our expulsion from Uganda but a host of other factors played a role. Some immigrated to escape discrimination or tyranny; others to forge a better life for their children; and still others simply because of a desire for adventure or change.

The entrepreneurial state of mind, dedication to hard work, and respect for education demonstrated by the Ismailis who emigrated from India to Africa have served their descendants well in their quest for success in the western world.

The population of Canada includes about 80,000 Ismailis, and that of British Columbia approximately 12,000. Our inclusion in Canadian society has certainly expanded the cultural mosaic of the nation. The Aga Khan has instructed us to embrace our adoptive county, and to contribute to Canadian society as best we can.

My Ismaili community has shown a remarkable ability to adapt to different cultures, and particularly to western ways. What better evidence than my nephew, Noah, whose ambition is to play in the National Hockey League.

In British Columbia, Ismailis have had a significant economic and social impact. To cite just a few examples, the Lalji family, from Uganda, owners of The Larco Group of Companies, are fabled real estate entrepreneurs who are among the richest families in Canada. Mobina Jaffer is a member of Canada's Senate. Her father, Sherali Bandali Jaffer, enjoyed enormous success as a poultry farmer. Abdul and Shamin Jamal established fourteen privately owned senior retirement homes. Noordin and Farida Sayani own several Executive Hotels & Resorts. Farhan Lalji is a cool television sports reporter for TSN. Dr. Shafique Pirani, who fled from Uganda when he was fifteen years old, is an orthopaedic surgeon in New Westminster, British Columbia. He is the prime mover and shaker behind, and the director of, the Uganda Sustainable Clubfoot Care Project funded by the Canadian International Development Agency and Enable Canada. In Uganda, about 1,000 infants each year are born with a clubfoot. The goals of this project are to "raise awareness of the clubfoot deformity throughout Uganda," and to train "local healthcare personnel to provide treatment with a method that is socially acceptable and economically viable for Uganda." Dr. Pirani has spent time in Uganda doing just that.

The Aga Khan's Remarkable Friendship with Canada

Aga Khan IV himself has nurtured close ties with Canada for many years. On behalf of our community, he has remained ever grateful to Prime Minister Pierre Trudeau and Canadians for welcoming so many Ismailis after the expulsion. Canada, in turn, has expressed its gratitude to the Aga Khan for his extraordinary humanitarian and unification efforts.

In June, 2005, in Ottawa, Ontario, Her Excellency the Right Honourable Adrienne Clarkson, Governor General of Canada, presided over a ceremony investing His Highness the Aga Khan as an honourary Companion of the Order of Canada. He received this high honour in recognition of a "lifetime of outstanding achievement, dedication to the community and service to the nation."

The citation lauded the Aga Khan for:

> ...personifying cherished Canadian values. His Highness the Aga Khan has devoted his life to protecting the environment and alleviating human suffering due to poverty. Imam of the Shia Imami Ismaili Muslims since 1957, he has guided the spiritual growth of his followers, teaching compassion and tolerance by example. In 1967, he launched his foundation, the Aga Khan Development Network, with branches in countries around the world, including Canada. Recognizing our nation's compassionate nature, he cites Canada as a role model for the world and has selected Ottawa as the home of a new global centre for pluralism.

In July 2007, on his Golden Jubilee tour, Aga Khan IV graced us with his presence in Vancouver. On his arrival at the Pan Pacific Hotel, ecstatic smiling crowds, bolstered by a Scottish marching bagpipe band, greeted him. About 125,000 well-wishers from British Columbia, and 15,000 from outside the Province, gathered in record temperatures to welcome Aga Khan IV to BC Place Stadium. Canadian, British Columbian, and Ismaili flags waved everywhere. Our community earned well-deserved accolades as an impressive number of volunteers turned out to organize and supervise the event.

In December 2008, on another official visit to Canada during his Golden Jubilee, the Aga Khan, accompanied by Canadian Prime Minister Stephen Harper, opened the Delegation of the Ismaili Imamat, located on Sussex Drive in Ottawa. The complex is the first of its kind, and will be the centre of operations for the humanitarian work of the Aga Khan Development Network.

My own City of Burnaby benefitted from the generosity of the Aga Khan during his Golden Jubilee tour. The Aga Khan met with the Burnaby mayor, and agreed that the Aga Khan Development Network would fund, design, and construct a contemplative nature park on land owned by the city.

In May, 2010, the Canadian Parliament further honoured Aga Khan IV by naming him an honourary citizen of Canada. Only four other persons have received this distinction. They are Raoul Wallenberg, the Swedish diplomat and Holocaust hero (posthumously); Nelson Mandela, former President of South Africa and Nobel Laureate; the Dalai Lama; and Aung San Suu Kyi, a Burmese pro-democracy activist and Nobel Laureate who spent close to twenty years under house arrest in her native country. Prime Minister Stephen Harper, in bestowing the award upon the Aga Khan, stated:

> As you yourself said, Your Highness, we cannot make the world safe for democracy without first making the world safe for diversity, If I may say, sir, you sound like a Canadian.... And in fact, you are.

On that same visit, Aga Khan IV and Prime Minister Stephen Harper met in Toronto to turn the sod for construction of the Ismaili Centre, Aga Khan Museum, and adjacent parkland in the Don Mills area. The estimated cost of the cultural centre, museum, and park is about (Can) $300,000,000. The complex is to include a Jamatkhana as well as facilities for intellectual engagement, public dialogue, learning, bridge-building, and social and cultural gatherings.

In Canada, the "World Partnership Walk," an event which takes place under the auspices of the Aga Khan Foundation Canada, raises funds and increases awareness to fight global poverty. Over the years, thousands of concerned Canadians have participated in this cause which assists some of the world's poorest communities. The walk takes place in May each year, and, in Vancouver its venue is Stanley Park.

Whatever became of...

As for my family and friends, we lost contact with many of them in the aftermath of expulsion. But, because the Ismaili community is so close-knit, we have been able to track down quite a few, some by design and others by happenstance.

After my visit at Heathrow with my childhood friend, Maira Butt, I lost track of her for a few years but was recently able to re-establish contact. She lives in London and has three children. Her son-in-law, Aamir, visited with our family during a business trip to Vancouver, and I've been lobbying for Maira to come to Vancouver for a vacation.

Tazmina Pradhan, who used to belt out Engelbert Humperdinck, Elvis Presley and Tom Jones songs with Maira and me, moved to England after expulsion. She is a dietician. She married Bill Crisp, a surgeon, and they have two sons, Nicholas Hussein and Rehman Simon. Tazmina's reconciliation with her Ugandan roots was somewhat different from mine. Here is her story in her own words:

> As I had left Uganda earlier than my friends, I had unfinished business and ghosts to lay to rest. Circumstances furnished me with the perfect opportunity. In 2007, I joined Rotary, an international charitable organization. At the same time, my children's school linked with a vocational college for AIDS orphans in Jinja—a coincidence or divine providence? I met the Head of the school, and began to build a network of friends while helping to raise funds for them through both school and Rotary.
>
> In 2008, my club adopted The Bujagali Trust, an educational charity supporting schools, orphanages, and individual pupils in and around Jinja. Since then, I have visited Uganda to deal with family property and to meet with the people we are supporting in education. Each time I return, the homecoming gets better. The ghosts have gone, and sun shines bright!

Tazim Pabani, aka "Cackles," also found refuge in England, and entered the nursing profession. She married Ken Shirley, and they have one daughter, Mari.

On my first trip back to Uganda, I had run into a gentleman named Salim Thobani, and found, to my astonishment, that his wife was Fatima Velji. During my London/Sardinia expedition, I reunited with Fatima, and spent the weekend with her at her home in Kensington. Fatima, who had remained in contact with Tazim, invited her to our reunion. Tazim is still a worldclass giggler, and we had a super time together. Just a few years ago, Tazim, Ken, and Mari visited us in Burnaby on their way to a vacation in Alaska.

Nazlin, Tazim and Fatima

Sabira Manek, who was such an evil influence on innocent me, forcing me to ride on her friend's motorbike in Jinja, is a talented interior designer and artist who lives in Rotterdam. She also puts out quotes on Twitter. My personal favourite is, "You must have crossed the river before you may tell the crocodile he has bad breath." I hope this admonition does not mean she has given up her wild ways, and become more cautious.

Another wild child from my youth, Nilam Ramji, whose parents banished her to boarding school in Kampala, moved to Toronto, and I have lost touch with her.

Nasreen Adatia, whose architect father designed our home at 7 Nalufenya Road, is a resident of the Lower Mainland, happily married, with two children. We run into one another now and again.

To my regret, I lost touch with Janet Anderson, my expatriate British friend from the Amber Club, when she returned home to England, and I have never caught up with her.

Yasin, Bapa's comptroller, and his wife who performed magic tricks for me as a child, fled to Great Britain with their sons but, sadly, they both died not too many years later.

Auntie Maisy, the midwife and family friend, who helped deliver all of us, moved to England after expulsion to live with one of her sons. Her other son settled in Canada, and became a priest in Ontario. A few years after we arrived in Vancouver, Auntie Maisy came to visit her son, and then, to our delight, continued on to visit us. She died several years ago.

When the Jogia family of jewellers, who owned the store in Jinja where Ma bought most of her jewellery, was expelled, they immigrated to England where they established a grand and well-known jewellery store in Wembley that took up most of a city block. They were close family friends, and I've kept in touch with them.

Rozina Shariff (sister of Mansur Shariff), who shared quarters with Zebby and Almas at Mrs. Hookway's boarding house, has suffered a lot of tragedy in her life. Her mother was ill, and Rozina used to escort her to the Mulago hospital in Kampala for treatment. One day, the equipment broke down, and they were forced to wait for the technician, Milan Xeno, to arrive. That worked out rather well because Rozina later married him. They lived in Jinja, Kampala, Tanzania, and then Australia where Milan died of cancer.

Abdul and Roshan Jaffer, who owned the fabric store in Kampala now live in North Vancouver, and are still family friends.

I've mentioned that Dr. and Mrs. Thakkar divide their time between Kent and Mumbai; that Shefali married Kishore Popat, a physician, and lives in California with him and their two sons; and that Chinchu resides in London with her parents. Believe it or not, their foul-mouthed parrot, Cuckoo, who swore in Gujarati, moved to India and then London with them. She lived for forty-five years, and died just recently.

Chinchu works, on behalf of thalidomide survivors, through a British organization called *Stop the Tears*. The tragic story of thalidomide began with a German company which marketed the drug internationally from 1957 to 1961. Heralded as a safe drug, pregnant women ingested it as a sleeping pill and to counteract morning sickness. The company withdrew the drug from the market when evidence of its terrible consequences became apparent but it was a classic case of "too little, too late."

Sixty to ninety percent of the women who took the drug miscarried. The 15,000 to 20,000 babies who survived suffered from colossal birth defects and massive deformities. About one third of the survivors are still alive, and are now in their fifties.

I've already described my exquisite reunion with Shenaz Khimji in Geneva.

Our cousin, Noorali Mohamed, who conspired with Ma to introduce Rustam to Zebby, and his wife, Noorjahan, who is Rustam's sister, are now enjoying retirement. They worked their fingers to the bone for many years on a poultry farm they owned in Abbotsford. As well as Shenin, they have two other daughters, Nina who lives with her family in Seattle, and Alshamsh who resides with her family in Abbotsford.

My cousins, Gulbanu and Mariam, who used to travel from Tanzania occasionally to visit us in Jinja are both still alive. Gulbanu and her family live in Port Moody, British Columbia and Mariam and her family reside in Denver, Colorado.

Bapa's nephew, Ramzan, is an elderly widower who lives in Richmond, British Columbia with his son, Arif, and daughter-in-law, Shaida. Arif is an executive with a prominent developer, and his wife, Shaida, is a school teacher. They have one son, Rahim. We keep in close contact with them, and, for the past twenty years or so, Ramzanbha, Arif, Shaida, and Rahim have celebrated Christmas with us at our home. I know we're Ismailis but, as I have said before, we never miss an opportunity for a celebration.

Sadly, Nasim Charania, who came to Canada with Almas, passed away several years ago, and her brother, Badrudin Charania, who was Bahadur's best man, died a few years ago. His widow, Zarin, and his son, Alnoor, are good family friends, and we see them often at the mosque. Alnoor is an actuarial who worked for the Jubilee Insurance Company in Nairobi for several years. He donates generously of his time to the Ismaili community.

Mariam Masi, who is now eighty-eight years old, still lives in Birmingham but a major stroke has severely crippled her. Of her children, Shenin lives in London; Shelah runs a confectionary store in Birmingham; Karim, who is the spitting image of Nanabapa, and Yasmin reside in Kitchener, Ontario; Azmina is an occupational therapist in Nottingham; Iqubal has remained in Birmingham, where Mariam Masi lives with him and his wife, Sabira; and Mehboob also lives in Birmingham, with his wife, Najwa. Mehboob is retired but was a successful businessman who ran homes for the elderly.

I had long since lost touch with my darling Gita Gosai from my Stoke Newington school days, and would have given my eye teeth to find her for one more rousing chorus of *Harambe, Harambe*. Miraculously, I recently found her living not too far from where we resided back in the day. Her name is now Gita Mehta, she is a nurse, her husband is a commercial banker, and they have one daughter, Priya. We plan to re-unite sooner rather than later.

I cannot leave this chapter without an update on where my beloved Jinja is now but, sadly, it is not in a good place. The streets of Jinja are bustling with Africans going about their business but sightings of folks of other races are rare. The streets and shops appear to be unmaintained since our departure in 1972. Some of the stores are now a garish red, blue or orange, signifying the colours of telecommunication providers, and stand out like sore thumbs. The closure of the railway line, which ran behind the industrial complexes on Home Road, has allowed squatters to throw up shacks, in which they now reside, along the line. The bridge over the Owen Falls Dam is in desperate need of repair and maintenance.

On a more positive note, Jinja now boasts several restaurants including a coffee house, pub, Internet cafe, and Thai food establishment; and, the Crested Crane Hotel is open for business. The town also has a tourism website, and advertises recreational pursuits, such as rafting below Bujagali Falls and all-terrain vehicle adventures.

I always try to look at our expulsion from a "glass half full" perspective. And, that is not hard to do when I think about all the wonderful reunions I have enjoyed with family and friends through the years.

CHAPTER THIRTY-THREE
A Potpourri of Reflections and Aspirations

My Family and Me Today

Many people have asked me why I don't buy a condo for myself in trendy Yaletown or chic Coal Harbour in cosmopolitan Downtown Vancouver. My answer is twofold.

The negative aspect is that I have a phobia about being alone at home, and, as a result, I don't think I could ever bear to live on my own. I know my fear is irrational but it stems from my childhood in Jinja where the dangers of home invasions, assaults, and kidnappings always lurked in the shadows of our everyday lives.

On a more positive note, my answer, quite simply, is that I'm happy where I am. Our home is "action central." It's almost always a whirlwind of activity. In addition to those of us who actually live there, at any given time we have relatives or visitors, or friends of relatives or visitors, passing through, dropping in for a meal, or staying with us. I especially love the fact that my family and I have treasured friends of every race, ethnicity, religion, and age.

As an example, one evening Almas and I were looking forward to a quiet dinner with our friend Susan. However, by the time dinner rolled around, our family room and kitchen were rollicking with guests. Zebby and Rustam arrived with care packages of food. Natasha, Nashina, and their friend, Liza, dropped in. Margaret showed up to take notes for our book, and Susan rolled up her sleeves to help Almas who was frantically preparing food. Even Bob, our contractor, showed up. He had just stopped by for a cup of tea but we convinced him to stay for dinner. So, at the drop of a hat, we were entertaining Ismailis, Hindus, Jews, Christians, older people, younger people, nutmeg-skinned Indians, Liza who is Japanese and Indian, and a couple of pasty white girls.

Occasionally, in my family, we bicker but, surprisingly, not often. I know that some people think my crowded family life has marred my chance to marry but the truth is that I have simply never met the "man of my dreams." Although I regret my single status once in awhile, my life has been so rich, and my part in helping to raise my nieces so fulfilling, that I waste little time fretting about what might have been.

And, now that we're all getting older, I cherish my family even more. Bahadur has undergone back surgery, and has some ongoing health problems. Arthritis is hobbling Zubeda but we all feel that her constant exercise in the kitchen, preparing our meals, keeps her supple. Bahadur and Zubeda fly down to Ontario frequently to visit Narmin and her family. They also take an extended vacation each year. Bahadur made a pilgrimage to Kakira in 2005 to spend time with Suru Madhvani and Bahadur and Zubeda have recently come back from a vacation in Uganda during with they again stayed with Suru.

Rashida gave us a good scare in October of 2004 when breast cancer almost toppled her but she endured the treatment, and came through with flying colours. Rashida is dedicated to exercise, and takes a brisk walk almost every day. Mansur, knock on wood, enjoys good health. Rashida and Mansur have recently sold their home and are awaiting the completion of their condominium in Burnaby. They have used their "homeless" state to travel and have just returned from visiting with Mansur's family in Pakistan.

Zebby and Rustam still like to travel. Unfortunately, though, they have experienced some troubling health problems. Rustam suffered a mild stroke but recovered without permanent damage. Then, just as Rashida was overcoming her illness, Zebby came down with breast cancer, too. Also like Rashida, she gutted her way through the treatment, and is now cancer free but she has been in constant pain from a back ailment, and has recently undergone surgery.

Nizar lives in his own world. He reads, watches television, and listens to music. But, he possesses a sharp wit and an engaging sense of humour, and is content with his life. He is not a keen traveller but has over the years visited with Mariam Masi and her family in Birmingham and taken an extended trip to India and Dubai with Mansur and Rashida. He adores his great-nephews and great-niece, and they him. The only trouble on his horizon is that, like Bapa, he is afflicted with diabetes.

Almas still works at her hair salon, and loves her clients. Other than that, she is much more of a homebody than I, and still takes great pleasure in her cross-stitch, needlepoint, flower arranging, cooking and gardening. In her cross-stitch pieces, Almas depicts African and Japanese motifs along with children's themes. Her work is exquisite. She indulges a passion for collecting sarees, and has quite the eye for them. Unfortunately, she suffers from rheumatoid arthritis.

Recently, our friend, Susan Jaffe, died suddenly and far too soon. Susan was so dear to my family and me, and we shall treasure always her kindness, thoughtfulness, generosity, and incandescent spirit. At her funeral service at the Schara Tzedeck Jewish Cemetery, Susan's son Joel paid us a priceless compliment when he said, "My sincere thanks to the Rahemtulla family for their unending love and support for my mother. Weddings, funerals and family events, she participated in all of them. In fact, Susan was at the Rahemtulla household so often, we considered having her mail forwarded there!" We shall miss her.

I tend to be more exuberant than my siblings, perhaps because I was the spoiled youngest child. I'm still a chatterbox, and I'll talk to anybody about anything. I would say that my best characteristic is that I value my friendships enormously, and I think I'm a good friend. I'd be quite happy, in fact, if that were my epitaph. Probably my worst character flaws are that I'm sometimes a bit too righteous, and I'm prone to volatile temper flare-ups. Now that I think about it, I'm much like Bapa in that way.

I'm also like Bapa in that I've never suffered from the "imposter syndrome" with regard to my career. Bapa had a confidence about him, and was always looking for the next challenge. I'm that way as well. I don't think I have more skills than anyone else, and I certainly don't think I'm smarter. More to the point, my nomadic life style has forced me to adapt to different circumstances quickly, and the terror we faced in Uganda makes pretty much anything else look like a walk in the park.

I'm passionate about dogs. After all these years, I'm still capable of shedding a tear for my darling, Mickey, mowed down by a taxi driver in Jinja, and Anais, who briefly shared our home but proved antagonistic toward my tiny nieces.

I'm not going to adopt another doggie until I retire but, meanwhile, Bailey Omar is the joy of my life. He is Zebby's "child" but he spends virtually every weekend with me. One family member or another is constantly driving back and forth to fetch Bailey from Zebby's or to return him. Bailey Omar is a nine year old Shih Tzu Poodle we have had since he was a puppy. On Saturdays and Sundays, he is my constant companion, and travels everywhere with me. I love him to death.

Bailey Omar

One reason Margaret and I are such good pals is because she is equally goofy about the canine species. We used to play tennis together, and, while we were playing, her dog, Buster Cornelius, would sit in his fancy pram. I saw nothing at all odd about that. Her current little guy, Charlie, a Yorkie, loves to come over to our house, and feels quite at home. He particularly likes to supervise Zubeda while she's cooking. Bailey Omar thinks he's human and ignores Charlie who Bailey sees as just a dog but Charlie's pretty laid back, and he's cool with that.

I sometimes wonder where I would be had I remained in Uganda. Likely, I would have joined Bapa, Bahadur, and Nizar in running Jubilee Ice & Soda Works, and helped them to expand the business to other parts of Africa. Or, I might have landed in the London financial world.

Our Religion Today

Our Ismaili faith remains at the core of our lives. Normally, we worship and socialize at the Burnaby Lake Jamatkhana. But, for special services and weddings, we have the privilege of attending the renowned Darkhana Ismaili Jamatkhana and Centre on Canada Way.

Bruno Freschi, a local but internationally known architect who was responsible for Expo 86 and the Telus Science Centre, designed this exquisite Jamatkhana. In 1985, then Canadian Prime Minister Brian

Mulroney, in the presence of His Highness the Aga Khan, participated in the opening ceremony.

Set against the backdrop of the snow-peaked North Shore mountains, the three-storey octagonal structure of cast-concrete is, in good part, sunk below ground. The design of the richly decorated bordered windows complements the style of the building. The main entrance features solid oak doors inlaid with brass strips. Abstract calligraphy adorns the tile work, windows, carpets, and wood screens. Splendid copper domes sit astride the prayer hall.

Bruno Freschi stated that:

> Materiality, the exposure of earth materials, concrete, sandstone, and marble gives a material presence and permanence, symbols of a 'timeless' foundation for the Ismaili community.

And Aga Khan IV, in his speech at the opening ceremony, said:

> The new building will stand in strongly landscaped sur-roundings. It will face a courtyard with fountains and a garden. Its scale, its proportions and the use of water will serve to create a serene and contemplative environment. This will be a place of congregation, of order, of peace, of prayer, of hope, of humility, and of brother-hood. From it should come forth those thoughts, those sentiments, those attitudes which bind men together and which unite.

As well as giving a sense of permanence to our religion, our Jamatkhanas serve to bind our community together socially. Many of the families who worship at them have ties of friendship that travel back several generations to Uganda and even to India.

I can think of no better way to conclude my commentary on Ismailism than to set forth, in his own words, the thoughts and vision of His Highness, Aga Khan IV:

> In the troubled times in which we live, it is important to remember, and honor, the vision of a pluralistic society. Tolerance, openness and understanding towards other peoples' cultures, social structures, values and faiths are now essential to the very survival of an interdependent world.

> I think what's important is to hope and work for and pray for a cosmopolitan civil ethic where the unity of the human race becomes an ethical purpose for all faiths.

Charitable Works

I hesitate to even mention the charitable works in which I've participated because they are so insignificant in the great scheme of things. But, my friends have convinced me to do so in case someone reading about them should get the urge to become involved in some charitable or community cause.

One simple thing that anyone can do is to undertake random acts of kindness. My friend, Jan McLeod, and I sometimes took beggars from the Vancouver streets into McDonald's for breakfast or lunch. We became rather fond of one particular elderly man. One time, Jan noticed that he was without shoes so she promptly went into Eaton's Department Store, and bought him a pair. On another occasion, I noticed that he wasn't feeling well, and had a fever. I gave some money to the staff at McDonald's, and asked them to feed my friend. I did that for others as well but, most of the time, the staff wouldn't take the money. They just fed the fellows for free.

At the start of my banking career, I belonged to Junior Achievement. For four or five years, under its auspices, I went to local high schools once a week to help train students to better understand business and economics.

For a few years, while I was in Private Banking, I sat on the Board of MOSAIC, a non-profit organization dedicated to helping immigrants become self-sufficient. I also sat on the Board of Pacifica, a drug and alcohol recovery facility, and on the Aga Khan Economic Planning Board in Vancouver.

My banking friend, Anne Lippert, has roped me into assisting with a good many major fund drives and other initiatives, sponsored by the Salvation Army, over the years.

Thoughts for the Future

I thoroughly enjoy my job, and expect and hope to work for several more years but I have some long-range retirement goals in mind. Two of them are pretty simple. I want to finally find the time to indulge my passion for reading, and I want to work with an organization that rescues or helps dogs in need.

My third retirement goal, though, will be somewhat more challenging. Historically, at Jubilees celebrating significant anniversaries, the adherents of the Aga Khans have given them their weight in gold and silver. However, Aga Khan IV, on the occasion of his fiftieth Jubilee, requested of his followers their commitment in "time" and "knowledge."

So, I hope to have the honour of volunteering my time and knowledge to the Aga Khan Development Network which "focuses on health, education, culture, rural development, institution-building and the promotion of economic development," and "is dedicated to improving living conditions and opportunity for the poor, without regard to their faith, origin or gender." My aspiration is to utilize the lending skills I acquired during my tenure at the Royal Bank by working in micro-finance, which is the provision of small loans to poor people without collateral. More specifically, I hope to work in-country helping to set up microcredit infrastructures.

As the Aga Khan has said, by assisting the poor through business, we are developing protection against extremism.

Closing Reflections

India, the land of my parents and ancestors, mysterious and alluring, fascinates and enthrals me. Uganda, and especially Jinja, the Place of Flat Rocks, will forever hold my heart. My experiences in Great Britain helped to mould me. But Canada, the country that gave my family shelter and boundless opportunities, commands my love, loyalty, and gratitude.

My priceless friends on all four continents have shown me the remarkable similarities of our shared experiences. I'm convinced that most people, one on one, would find that they share more connections than differences.

Tragedy and pain have certainly touched my life. I have been forcibly wrenched from my home and country; I have mourned the deaths of my Nanima, Nanabapa, Ma, Bapa, and newborn niece, Fatima; and I have experienced petty but hurtful discrimination on three continents. But, my cornucopia of good fortune far outweighs any tribulations I have suffered. My family is my bulwark; my friends are stalwart; and my faith sustains me. I have received personal benedictions from Aga Khan IV. I could not have dreamed of a better career path than the one I have enjoyed. Nor could I have imagined a better goal than designing and helping to bring to fruition a perfect home for my family.

I have captured buckets of katydids raining from trees in Jinja; picnicked near the River Nile; hawked shoes in Petticoat Lane; careened about on camels in Karachi; watched elephants cavorting in Kenya; cruised the backwaters of Kerala; clambered along Guernsey's cliff top trails and country lanes; sated my craving for shopping in New York, Paris, and Rome; and gorged on Knickerbocker Glories in Kampala, Nairobi, and London. And, hopefully, I have paid my good fortune forward along the way.

On balance, I can liken my unparalleled blessings to the inscription "RSVP" carved by Bugandans on their bark cloth invitations to village celebrations. "Rice and Stew Very Plenty!"

GLOSSARY

Aga Khan	Commander-in-Chief
askari	night watchman or policeman (Swahili)
ayah	nanny or maid (Swahili)
baksheesh	offering of money or tip to a beggar (Swahili)
banyani	Hindu (Swahili)
bapa	father (Kutchi)
bhabhi	sister-in-law (Kutchi and Gujarati)
bhajia, ondhwo, chevro, ganthia	Indian savouries
bhel-puri	snack of puffed rice, cubed potatoes, tamarind sauce, roasted peanuts, chopped onions and tomatoes, green chillies, coriander, and chutney
bhunga	round dwelling constructed of stone, mud, and dung
biryani	curried chicken or beef served on a bed of rice with sauces
bismillah al-rahman al-rahim	In the name of Allah the most beneficent and the most merciful
boma	corral (Swahili)
bwana	mister or sir (Swahili)
chandlo	yellow mark (Gujarati)
chor	thief (Gujarati)
chotaro	derogatory word used to describe a mixed race child
dadabapa	paternal grandfather (Kutchi and Gujarati)
dadima	paternal grandmother (Kutchi and Gujarati)
dhow	triangular-sailing vessel
Diwali	Hindu festival of lights
diya	small clay pot lit with oil (Gujarati)
duka	small shop (Swahili)
dw'a	prayer
Eid Mubarak	Blessed Eid
Eid ul-Adha	Muslim festival to mark the homecoming from the annual pilgrimage to Mecca
Eid ul-Fitr	Muslim festival at the conclusion of the fast after Ramadan
firman	written edict from the Aga Khan
gilli-danda	primitive form of cricket (Gujarati)

ginan	devotional hymn
gomezi or basuti	colourful native dress (Swahili)
hakuna matata	no problem (Swahili)
halal	Islamic term for food that is permissible to eat
Harambe, Harambe	all pull together or pulling together (Swahili)
hijab	burka or head covering used by Muslim women
Holi	Hindu festival - people throw coloured water at one another
Imamate	spiritual leadership
Imam	leader
Ithnasheri	largest branch of Shi'a Islam
Jama Masjid	place of worship for followers of Islam
Jamatkhana	Ismaili mosque
jambo, bwana	hello, mister (Swahili)
jambo, mama	hello, lady (Swahili)
kabaka	king (Swahili)
kamadia	assistant or accountant
karanga	roasted peanuts (Swahili)
kasuku	parrot (Swahili)
katha	brown powder
khechri	hodgepodge of lentils and rice boiled together (Kutchi and Gujarati)
khobo	groom's father offering a tray of coins to the bride
kitenge	cotton fabric with African designs
kondo	armed thief (Swahili)
Khushyali	celebration
Kutchi	dialect spoken by people from Kutch
laddu, paak, paara, halwo, jalebi	Indian sweets
ma	mother (Kutchi)
maharaj	Hindu priest
mama	uncle from mother's side of the family Kutchi and Gujarati
mandwo	similar to a wedding shower (Kutchi and Gujarati)
manyatta	village enclosure (Swahili)
marefu	tall (Swahili)
masa	mother's sister's husband (Kutchi and Gujarati)
masala chai	spiced tea (Kutchi and Gujarati)
masi	mother's sister (Kutchi and Gujarati)

maskini	beggar (Swahili)
matooke	cooked green bananas (Swahili)
matoongi	clay pot to store drinking water (Swahili)
mehndi	henna (Kutchi and Gujarati)
mericani	cloth woven in Massachusetts
mogo	cassava root (Swahili)
mukhi	guardian
mukhwas	mixture of seeds and nuts, freshens breath
mullah	Muslim religious leader
nanabapa	maternal grandfather (Kutchi and Gujarati)
nanima	maternal grandmother (Kutchi and Gujarati)
Navroz	Muslim New Year
Navroz Mubarak	congratulations on the auspicious occasion of Navroz
nyama choma or mishkaki	barbequed meats (Swahili)
oudh	perfumed chips of wood burnt on coals to release fragrance
paanwalla	vendor selling paan (leaves containing beetle nut, etc.)
pacheri	scarves (Kutchi and Gujarati)
paw paw	papaya (Swahili)
pimbo	baton (Swahili)
Qur'an	Koran
Raksha Bandhan or Rakhi	Hindu tradition - sisters tie fancy glittering bracelets on their brothers wrists
Ramadan	ninth month of the year in the Islamic calendar
rann	desert
rotli	unleavened bread made from stone ground whole meal flour (Kutchi and Gujarati)
sagri	coal burning stove (Kutchi and Gujarati)
samosa	pastry stuffed with beef, chicken or vegetables
saree	Indian garment worn by woman
sav	sweet vermicelli dish (Kutchi and Gujarati)
senene	grasshopper (Swahili)
shamba	garden (Swahili)
sharia	Islamic law
sherbat	similar to a milkshake (Kutchi and Gujarati)
shuka	colourful piece of cloth (Swahili)
sokoni	open air market (Swahili)

supari	betal nut (Kutchi and Gujarati)
Surah Ya-Sin	portion of the text of the Holy Qur'an
thepla	type of cookie (Kutchi and Gujarati)
tukmaria	basil seeds (Kutchi and Gujarati)
ugali	popular staple food among Africans in Uganda
wahindi	slang for Asian (Swahili)
waragi	alcoholic drink made from sugar cane (Swahili)

APPENDIX

The following is a write-up that was appended to a study on Jubilee Ice and Soda Works conducted by Price Waterhouse Africa:

Price Waterhouse Africa

CONCEPT AND PROFILE OF FOUNDER

Jubilee Ice and Soda Works was initially formed and developed by a Ugandan Asian in the early 1940's.

Not much is known about the **Rahemtulla family** or the founder of Jubilee Ice, **Mr. Mohamed Rahemtulla,** or their present whereabouts since their forced expulsion out of Uganda during the brutal regime of Idi Amin.

A long time employee of Jubilee Ice who had worked closely with **Mr.Rahemtulla** has provided a few details that we feel should be inserted here.

Mr. Rahemtulla, a man of pioneering spirit came to Uganda during the early 1920's and is known to have travelled by Steam ship from India to Mombasa in Kenya and thereafter by foot to Jinja. Upon arrival in Jinja, he stayed behind whilst the rest of his travelling party went onwards.

Mr. Rahemtulla developed a small makeshift Soda Manufacturing plant in his kitchen whereby after returning home from his labouring job, and uptill late at night the soda mixture prepared by his wife was bottled. A limited production of 25 to 30 crates was made on a daily bases with sales ex-home.

The Jubilee soda after a few years became a popular drink in the Busoga District. As demand increased, it was evident that a modern Soda manufacturing and bottling plant had to be built. This was done in the early 1940's by **Mr. Rahemtulla** that is the present plant.

As Jubilee production increased so did the market whereby Jubilee was gaining in roads to the branded drinks like Coca Cola and Pepsi, and a threat. The branded drinks, to force Jubilee out of competition, instigated a move whereby supplies of carbon dioxide to Jubilee Soda was cut off.

This did not deter **Mr. Rahemtulla** who at once set up a carbon dioxide plant . The gas derived by burning crude oil that produced carbon monoxide that was refined and separated to carbon dioxide gas.

By 1956 Jubilee Soda was making enough carbon dioxide gas to supply the rest of the bottling plants in Uganda. Up to present Jubilee is the sole producer of carbon dioxide gas in Uganda and Uganda should be thankful to **Mr. Mohamed Rahemtulla,** a man of vision and true pioneering spirit.

NOTES

CHAPTER 1: MY ISMAILI AND INDIAN HERITAGE

1. The discussion of Ismaili history draws upon several sources including: Daftary, Farhad. *A Short History Of The Ismailis*. Edinburgh: Edinburgh University Press, 1998; Daftary, Farhad and Zulfikar Hirji. *The Ismailis: An Illustrated History*. United Kingdom: Azimuth Editions in association with The Institute of Ismaili Studies, 2008; Levinson, David and Karen Christensen, ed. *Ismaili Sects—South Asia. Encyclopedia of Modern Asia*, Vol. 3, pp. 185-187. New York, 2002.

2. The descriptions of India, the Gujarat, Bhuj, and Madhapur draw upon several sources including: Davies, Gill. *Spirit of India*. Bath: Parragon Publishing, Queen Street House, 2008; Singh, Sarina, Arnold Barkhordarian, Charlotte Beech, Joe Bindloss, Susan Derby, Anthony Ham, Paul Harding, Abigail Hole, Patrick Horton, Grace Pundyk, Lucas Vidgen. *Lonely Planet: India*. Lonely Planet Publications Pty. Ltd., 2003; and, particularly, Tyabji, Azhar. *Bhuj*. India: Mapin Publishing Pvt. Ltd. in association with Environmental Planning Collaborative, 2006. Green Township, New Jersey: Grantha Corporation, 2006.

CHAPTER 2: OUTWARD BOUND TO THE DARK CONTINENT

3. The discussion of the early history of East Africa and description of Uganda draws upon several sources including: Davies, Gill. *Africa Natural Spirit of the African Continent*. Bath: Parragon Publishing, Queen Street House, 2007; Fitzpatrick, Mary, Tim Bewer, Matthew D. Firestone. *Lonely Planet: East Africa*. Lonely Planet Publications Pty. Ltd., 2009; Meredith, Martin. *The Fate of Africa: From the Hopes of Freedom to the Heart of Despair*. New York: Public Affairs, a member of the Perseus Books Group, 2005; Roberts, A.D, ed. *The Cambridge History of Africa*, volume 7, 1905–1940. Cambridge: Cambridge University Press, 1986.

CHAPTER 13: UGANDA'S GROWING PAINS

4. The discussion of Uganda's economic and political growth, Ugandan independence, Milton Obote, and the Indian experience during this period draws upon several sources including: Melady, Thomas and

Margaret Melady. *Idi Amin Dada: Hitler in Africa*. Kansas City: Sheed Andrews and McMeel, Subsidiary of Universal Press Syndicate, 1977; Melady, Thomas and Margaret Melady. *Uganda: The Asian Exiles*. Maryknoll, New York: Orbis Books, 1976.; Meredith, Martin. *The Fate of Africa: From the Hopes of Freedom to the Heart of Despair*. New York: Public Affairs, a member of the Perseus Books Group, 2005; Roberts, A.D, ed. *The Cambridge History of Africa*, volume 7, 1905–1940. Cambridge: Cambridge University Press, 1986.

CHAPTER 14: THE ADVENT OF EVIL

5. The discussion of Idi Amin draws upon several sources including: Meredith, Martin. *The Fate of Africa: From the Hopes of Freedom to the Heart of Despair*. New York: Public Affairs, a member of the Perseus Books Group, 2005; Roberts, A.D, ed. *The Cambridge History of Africa*, volume 7, 1905–1940. Cambridge: Cambridge University Press, 1986; and Melady, Thomas and Margaret Melady. *Idi Amin Dada: Hitler in Africa*. Kansas City: Sheed Andrews and McMeel, Subsidiary of Universal Press Syndicate, 1977.

CHAPTER 16: SURELY, IT CAN'T BE TRUE

6. The discussion of the expulsion proclamation and its consequences, and the Indian diaspora, draws upon several sources including: Marks, Kathy. *The New Britons: How Uganda's dispossessed became model citizens*. The Independent News, *19 September 1997;* Melady, Thomas and Margaret Melady. *Idi Amin Dada: Hitler in Africa*. Kansas City: Sheed Andrews and McMeel, Subsidiary of Universal Press Syndicate, 1977; and Melady, Thomas and Margaret Melady. *Uganda: The Asian Exiles*. Maryknoll, New York: Orbis Books, 1976.

7. The discussion of the backlash against Indians in Great Britain led by Enoch Powell; the quotation by Enoch Powell; the passage and consequences of the Commonwealth Immigrants Act, 1968; the seeking of redress from the European Commission of Human Rights; the damning report of the European Commission of Human Rights; and the quotation by Lord Anthony Lester is based solely upon: Lester, Anthony. Lecture. *East African Asians Versus The United Kingdom: The Inside Story*. October 23, 2003. This lecture draws heavily upon Lester, Thirty Years on: the East African Case revisited, Public Law [2002] PL Spring Pages 52–72.

CHAPTER 21: THE WONDERS OF KENYAN SAFARIS

8. A helpful source was Sassi, Dino. *Maasai*. Kensta, Nairobi: Mr. Pravin Shah, 1979.

CHAPTER 25: GOOD FORTUNE RAINS DOWN ON UGANDA

9. The discussion of the Madhvani family draws upon several sources including: Becker, Robert and Nitin Jayant Madhvani, ed. *Jayant Madhvani*. London: Privately printed. Designed and produced by The Folio Society Ltd., 1973.

BIBLIOGRAPHY

Becker, Robert and Nitin Jayant Madhvani, ed. *Jayant Madhvani*. London: Privately printed. Designed and produced by The Folio Society Ltd., 1973.

Daftary, Farhad. *A Short History Of The Ismailis*. Edinburgh: Edinburgh University Press, 1998.

Daftary, Farhad and Zulfikar Hirji. *The Ismailis: An Illustrated History*. United Kingdom: Azimuth Editions in association with The Institute of Ismaili Studies, 2008.

Davies, Gill. *Spirit of India*. Bath: Parragon Publishing, Queen Street House, 2008.

Davies, Gill. *Africa Natural Spirit of the African Continent*. Bath: Parragon Publishing, Queen Street House, 2007.

Fitzpatrick, Mary, Tim Bewer, Matthew D. Firestone. *Lonely Planet: East Africa*. Lonely Planet Publications Pty. Ltd., 2009.

H.R.H. Prince Aga Khan III. *Islam: The Religion of my Ancestors*. Courtesy: The Shia Imami Ismaili Tariqah and Religious Education Board for Pakistan.

Lester, Anthony. Lecture. *East African Asians Versus The United Kingdom: The Inside Story*. October 23, 2003. This lecture draws heavily upon Lester, Thirty Years on: the East African Case revisited, Public Law [2002] PL Spring Pages 52–72.

Levinson, David and Karen Christensen, ed. *Ismaili Sects—South Asia*. *Encyclopedia of Modern Asia*, Vol. 3, pp. 185-187. New York, 2002.

Marks, Kathy. *The New Britons: How Uganda's dispossessed became model citizens*. The Independent News, 19 September 1997.

Melady, Thomas and Margaret Melady. *Idi Amin Dada: Hitler in Africa*. Kansas City: Sheed Andrews and McMeel, Subsidiary of Universal Press Syndicate, 1977.

Melady, Thomas and Margaret Melady. *Uganda: The Asian Exiles*. Maryknoll, New York: Orbis Books, 1976.

Meredith, Martin. *The Fate of Africa: From the Hopes of Freedom to the Heart of Despair*. New York: Public Affairs, a member of the Perseus Books Group, 2005.

Roberts, A.D, ed. *The Cambridge History of Africa*, volume 7, 1905–1940. Cambridge: Cambridge University Press, 1986.

Sassi, Dino. *Maasai*. Kensta, Nairobi: Mr. Pravin Shah, 1979.

Singh, Sarina, Arnold Barkhordarian, Charlotte Beech, Joe Bindloss, Susan Derby, Anthony Ham, Paul Harding, Abigail Hole, Patrick Horton, Grace Pundyk, Lucas Vidgen. *Lonely Planet: India*. Lonely Planet Publications Pty. Ltd., 2003.

Tyabji, Azhar. *Bhuj*. India: Mapin Publishing Pvt. Ltd. in association with Environmental Planning Collaborative, 2006. Green Township, New Jersey: Grantha Corporation, 2006.

FAMILY TREE

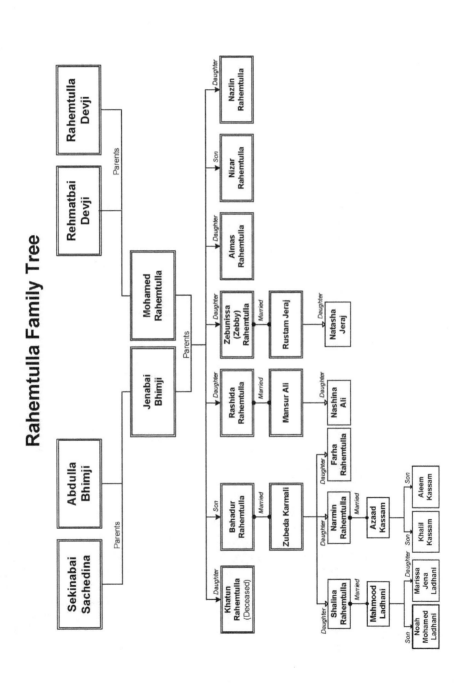

Rahemtulla Family Tree